CW00544213

ESPAÑA

About the author

Giles Tremlett is a prize-winning historian, author and journalist based in Madrid, Spain. He has lived in, and written extensively about, Spain almost continuously since graduating from Oxford University thirty-five years ago. He is Visiting Fellow of the Cañada Blanch Centre at the London School of Economics, writes opinion and long form reportage for the *Guardian* and is a former Madrid correspondent for *The Economist*.

GILES
TREMLETT

ESPAÑA

A BRIEF HISTORY OF SPAIN

BLOOMSBURY PUBLISHING
NEW YORK • LONDON • OXFORD • NEW DELHI • SYDNEY

This is an Apollo book. First published in the UK in 2022 by Head of Zeus Ltd, part of Bloomsbury Publishing Plc

First published in the US in 2022 by Bloomsbury Publishing Inc.

BLOOMSBURY, BLOOMSBURY PUBLISHING and the Diana logo are trademarks of Bloomsbury Publishing Plc

Copyright © Giles Tremlett, 2022

The moral right of Giles Tremlett to be identified as the author of this work has been asserted in accordance with the Copyright, Designs and Patents Act of 1988.

All rights reserved. No part of this publication may be reproduced, stored in a retrieval system, or transmitted in any form or by any means, electronic, mechanical, photocopying, recording, or otherwise, without the prior permission of both the copyright owner and the above publisher of this book.

9 7 5 3 1 2 4 6 8

A catalogue record for this book is available from the British Library.

Library of Congress cataloging-in-publication data is available.

ISBN (UK HB): 9781789544374
ISBN (US HB): 9781639730575
ISBN (E): 9781789544398

Designed and typeset by Francesca Mangiaracina

Colour separation by DawkinsColour

Maps by Jamie Whyte

Printed and bound in Spain by Gráficas Estella

Head of Zeus Ltd
First Floor East
5–8 Hardwick Street
London EC1R 4RG, UK

www.headofzeus.com

BLOOMSBURY PUBLISHING
Bloomsbury Publishing Inc.
1385 Broadway
New York NY 10018, USA

www.bloomsbury.com

To two fellow new Spaniards,
Lucas and Samuel Tremlett,
and two old teachers,
Peter Carter (in memoriam)
and Oliver Ramsbotham.

Contents

CANTABRIAN SEA
Gijón
Santander
A Coruña
Oviedo
Covadonga
Bilbao
Santiago de Compostela
Finisterre
Priaranza del Bierzo
Vitoria-Gasteiz
León
Atapuerca
Las Médulas
Burgos
Valladolid
Torsedillas
DUERO
Gormaz
Oporto
Arévalo
Salamanca
Brieva
Alba de Tormes
MADRID
TAJO
Aranjuez
Talavera de la Reina
Toledo
Ocaña
ESP
PORTUGAL
ATLANTIC
Medellín
Mérida
Badajóz
Ciudad Real
GUADIANA
LISBON
Valdepeñas
Navas de Tolosa
Alcolea
Bailén
Córdoba
GUADALQUIVIR
Jaén
Huelva
Seville
Granada
Alhama de Granada
Ronda
Málaga
Cádiz
Algeciras
Ceuta
OCEAN

FRANCE
Bayonne
Hendaye
PYRENEES
Pamplona
ANDORRA
EBRO
Figueres
Empúrion
Girona
Zaragoza
Bruch
Barcelona
Tarragona
Sant Carles de la Rápita
N
Mahón
Palma de Mallorca
JÚCAR
Valencia
Albacete
Ibiza
Elche
Alicante
Murcia
Cartagena
0
100
200
KM
SPAIN
MAIN TOWNS, RIVERS AND MOUNTAIN CHAINS
ALGERIA

Introduction

We could choose any moment just before a football match featuring Spain's national team but let us start with the 2010 World Cup final at the Soccer City stadium in Johannesburg, South Africa. The game will end in victory thanks to an extra-time goal by Andrés Iniesta, provoking an outpouring of national jubilation and pride. *La Roja* – The Reds – were the champions of the world. In soccer-mad Spain, there was euphoria.

Before the match started, however, television viewers around the world were puzzled. When the national anthems were played, the Netherlands players shouted out the words to The Wilhelmus, which is said to date back to 1572 and commemorates William of Orange, the leader of the Dutch revolt against Spanish rule. They sang about their country's 'guiltless blood', 'faithful warriors' and 'steadfast hearts'. In contrast, Iniesta, Xavi, Puyol and the Spanish squad merely hummed. Their national anthem has no words. Why is this? Because Spaniards disagree so profoundly about their own history that they dare not put words to it. They cannot conjure up that treacly mixture of geography, history, folklore and bombast that is the essence of such anthems. National pride cannot be put to words.

Spain has no 'national story' that it can celebrate in comfort. That makes it almost unique. Other nations build narratives based on history, myth and saccharine sentimentality. Some, like Germany,

↑ Andrés Iniesta scores the winning goal for Spain in the 2010 World Cup football tournament in South Africa. Spaniards were proud, though disagreements over history meant they had no words for their national anthem.

add historical guilt, or responsibility. These narratives are rarely factually honest but channel a people's emotional attachment to nation. At its best, this creates community. At its worst, it causes war.

Either way, such stories eventually form part of history itself, since the way people see themselves shapes their actions. Ardent Spanish nationalists claim they inhabit the 'oldest nation on earth'. That is wrong, but there is no doubt that Spain has existed more or less in its current geographical format for longer than most countries. So why the difficulty with a national narrative? This short history argues that disagreement about the past is, in itself, part of that narrative. Spain, in other words, has struggled constantly to fuse together a fractured soul.

I am a British-born, recently nationalized 'new' Spaniard, still imbued with a convert's enthusiasm (rather like the *conversos* to

Christianity who appear later in this book), but this is not an attempt to supply Spain's missing national story. I will, however, challenge simple stereotypes (including some beloved by Spaniards themselves) about a people deemed passionate, hot-tempered, party-loving, lazy, Quixotic or violent – except where those views have helped to shape history itself.

The Iberian Peninsula – which Spain shares with Portugal – stands on three of Europe's most significant geographical frontiers. Two of these are clear on any atlas: the first separates the Mediterranean from the Atlantic; and the second divides Europe from Africa. The third frontier is only revealed when we draw onto our atlas the circular winds and currents of the Atlantic Ocean. Where Romans saw the world's western edge at Finisterre on Spain's north-western Atlantic coast, those winds and currents actually link Europe to the American continent. That is how Christopher Columbus 'discovered' the Americas and could return to explain what he had done. It is also why Spain (or, rather, Castile – the most powerful of the kingdoms that eventually formed a single country) conquered so much of it, creating the world's first global empire in the sixteenth century.

Spain's position on Europe's south-western corner, then, exposes it to cultural, political and actual winds from all quadrants. Africa is a mere nine miles away to the south across the Strait of Gibraltar, clearly visible from the wind-surfing beaches of Tarifa. The Mediterranean – a vast and ancient community of its own – connects it to the cultures of Phoenicians, Greeks, Jews, Carthaginians and Romans as well as to the Arab and Muslim lands of the Near East or the Maghreb. In the north, the Pyrenees mountains anchor it to Western Europe. The Atlantic and Mediterranean coastal paths on either side of those mountains have allowed species, cultures, trade, trends and peoples to flow north and south.

Although Spanish history is full of attempts to resist 'foreign' influences or outright invasions, these often failed. Opposition gave way to assimilation. Romans, Visigoths, Christians, Muslim 'Moors' and Jews in Spain were frequently, in fact, neither invaders nor foreigners. They were native 'Spaniards' whose families became religious or cultural converts or had lived there for many generations.

Men from the Russian steppe were among the first to arrive from the north and the only ones to provoke genetic turmoil, since they mostly wiped out autochthonous males between 2500 and 2000 BC. Berber Muslims invaded almost the entire country in the eighth century AD. Sun-seeking twentieth-century European tourists in their cars, planes and caravans became another sort of invader, bringing change to Spain's culture, social mores and politics. Migrants from Latin America added another twist to the story at the beginning of the twenty-first century, reversing a centuries-old trend in the opposite direction.

Spain is both a cornerstone of Europe and one of its great pivots. At times, like a weathercock, the direction it takes is dictated by external forces. Storms blow in (Romans, Visigoths, Christianity, Islam, Habsburg monarchs, American silver, Bonaparte's armies, bikini-clad tourists), and Spain changes. At other times, it grasps the mechanism that controls the swivel to shape not just its own political and cultural destiny, but that of Europe or other parts of the world.

Its translators' school in Toledo fuelled a return to intellectual and scientific thought after the fallow years of the early Middle Ages by bringing Greek learning (with Indian, Persian and Arab improvements) back to Europe. Columbus and the conquistadors who followed him not only brought often lethal change to the peoples of the American continent but also began one of the most remarkable interchanges of plant and animal species (and deadly diseases, whether sexually transmitted or not) the world has ever seen. Spain exported the modern novel, 'invented' by Cervantes, and did much to spread formal education, especially of elites, through the work of the Jesuits. Less gloriously, it also expelled the Sephardic Jews and, later, its home-grown Muslims – while pursuing Christians for the slightest hint of unorthodoxy. The first African slave to reach the Americas travelled on a Spanish boat, and many of the last were shipped by Spaniards to their colony in Cuba.

Just as geography placed Spain at a global crossroads, so it also, paradoxically, turned it into a fortress. The Iberian Peninsula is a massive, towering block of rock bolted to Europe's south-west corner. It would be Western Europe's largest country if Portugal did not also occupy one-sixth of it. Spain is Europe's second-highest country, after only Alpine Switzerland (and, on average, almost twice as high as France or Germany). Most of it sits on the vast, high tableland known as the *meseta*. This is surrounded by often narrow strips of low-lying coastland onto which much of Spain's population is now squeezed. Today, only two of Spain's ten largest cities – Madrid and Zaragoza – are not on these coastal flatlands, and more than half of Spaniards live in seaside provinces (including the Canary and Balearic Islands).

The change between gentle coastland and rugged interior is so abrupt in places that mainland Spain's highest peak, the Mulhacén of the Sierra Nevada, lies just 35 kilometres from the southern coast, while the northern Picos de Europa loom above the Cantabrian Sea, reaching a peak just 25 kilometres inland. The *meseta* is cut up by deep river valleys and long, impenetrable mountain ranges that the nineteenth-century British traveller Richard Ford called 'moats and walls'. Until these obstacles were bridged or bored through in the twentieth century, they kept Spaniards separate and distinct from one another. From north-west Galicia, for several centuries, communication with Cuba was more fluid than with, say, its desert-like opposite corner of Spain at Almería. This tension, between the many, inward-looking 'little Spains' of a harsh interior with a continental climate of short, blistering summers separated by long, freezing winters and the globally connected, temperate coasts (as well as the valleys leading down to them) has done much to shape

↑ The Mulhacén in the Sierra Nevada near Granada is, at 11,414 foot, the highest peak on mainland Spain, with views across the Mediterranean to Africa. Spain's rugged, impenetrable terrain has shaped its history.

Spain's history. The cultural and political waves that crash onto its shores often take a long time to penetrate its rock-like interior.

The early twentieth-century Spanish philosopher Miguel de Unamuno was right when he declared that 'the Castilian soul was great when it exposed us to the four winds and spread throughout the world', but that this withered whenever the windows were slammed shut to keep out those same winds. A continuous process of cultural mixing has provided moments of hybrid vigour that reveal themselves in everything from architecture, art and agriculture to philosophy or flamenco music. At other times when Spain has denied its cross-cultural personality, it has required a monstrous effort (the Inquisition, say, or mass expulsion of Jews and Muslims, or Francoist dictatorship and autarky) to fashion a 'pure' national identity. At such times, Spain's self-myths of national resilience in the face of foreign aggression based on envy are dusted off and presented as unassailable truths. This always, in the end, fails – just as attempts to homogenize Spain's internal identities and languages (of Catalans, say, or Basques) are doomed to disaster. This tension, between the idea of Spain as a single, pure and homogeneous entity that can only be corrupted by the outside world and of a place of many identities continually refreshed by Unamuno's four winds, has never been resolved. It has, in fact, often been one of the driving forces of its history. Hence the lack of a national narrative, or an anthem.

These themes will reappear constantly though the coming pages. Let us, however, leave facts for later and start with myth. The history of a country depends also on how its own people have imagined it. Spain is no exception.

1
Uncle Hercules and the Pit of Bones

The wife-killer and child-murderer known to the Romans as Hercules purged his considerable sins with twelve, famously harsh tasks. Some of these, the original Greek mythology says, were performed in the 'far West', at the edge of the known world. Since what we now call the Atlantic Ocean formed that world's western boundary, this was later identified as Spain, or Iberia – Europe's bulging south-western peninsula, which is shared with Portugal. On one of these trips, Hercules (or Heracles, as the Greeks called him) was frustrated to find a pair of mountains barring his way. Because he was so strong, he pushed them aside, accidentally connecting the Mediterranean to the Atlantic and creating the Strait of Gibraltar. The twin Pillars of Hercules, by this reckoning, are the Rock of Gibraltar and, opposite it, the Moroccan mountain of Jebel Musa. Beyond them and over the horizon to the west lay Atlantis, or so Plato said, while Renaissance writers claimed the pillars also bore a warning sign that read 'Non Plus Ultra', or 'There is nothing beyond this'.

⇠ The mythical figure of Hercules has long been associated with Iberia, where he carried out some of his legendary twelve labours. Julius Caesar wept when he visited the now disappeared Temple of Hercules in Cádiz. The Romans also named the lighthouse they built at La Coruña in the first century the Tower of Hercules.

Hercules' connection to Spain was elaborated on over centuries, as writers sought a national narrative stretching back to the foundational myths of western civilization. According to early versions, a nephew called Hispano travelled with him, and since the inhabitants of Iberia were an unruly rabble, Hercules made him their king, thereby founding a country. Today's 'Hispanics' owe their ethnic label to the nephew or, rather, to the inventors of these stories. Spain itself derives from his name, which some wrote as 'Espan' – just a tilde accent mark and a vowel away from 'España'.

In the Middle Ages, Spanish monarchs (or their chroniclers) liked to claim descent from Hercules (and, hence, from his father, Zeus – known as Jupiter to the Romans). The legendary strongman was later deemed to have sown Spain with monuments and cities – from the great Mediterranean port city of Barcelona to the vast stone aqueduct at Segovia, the ancient lighthouse at La Coruña and, even, the university in Salamanca. Today, his columns decorate the Spanish flag and *La Roja*'s shirt. They were once also incorporated onto Spain's colonial silver piece of eight (or 'Spanish dollar'). One column allegedly remains in the centre of the US dollar's '$' symbol (previously a '$', with two vertical columns) since this was originally modelled on the widely used Spanish coin, which remained legal tender in the United States until 1857.

The Herculean myth tells us much about Spain, or how it has viewed itself. Here is a remote corner of Europe (in Greek and Roman times) that borders the scary unknown but which was endowed by the ancients with their (and Europe's) civilization. That has often invited another question. Was Spain always an active, contributing part of that civilization or was it an untamed borderland – Europe's wild west? Even today, in other terms and with little basis, Spaniards ponder this question during moments of introspective glumness, while being immensely offended if any outsider does the same. Painful self-questioning, in fact, has been part of Spanish discourse for a good four centuries.

Hercules provides a convenient, if fictitious, explanation of Spain's prehistory. The story of his pillars already points to the intimate connection between Africa and Spain. From the upper reaches of the Rock of Gibraltar, indeed, Africa is almost always clearly visible. The monkeys here are called Barbary apes, like the pirates who once lived on the opposite shore. In fact, Africa can be seen from a whole stretch of Spain's coastline, its lights twinkling in the dark.

The narrow corridor between the two continents was last walkable around 5.3 million years ago, after the Mediterranean had gradually dried out over several hundred thousand years. The Atlantic Ocean was held back by a kilometre-high buttress, which slowly gave way (unless, that is, Hercules knocked it over). Some scientific reconstructions see water flooding through in a torrent the size of one thousand Amazon rivers, producing a biblical flood that refilled the Mediterranean by up to 10 metres per day. Other scientists see a more gradual in-flow, but all agree that an event known as the Zanclean Deluge cut Iberia off from Africa. Ice ages later lowered water levels by up to 100 metres, narrowing the channel and dotting it with islands. Fossils and stone tools found at the Victoria Cave and Black Cave sites near Cartagena, south-east Spain, in 2016 suggest that this may have allowed some early hominins (as we now call existing and extinct human lines and their immediate ancestors) to island-hop into Iberia from Africa. These were previously thought only to have entered Europe from Africa at the eastern end of the Mediterranean, but this may be the first example of what historian Simon Barton described as the Strait of Gibraltar acting 'less as a barrier than as a bridge'.

Whatever the truth about how they arrived, knowledge of hominins and human prehistory in Spain starts in a series of caves at Atapuerca, in gently rolling countryside near Burgos in the northwest of the country. The ancient limestone caverns here form one of the world's most remarkable archaeological sites – a place that gives up secrets, year after year, enriching our knowledge of prehistory.

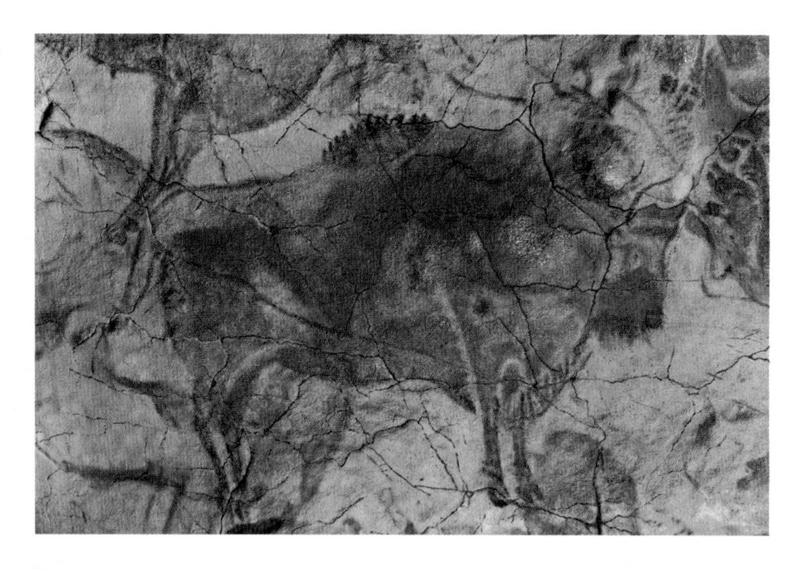

↑ The cave paintings of Altamira and the fossils of Atapuerca help illuminate the prehistory of Spain and how Iberia became a European refuge during the Ice Age.

For this is where some of the 'earliest and most abundant evidence of humankind in Europe' has been found, according to UNESCO, along with artefacts that rewrite history.

The site's discovery was unwittingly caused by British businessman Richard Preece Williams, founder of the soon-to-fail Sierra Company Limited, who built a coal-carrying railway line through a deep cutting in the 1890s. The cutting sliced through sediment-filled caverns full of fossils and prehistoric remains. The railway line closed in 1920, by which time it was already attracting fossil-hunters, and the area had become famous for cave paintings and the teeth of ancient cave bears. In 1976 a fossil-hunting student found a 400,000-year-old human jawbone, and the true importance of the site began to be revealed. When hominin bones from 800,000 years ago appeared in the 1990s, they were hailed as the first evidence of a new 'missing link' species, the Homo antecessor (literally 'pioneer human'), and made the front cover of the scientific journal *Nature*. These hominins had remarkably similar facial features to Homo sapiens, though research now suggests they were a prior offshoot rather than a common link to the Neanderthals. The appearance of hominins here was pushed even further back in time when, in 2007, teeth and jaw fragments from 1.3 million years ago were found. At the time, they were the oldest hominin fossils to have been discovered in Europe.

A 13-metre-deep pit along the cutting – the Pit of Bones – contains not just animal remains but also the world's largest collection of ancient hominin fossils from around 430,000 years ago. These hominins butchered animals, and each other, with rudimentary tools, practising cannibalism. When a red-and-brown quartzite axe-head known as Excalibur was found buried amongst the bones of twenty-eight individuals from the Homo heidelbergensis line in 1998 it generated excitement and controversy in equal measure. If the axe-head had been placed there deliberately as a burial gift, then it was the first known instance of ancient 'humans' indulging in a symbolic or ceremonial activity. That makes it the first proof of the spark of creativity that defines our species, or so those who discovered Excalibur claimed.

In the fog of prehistory, it is easy to dream of origin stories. Excalibur is open to multiple interpretations (it may, after all, simply have slipped from a ham-fisted hominin's hand). Together with Homo antecessor, however, Atapuerca proves that Spain – which largely remained habitable during the ice ages (and became a refuge for groups from frozen-over parts of Europe, which helps explain Spain's broad genetic mix) – has a continuous hominin history stretching back over a million years.

As for how these people lived, well we have been given only brief glimpses of their habits – like the Atapuerca axe-head. Neanderthals and Homo sapiens mingled briefly. Stone Age people, with their rudimentary tools, came in waves, setting a pattern for the future by arriving from different directions and continents.

First, they brought the Aurignacian culture from continental Europe and the East, then the Solutrean cultures of North Africa and then Magdalenian culture, again from across the Pyrenees. Europe, in other words, met Africa in Iberia.

A tomb found recently in a field of olive trees at Castillejo del Bonete near Ciudad Real (in central Spain) contains the bones of a couple with startlingly different DNA – a man from the Russian steppe and his Iberian wife. They are evidence of a 500-year period in the Bronze Age, when a long, drawn-out 'invasion' (as settlers, immigrants or occupiers) by such men saw them somehow sideline autochthonous males, whose Y chromosomes were almost totally replaced.

In 1897, a hoe-wielding farm-boy found a life-size limestone bust of an elegant Bronze Age woman buried in a field near Elche, in eastern Spain, 10 kilometres inland from the Mediterranean Sea. Laden down with chunky jewellery and with two large, wheel-like coils covering her ears, the exotic lady with delicately sculpted lips was originally assumed to be a Moorish princess. She appears lost in thought, her fine features tensed into a reflection on the mysteries of life or, more probably, death (given that she doubles as a funeral urn).

The Lady of Elche, as she became known, spent the first weeks after the discovery casting her inquisitive gaze along a local street from the balcony of the landowner's townhouse. A few weeks later, however, she disappeared. A sharp-eyed French archaeologist spotted her while visiting to see Elche's medieval, chanted Mystery Play, which is still performed at the Basilica of Santa María every 14 and 15 August. The Frenchman immediately realized her unique value and persuaded the Louvre Museum in Paris to buy the bust at considerable expense.

The remarkable 56-centimetre-high Dama de Elche, once described as boasting 'the best lips in antiquity', now sits in Madrid's National Archaeology Museum, where researchers have scraped out fourth- or fifth-century BC funeral ash from a cavity in the back. The 65-kilo Lady is a cultural hybrid, who nominally belongs to one of the main Bronze Age cultures of Spain – the mostly coastal and Mediterranean Iberians. Their lands included Elche, while their origins in either Africa, Europe or further east in the Mediterranean basin remain unclear. They shared Iberia with Celts, whose culture and peoples had spread across the Pyrenees from further north in Europe to occupy the west and much of the *meseta*. Between them, in a large, curving stretch of land that stretched from the north of modern-day Madrid and swept east and south towards Elche, lay a third group of Celtic-style tribes, confusingly called the Celtiberians by the Greek geographer Strabo.

In simplistic terms, the Iberians were the cultural sophisticates of the coast, living in fortified towns or villages and exposed to the influences of the eastern Mediterranean and Africa. The Celts, meanwhile, battled the elements and hardship of the interior, grazing cattle and eventually adopting iron. They also prospered in the Atlantic north-west, with its plentiful rain and abundant seafood, from where, local Galician legend has it, they eventually conquered and settled Ireland in a single day.

The Lady of Elche shows how Spain's Mediterranean coast was already a cultural melting pot by around the fourth century BC. Her fibula broach is pure Iberian, while the long, dangling earrings belong to the already mixed culture of the Celtiberians. She appears to represent, however, a priestess serving a Spanish version of the goddess Tanit (from Carthage, in Africa). Some experts also detect Greek and Phoenician elements. The influences, then, of Africa, the Mediterranean and Europe all meet in this 65-kilo block of sculpted limestone – a potent symbol of Spain as a place of encounter.

Those encounters had begun to take a settled, physical presence as the great trading nations of the eastern Mediterranean – the Phoenicians and Greeks – pushed west looking for gold, metals and business. The sea-faring Phoenicians from the Asian coastline

of the Mediterranean arrived first, founding Western Europe's first proper city at Cádiz eleven centuries before Christ, on an easily defended island by the mouth of the River Guadalete. It was the final trading post in a chain that stretched along the shores of North Africa, around the Levant and on to Cyprus and Crete. This, once more, was mythical Hercules territory, close to both his pillars and the Gates to Hades (said to be located near the Río Tinto river in Huelva, whose orange and red, metallic waters were both a source of wonder and a sign of valuable metal deposits). The Phoenicians' original neighbours were a mysterious and heavily romanticized Spanish culture, the Tartessians, who mined gold and other metals. The Phoenicians spread along both the Atlantic and Mediterranean coasts as well as up the broad, fertile Guadalquivir valley to occupy parts of what are now the provinces of Seville, Cádiz and Huelva. They left behind tantalizing scraps of a written language, mainly in short inscriptions in Iron Age burial sites. Strabo identified their successor people, the Turdentians, as

> the wisest of the Iberians; and they make use of an alphabet, and possess records of their ancient history, poems, and laws written in verse that are six thousand years old, as they assert. The other Iberians also use an alphabet, though not letters of one and the same character, for their speech is not one and the same.

The most spectacular legacy of this apparently wealthy and sophisticated culture are the twenty-one gold pieces that make up the Carambolo Treasure from the seventh century BC, which includes bracelets, a necklace and studded plaques of gold. They were dug up by workmen at a pigeon-shooting club just outside

← The elegant Lady of Elche shows Carthaginian, Greek and Celtiberian elements, reflecting the mix of cultures that had already occurred when she was carved out of limestone in the fourth century BC.

Seville in 1958. Once again, the golden relics show cultures flowing into one another and mixing, since the precious metal is locally mined while the techniques are Phoenician (just as some written Tartessian characters resemble Phoenician writing).

The Phoenicians, indeed, spread their influence slowly through southern Spain and up the east coast, reaching as far as the Balearic island of Ibiza. The Greeks, meanwhile, arrived six centuries before Christ and set up a first trading post – a satellite of their Marseilles colony – at Emporion in Catalonia, 30 kilometres south of the French border. They then extended their network further south, establishing several outposts near the mouth of the Júcar river, just south of Valencia. To them there was no such thing as 'Spain' – or Hispania, as the Romans would call it – since they spoke of 'Iberia'.

Although the seaside ruins of Emporion can be visited today, one does not need ancient artefacts to appreciate the lasting impact that the Greeks and their Phoenician trading rivals had on Spain. Between them, they brought olive trees and commercial vines, plants that altered the agriculture and landscape of the peninsula, remaining with us today.

Five or six centuries before Christ, then, Iberians and Celts represented an intertwining of north and south, while sophisticated and adventurous trading peoples from both the southern European and North African cultures of the Mediterranean were established along Spain's coastline. The people of Iberia remained, however, a hotchpotch of tribes, settlements and cultures that overlapped and rubbed along, or not. The west, meanwhile, remained the outer limit of the known world, a watery grey horizon beyond which monsters and legends lay.

2
Elephants, Carthaginians and Romans

The thirty-eight war elephants who plodded north towards the eastern end of the Pyrenees in 218 BC were an unusual and awe-provoking sight. The lumbering grey animals accompanied troops led by an ambitious and talented Carthaginian general called Hannibal, who had spent much of his young life in Spain. Famously, they were heading for Rome, as the two great powers of the western Mediterranean clashed once more in the Second Punic War.

Mighty Carthage had been defeated in the First Punic War by an ambitious and expansive Roman republic twenty-three years earlier. Their long-running, epic power tussle pitched a European power against an African one, since Carthage was near modern-day Tunis and controlled much of the north coast of Africa, as well as former Phoenician outposts in Iberia like Cádiz, Málaga (Malaca) and Sexi, south of Granada.

In 236 BC, an enterprising Carthaginian general called Hamilcar, known also as 'Barca' (the 'Thunderbolt'), had crossed into Spain, determined to enlarge Carthage's threatened empire and exact revenge on Rome. The Roman historian Titus Livy claimed that Hamilcar's nine-year-old son, Hannibal, begged to be allowed to go with him. Another tale has his father holding the boy over the body of a victim being sacrificed to the gods and making him pledge that 'as soon as age will permit ... I will use fire and steel to arrest the destiny of Rome'. Hannibal nevertheless stayed in Carthage, while dreaming of Spain and joining his father.

Since the Carthaginian fleet had been destroyed in the First Punic War, Hamilcar made his army march along the coast towards the Pillars of Hercules. From there it was easy to ship his soldiers across the strait to Carthaginian-controlled Cádiz. He then set out to take control of the gold and silver mines of the Sierra Morena, overlooking the Guadalquivir valley, before fighting his way through southern and eastern Spain. When Hamilcar accidentally drowned, his famously beautiful son-in-law Hasdrubal the Fair took over and demanded that the nineteen-year-old Hannibal be sent to him. Hasdrubal extended the Carthaginian zone through clever deal-making with Iberian chiefs and founded the eastern port city of modern Cartagena (Qart Hadasht) before an Iberian prisoner murdered him in 221 BC and twenty-six-year-old Hannibal took over. The young general inspired the same devotion among the troops as his father, from whom he had inherited 'the same determined expression, the same piercing eyes, the same cast of features'.

Rome looked on nervously as the Carthaginians pushed north, turning the swathe of Spain that they controlled into their largest territory. If Hannibal reached the eastern Pyrenees, he would be as close to Rome as to Cádiz – though the lands of the Gauls lay between them. A frontier between the Carthaginian and Roman zones of influence and future conquest had been agreed in 226 BC, running along the River Ebro. The port of Saguntum, down the Mediterranean coast near modern-day Valencia, had been declared a free city, but soon begged for the protection of Rome. With Hannibal in charge, however, Rome began to wonder if agreements about frontiers and protected cities would be respected.

Hannibal was bloodthirsty and brilliant, rampaging across Spain and driving inland onto the *meseta* to defeat its tribes and dominate a region bigger than Carthage itself. In one famous battle, his men massacred an army of Carpetani – Celts from the central zone of Toledo and Madrid – whose soldiers were ambushed as they waded across the Tagus river. In the panic, said Livy, many 'were swept down the river, some were carried by cross currents to the other side where the enemy were, and were trampled to death by the elephants'.

When Hannibal sacked wealthy Saguntum in 219 (after the resolute defenders had landed a javelin in his thigh), he ordered the massacre of all its adult males. This victory against a city that had eventually sought the protection of Rome gave him control of the last unconquered lands south of the Ebro, making him lord of much of Spain. For good measure and to cement an alliance, he had already married an Iberian princess called Imilce, from the Oretania tribe of La Mancha. Just as the Phoenicians from the Asian 'Levantine' coastline of the Mediterranean had first introduced the sophisticated cultures of that region to continental Spain, so it was another non-European power, Carthage, that first consolidated rule over a great part of Spain. This also, however, broke the treaty with Rome, set the tectonic plates of Mediterranean power spinning, and sparked the seventeen-year Second Punic War.

Initial Roman attempts to provoke rebellion and resistance in Spain failed. The Iberian Volciani of modern-day Catalonia told Roman envoys that, after seeing what had happened to the people of Saguntum, they would be mad to oppose Hannibal. 'Look for allies where the fall of Saguntum has never been heard of,' they advised. 'The nations of Spain see in the ruins of Saguntum a sad and emphatic warning against putting any trust in alliances with Rome.'

Instead, Hannibal attacked. He set off across the Ebro and towards Gaul with his North African elephants (a now extinct subspecies that was about 3 metres tall to the shoulder). His army had honed its skills during twenty-three years of fighting in Spain, and many of its 52,000 soldiers were native Iberians or Spanish Celts (though 10,000 deserted or were sent home once they reached the Pyrenees). A further 15,000 Spanish soldiers equipped with small, round ox-hide buckler shields and including 870 'Balearic slingers', were dispatched to Africa to defend Carthage itself.

Rome expected to fight this war in Spain, but Hannibal's army surprised it by making an epic crossing of the Alps. He conquered much of Italy, accompanied by the handful of elephants who survived the Alpine passes, but never inflicted a definitive defeat on the Romans. Livy called this 'the most memorable war that has ever been waged', with Iberians recruited to fight on both sides. 'No states, no nations ever met in arms greater in strength or richer in resources,' he observed. 'And yet, great as was their strength, the hatred they felt towards each other was almost greater.'

Hannibal destroyed many Roman armies, but, ultimately, his adventure was a failure. Indeed, while he wandered Italy with his armies, the Romans went on the attack in Iberia – pushing the Carthaginians out by 206 BC. For the next nine centuries, Spain's history was dominated by its status as part of the Roman empire or as a place ruled over by the Romanized Visigothic regimes that followed.

Roman generals swept through Gaul in ten years and would take forty-five years to occupy much of Britain (recruiting Iberian troops to do so). They took 200 years, however, to take full control of Iberia. The barriers formed by powerful rivers like the Ebro and Duero and by long, high mountain chains played a major role once more. So did the numerous small tribes and groups that had to be co-opted or conquered, one by one. Some were notoriously obstinate. After a ferocious siege led by Scipio Africanus the Younger, the inhabitants of Numantia, a walled Celtiberian hill-town near Soria, central Spain, opted for mass suicide in 133 BC. The idea of 'Numantine resistance' – or fighting to the bitter end – has remained a Spanish concept ever since.

The Romans built 20,000 kilometres of straight (often paved) roads, magnificent infrastructure like the still-standing aqueduct at Segovia and the lighthouse at La Coruña and improved irrigation techniques. An efficient administration divided the peninsula that they called 'Hispania' into two provinces and then, gradually, into nine. Yet the network of Roman roads was far less dense than in, say, Britain, Gaul, Asia Minor or North Africa – another sign of Spain's impenetrable geography.

Looking across the Mediterranean towards Rome, Tarragona was initially the provincial capital of Hispania Citerior, or 'Hither Spain', governing the north and east, while Hispania Ulterior, or 'Thither Spain', covered the south and west. Tarragona became the wealthiest city of the eastern coast, thanks in part to its wines. More importantly, the Romans placed Iberia within a network of commercial relationships across the empire. This reached its maximum splendour under a Spanish-Roman – the emperor Trajan – in 117, by which time the Mediterranean was a Roman lake, providing vast trading opportunities. Trajan was not the only Spanish emperor, since both his cousin (and successor) Hadrian and the late fourth-century emperor Theodosius the Great also hailed from Iberia. The largely peaceful, twenty-one-year-long reign of 'benevolent dictator' Hadrian, which ended in 138, was described by historian Edward Gibbon as overseeing the 'happiest era in human history'. In Spain, the cultured emperor completely remodelled his birthplace of Itálica, outside Seville, and restored the temple to Augustus in Tarragona. In England, he famously built a 118-kilometre defensive wall from sea to sea in the north to keep out Picts. Theodosius, meanwhile, definitively split the empire into two by making the sons he had with his Hispano-Roman wife, Aella Flavia – Arcadius and Honorius – his heirs. Honorius thus inherited the western empire on his father's death in 395, while Arcadius (who had also been born in Spain) ruled over the eastern empire.

→ Romans tried to tame the natural ruggedness of Spain with roads and engineering feats like the aqueduct at Segovia, though progress was slow.

HORNO DE ASAR

A major road, the 1,500-kilometre Via Augusta, followed the path of what had once been known as the Herculean Road. It ran from Cádiz – where Julius Caesar wept when he visited the temple built at Hercules' supposed burial site – up the Guadalquivir valley, then over into the Júcar valley and north along the Mediterranean coast to Gaul and, ultimately, Rome.

By the third century, the Romans had also introduced Christianity. The new cult probably first arrived with legionnaires at their retirement colonies in the south, or as they travelled back from wars in the province of Mauretania (the northern, Mediterranean stretch of today's Maghreb countries where the Mauri, or Moors, came from). In Spain it would become a weapon in future wars of identity.

Occasional local uprisings did little to spoil three centuries of relative calm in which some Iberians, especially those living along the Mediterranean and in major river basins like the Guadalquivir, became thoroughly Romanized. Along the coastlines and up the valleys, as the presence of so many Hispano-Roman emperors suggests, this was a question of local people adopting a Roman identity rather than an invasion of settlers or conquerors. Interior Spain proved far more difficult, and many, especially in the north-west, were only skin-deep Romans. All, however, benefitted from imperial stability.

During the third and fourth centuries, as Rome itself struggled, elites abandoned cities for their rural estates. Wealth and security were now best maintained in the countryside. As the western empire fell further into decline in the fifth century, German barbarians – Vandals, Suebians and others – either invaded or were invited in to help the Romans control Iberia. The Suebians were among the first to form a break-off kingdom, ruling over Galicia and parts of modern-day Portugal from 410 until 584. Eventually the Romans called in the Visigoths – before collapsing and being replaced by the mid-470s across the rest of Iberia by their newest mercenaries. This was not as traumatic as it sounds.

The Visigoths were already Romanized themselves and were few in number. In the early days they were simply an armed elite that ran what historian Richard Fletcher called 'Roman Spain under changed management'. They became Christians, spoke Latin, administered the country like Romans and admired their cultural legacy. The sophisticated but increasingly lawless cities, however, continued to lose power to the great landed estates that were owned by Hispano-Gothic magnates with personal armies that monarchs came to rely on. Estates and cities, meanwhile, both lost access to their lucrative export markets in the former Roman empire. As central control weakened, and crime spread, free men increasingly sought the protection of these mighty lords. Faction-fighting broke out, allowing Byzantines serving the successful Emperor Justinian to make coastal land grabs in order to add to their Constantinople-based empire. They occupied a 500-kilometre strip in the south that ran from Cartagena to Medina Sidonia, near Cádiz, and was known as the Byzantine empire's 'Spanish province'.

A vigorous Visigothic king called Leogovild quelled most opposition, with his son Suinthila finishing the task of uniting Iberia in 624. By now, the old Roman city of Toledo, perched on a rocky loop above the River Tagus, had become the political and religious capital.

One major sticking point remained. The Visigothic magnates, and King Leogovild himself, were Arian Christians – who saw Christ as subordinate to God the Father – while the Hispano-Romans were obdurate trinitarian Catholics. In the ensuing stand-off, it was the Visigoths who gave in. Leogovild's son and heir, Reccared I, converted, and declared the kingdom to be Catholic in 589. There was initial grumbling and some bloodshed, but the issue was now settled.

A period of Visigothic splendour began. Ambitious law codes were written, intellectuals thrived, and the Visigoths intermarried with the Hispano-Romans, creating, at least amongst elites, a comfortably mixed society. The Visigoths became major contributors to the intellectual life of Latin Christendom. In part, this was because bishops were powerful figures, with lands, wealth and patronage of their own, but also because they remained in contact with the lively culture of Byzantium. There was also, however, an important Hispano-Roman tradition to build on (both the poet Martial and the mordant philosopher Seneca the Elder had been from Spain).

One remarkable man stands out. Saint Isidore of Seville came from one of the old Hispano-Roman elite families who thrived under the Visigoths. He was a churchman, politician, theologian, cornerstone of the early medieval church and incorrigible collector of wisdom. Isidore's achievements are so vast that, were his work not still available, it might be thought the stuff of legend.

Isidore came from a powerful Christian family, and his three siblings also became saints. His elder brother Leander helped convert Reccared to Catholicism and was his predecessor as Bishop of Seville, which is why they both now feature on the badges worn by Seville Football Club players. A second brother, Fulgentius, served as a bishop under the same king. Perhaps, however, none of the three brothers were quite as powerful as their sister, Florentina, who oversaw most of Spain's convents.

We know almost exactly the fullest extent of Visigothic knowledge – and so how the most educated people in seventh-century Spain viewed the world – because Isidore wrote it all down. His twenty-volume encyclopaedia, the *Etymologiae* or *Origins*, became medieval Europe's most popular textbook. Written over twenty-five years, it represents the limits of knowledge in the 'dark' early Middle Ages of Europe, since it distils everything from the surviving classical tomes of the period – including Aristotle – to the rules of punctuation.

This unique (for the time) compendium of knowledge covered astronomy, geography, history, theology, moral philosophy, arithmetic, literature, grammar, geometry, architecture, animals, plants, rocks and much more. It was so extensive, indeed, that some consider Isidore to be the internet's unofficial patron saint. The impact of this work was both brilliantly illuminating and destructive. Irish monks, who began reading it soon after his death at the age of eighty in 636, called it the 'Culmen' – or the culmination of all knowledge. Unfortunately, some of the original classical tomes it was based on were lost precisely because people stopped reading them once Isidore's extended 'crib sheet', with its potted versions, had been produced. Reading Isidore was much easier, and quicker, than struggling with the original. Quite remarkably, the *Origins* became a bestseller more than eight centuries later, following the invention of the printing press, with ten editions published between 1470 and 1530. Few authors in history have had such an impact.

Isidore is also one of the first Spaniards to write specifically about 'Spain' or – at least – Hispania. He includes an elegy to the mother country in his *History of the Goths, Vandals and Suebians* (yet another marathon project), praising Spain as 'the most beautiful land to the west of India'. Hispania, he says, is 'the ornament of the world ... rich in fruits, with copious grapes and joyous harvests'. Its climate, landscape and agriculture, were such that 'a long time ago, Golden Rome – that leader of peoples – desired you ... until the flourishing nation of the Goths, after numerous victories around the world, conquered and loved you and to this day keeps and enjoys you in the security of its royal rule'.

Isidore is praised as 'the last scholar of the ancient world', though it might be better to think of him as a walking library of ancient thought. His impact is felt even today, since he is also credited with inventing key punctuation marks – including the full stop, comma and colon. 'An utterance whose sense and grammar were complete would receive a dot at the top of the line, which would eventually migrate down to the bottom and become the full stop or period we know today,' scholar Florence Hazrat explains.

> An utterance whose sense and grammar were complete but accommodated expansion would get a dot in the centre: the future colon. Lastly, an utterance that was neither complete in sense nor in grammar would be marked off with a dot at the bottom, evolving into the comma ... Isidore's ideas circulated widely and, by the end of the same century, Irish monks had added spaces between words to his system of dots.

With the religious conformity brought by Isidore and others came a desire for purity. Jews had been a discrete but growing presence in Spain for at least five centuries and were its first monotheists. Isidore was amongst the first Spaniards to write down a challenge to what he considered the disingenuous nature of their faith, in *De fide catholica contra Judaeos*. More darkly, he was also part of a decision to ban them (and their Christian descendants, if these converted) from holding public office and to remove children from any 'false' converts who were really Crypto-Jews.

By the end of the seventh century, indeed, Jews had become a target – as they were around much of Christendom. Further laws were passed against them, including an obligation to convert, and orders were issued that deprived them of property or turned them into slaves. These draconian rules were carried out only partially, if at all. The future, nevertheless, looked grim for Spain's Jews, until, that is, Muslims saved them from Christian persecution.

3
Unlocking the Door – Al-Andalus

When the newly ascendent Visigothic king Rodrigo came to the ancient tower in Toledo in 710, he found twenty-seven padlocks on the door. Centuries earlier a monarch had locked a terrifying secret behind the door. Each consecutive monarch had obeyed his instructions to reinforce it with another padlock. Rather than add another one, as he was meant to, Rodrigo's curiosity got the better of him. What was inside the tower (or the 'House of Hercules', as some called it, assuming that the demi-god had been their first monarch)? Rodrigo tore open the padlocks and walked in. We can imagine a creaky, ancient door pushed open and throwing light into a previously darkened chamber. Paintings on the walls revealed scimitar-wielding Arab horsemen. A scroll tucked inside an urn on the table bears the words: 'Whenever this chamber is violated, and the spell contained in this urn is broken, the people painted on these walls will invade Spain, overthrow its kinds, and subdue the entire land.' Which is exactly what happened.

This, of course, is legend. It is also, however, an historical fact that Rodrigo (or 'Roderic') was the king who lost Iberia to the Muslims – since this was conquered outright by invaders from North Africa in the three years after 711. Perplexed Christians sought an explanation. Only God's wrath provoked by their sins or Rodrigo's excessive nosiness (or both) could provide that – unless they wanted to admit that they had been overrun by a better-organized, more militarily potent culture.

For the next three centuries most of Spain was ruled by Muslims, and a majority of Iberians eventually embraced Islam. In understanding the Moors, indeed, it is crucial to remember that they were mostly not of foreign blood. Just as the Hispano-Romans were ethnically more Hispanic than Roman, so the story of assimilation continued. That is why such a surprisingly modest amount of North Africa's genetic code is shared by modern-day Spaniards (one out of twenty Spaniards shares the E1b1b1b sub-haplogroup of most Berber Moroccans). More importantly, it also helps explain why Muslim kingdoms were so successful, occupying at least part of the country for the next eight centuries, while a clandestine Muslim population – the Moriscos – remained a significant presence until they were expelled in 1609.

It is remarkable to recall that, when a general called Tariq crossed the Strait of Gibraltar in 711, Islam itself was only eighty-nine years old. It had spread out from the Arabian Peninsula, racing along the northern coast of Africa and reaching deep into the Berber lands of what is now Morocco. Rarely has a new religion been so instantly successful.

Islam's rapid success in Spain is part of that wider story. The Spanish experience of Muslim expansion followed the pattern of what had happened in Morocco. In simple terms, Arabs ruled, while Berbers (whose name derived from the Latin for Barbarian) followed. By Arab standards, the Berbers were relatively uncultured, but they were formidable fighters. By 711, the Arab governor of North Africa for the Damascus-based Umayyad caliphate, Musa ben Nusayr (a seventy-year-old veteran general from the Yemen) had been sending raiding parties across the neck of the Mediterranean for several years. That year, however, his general Tariq led a much larger Berber army that landed near Gibraltar (originally named Jabal Tariq, or 'Tariq's mountain'). The following year he defeated and killed Rodrigo at a battle near Jerez, where the Visigothic king was supposedly betrayed by his own people.

Tariq struck north and east, sacking the capital, Toledo, and provoking such terror that wealthy families barely had time to bury their jewels before fleeing. Visigothic Spain, which had already fallen into civil war, was soon part of history. Musa became Iberia's first Muslim governor, and within five years new bilingual coins were being minted, with their Latin face identifying them as being from 'Hispania', while the Arab face called this 'Al-Andalus'. Rodrigo's image, meanwhile, was added to a fresco on a wall in the desert castle of Qusayr Amra, in what is now Jordan, that depicted half a dozen kings defeated by the caliph of Damascus.

In August 1858, a young girl called Escolástica Morales squatted behind some stones in a field 15 kilometres from Toledo. It had been raining hard, and the dry summer topsoil around what was then known as the Guarrazar spring had been washed away. As Escolástica crouched, she saw something glittering in the mud. The girl and her parents dug around and began to find jewels – sapphires, emeralds and pearls – along with bits of worked gold. They had discovered Visigothic Spain's most spectacular treasure trove – a collection of twenty votive crowns gifted by King Recceswinth and others to a basilica built on the spot in the seventh century. These had been buried in two large boxes, apparently to prevent them falling into Muslim hands.

The Morales family and others returned secretly over several days and nights, dropping jewels and bits of worked gold as they stumbled around in the dark and washed their loot in the spring. The haul included 243 sapphires from Sri Lanka, as well as a startling array of emeralds and pearls. The treasure was broken up, and parts of it carried off to France, but fortunately the most breathtaking pieces are now in Madrid's National Archaeology Museum, including a jewel-encrusted gold crown bearing, in hanging letters, the words '[R]ECCESVINTHVS REX OFFERE' – 'King Recceswinth presented this offering'.

The Moors had conquered Iberia and were besieging the French city of Toulouse by 720, just nine years after their arrival. It had taken the Romans two centuries to do this, but they had also constructed a well-articulated territory that was now far easier to occupy. There were roads to march along (the invaders called the Via Augusta 'al-Racif', or 'the paved way') and administrative networks passed on to the Visigoths by the Romans that were simple to deal with. The weaknesses that had emerged before they arrived, as power fractured in favour of landed magnates, also helped. These could make local deals that guaranteed lives, livelihoods, personal wealth and religious freedom in return for acknowledgement of Muslim rule.

Contrary to the popular idea of a hardcore of Celts, Iberians or Goths holding out in the north, the Moors reached and subdued at least part of the coast along the Cantabrian Sea. A Moorish governor called Munuza, indeed, installed himself in what is now the port city of Gijón, in Asturias. He likely received tribute payments from the locals until an Asturian leader called Pelagius (or Pelayo) rose up – possibly because he was being pressed too hard for money, or because Munuza had fallen for his sister and taken her off to Córdoba. 'This Pelayo was the first to rebel against them in Asturias,' according to the Albeldense Chronicle, written in Latin 140 years later. In 722, he lured a Muslim force sent to quash his rebellion into the treacherous, unfamiliar terrain of the Picos de Europa mountains and destroyed it somewhere near Covadonga. The sources are unreliable, but there is no doubt that a small Christian stronghold had emerged. It would, in time, become a serious problem for the new rulers of Iberia.

Pigs, church bells and images of saints may have seemed crude

→ The gold votive crown of seventh-century King Recceswinth is one of the finest examples of Visigoth art in Spain. The pearls, emeralds and sapphires came from as far away as Sri Lanka.

and offensive to the invaders, but non-Muslims were useful. They paid taxes, for one thing. Also, there were an estimated 4 million of them – far too many to expel and replace. Up to 200,000 Berbers, nevertheless, settled in a land that was geographically easy for them to adapt to; the soil promised good rewards, soldiers were constantly in demand, and relatives were a short distance away across the Strait of Gibraltar.

The Christians, soon known as *mozárabes*, remained a majority for about two and half centuries. As People of the Book (or fellow followers of faiths with monotheistic scriptures), both they and the Jews were allowed to continue practising their religions. *Mozárabe* derives from the Arabic for 'Arabized' and this eventually became the common language of much of Iberia, shared with Christians and Jews. A speculative historical estimate devised by historian Richard Bulliet assumes that the territory was half Muslim by 1000 and that 80 per cent of its people followed Islam by 1100. Christians avoided angering their Muslim masters, though a rare outbreak of apocalyptic defiance saw a small group deliberately challenge the boundaries of religious tolerance in ninth-century Córdoba in order to seek (and find) martyrdom. The first of them, known only as Isaac, provocatively tried to convert a Muslim religious judge, or *qadi*, and was hung by his feet.

What had once been a far-flung corner of the Roman empire initially became an even further-flung corner of an empire whose capital sat 2,400 miles away in Damascus, Syria – the seat of the Umayyad caliphs. When they were ousted by the Abbasids in a bloody revolt in 750 and the capital moved to Baghdad, the shockwaves travelled as far as Al-Andalus. Berber revolts against the Arab elites had already broken out, throwing Al-Andalus into prolonged turmoil. Now a young member of the Umayyad family called Abd al-Rahman, fleeing the bloodletting in Damascus, arrived and gradually imposed himself. In a process that took decades, his family became the emirs of Al-Andalus.

The Christian rebels of the north-west (in modern-day Asturias and Galicia), meanwhile, took advantage of an extended period of Muslim infighting to expand their area of control and to create a large, depopulated frontier zone. From now on there would be three bands of territory, of fluctuating size, in Iberia, with Muslims in the south, the half-empty frontier lands in the middle and Christians initially occupying a narrow strip to the north, but gradually pushing the boundary south to the River Duero (which runs into the Atlantic at Oporto, in Portugal) by 900.

The Umayyad era started a period of cultural glory which contrasted with Western Europe's status as an ignorant backwater of the Eurasian land mass. The emirs cultivated an image of distant, frightening but sophisticated rulers – surrounded by bureaucrats and protected by foreign mercenaries. The regime's new splendour was most visible in and around their capital at Córdoba. In 784, Abd al-Rahman I began construction of the vast mosque which still dominates the city's old quarter today. Successors increased it in size over the next 200 years until it became the second-largest mosque in the world. The original Muslim splendour continues to outshine the trappings of a Christian cathedral clumsily inserted between the hundreds of two-tone horseshoe arches perched on 856 columns sculpted from jade, marble and granite.

Unfortunately, much less remains of the even more impressive Madinat az-Zahra, or Resplendent City, begun by the blue-eyed Abd al-Rahman III in 936. He had declared himself caliph rather than emir, implying direct lineage from the Prophet Muhammad – though his mother and paternal grandmother were both Christians. The rival al-Madina al-Zahira, or Radiant City, was built nearby

→ The vast mosque at Córdoba reflects the glorious rise of Muslim Spain after Berber invaders crossed the Mediterranean to conquer Iberia in 711. They stayed for eight centuries.

on the opposite side of Córdoba five decades later by the powerful vizier and de facto strongman Ya'qub al-Mansur, known as Almanzor. The latter's regular raids into Christian territory over more than two decades were ruthlessly successful, bringing booty, slaves and prestige. The highest peak of the soaring Gredos range in central Spain still bears this Cordobese warrior's name. Relentless raiding saw Barcelona, Pamplona and Coimbra (in Portugal) sacked and the bells from the cathedral at Santiago de Compostela, in Galicia, transported to Córdoba, where they became glorified candleholders with torches planted inside them.

The new caliphate brought stronger rule, greater wealth and a golden age of culture and tolerance. Its capital, Córdoba, was by now Western Europe's largest city with a population of 100,000 people. Some 3,750 of these were enslaved people (often Europeans) at the caliph's court, where visitors were dazzled by a bowl of mercury that was rocked gently in order to send the sun's rays spinning around the throne room. Although Roman in origin, Córdoba was like a great and sophisticated Arab city that had been transplanted onto European soil – with hundreds of mosques, some eighty schools, paved streets, public fountains and sewers.

The greatest measure of Córdoba's cultural standing was the vast library built up by the second caliph, al-Hakem II, with the help of his (and his father's) Jewish financier Hasdai ibn Shaprut and a famously intellectual woman secretary and poet called Lubna. The twelfth-century Cordobese chronicler Ibn Bashkuwal described Lubna like this: 'She excelled in writing, grammar and poetry. Her knowledge of mathematics was also immense and she was proficient in other sciences as well. There were none in the Umayyad palace as noble as her.' Lubna is credited with travelling the world, seeking out rare manuscripts. If that is true, the results of her work (and of many other buyers, some possibly also women) were remarkable. The library's catalogue alone ran to more than 2,200 folios, divided into forty-four volumes. Other wealthy families vied to build libraries to impress their intellectual caliph, turning the city into a glittering centre of knowledge.

The idea that a woman could be behind one of the great cultural achievements of Al-Andalus is not entirely surprising. Al-Maqqari, writing in the seventeenth century, when Al-Andalus was already a lost paradise to Muslims, declared that 'the literary mastery of Al-Andalus was such that it was almost an instinct, which even women and children shared'. His list of poetesses included the ninth-century slaves Mut'a and Qamar who were known as *qiyan*, a slave category for women who were half-entertainers, half-courtesans. Lubna and a contemporary poetess belonging to Almanzor, known as Uns Al-Qulub, were almost certainly also slaves. Poetic ability, indeed, added to their value, with a Muslim king of Almería sending a blind envoy to weigh up the merits of the slave-poetess Gayat al-Muna. The philosopher Muhammad al-Kattani even set up a chain of *qiyan* schools, training slave-women in music and poetry and then selling them on at much improved prices. Poetesses were not uncommon in the Arab world but were a rarity in Europe, and the result, according to scholar Teresa Garulo, was that Al-Andalus generated 'quite possibly the most extensive production of female poetry in western Europe'. Their work was, to other Arab-speakers, often distinctively Andalusian, and they even dared write of love – that dangerous realm of human desire – drawing criticism from prudish eastern visitors.

The list of achievements is endless, since Al-Andalus briefly became – in the only slightly exaggerated words of one historian – 'a superpower'. The hill-top castle at Gormaz (near Soria) was Western Europe's biggest. A 'green revolution' that swept Muslim lands and transformed agricultural practices saw oranges, lemons, watermelon, pomegranates, spinach, artichoke, rice and sorghum established as crops. Some of the irrigation systems built to support this agricultural revolution survive around Valencia and Granada.

They appear to copy those constructed around Damascus and have proved long-lived, with Valencia's Water Tribunal – founded by the first caliph – still meeting every week eleven centuries later to adjudicate on arguments. Around 5,000 water wheels were reportedly working in the Guadalquivir valley alone, raising water out of rivers into irrigation channels or towns (in the fifteenth-century Queen Isabella insisted Córdoba's main wheel be stopped at night, since its squeaking kept her awake).

By the turn of the millennium, Islamic Spain had outstripped the rest of Europe in almost all aspects. 'For nearly a century Al-Andalus had been the richest, the best-governed, the most powerful, the most renowned state in the western world,' according to Richard Fletcher. Suddenly, however, it was not. Decline was dramatic and sudden. Al-Madina al-Zahira and Madinat az-Zahra – monuments that would rival the Alhambra in Granada were they still standing today – were ransacked or reduced to rubble over the twenty-three years between 1008 and 1031. That is how long it took for the caliphate to fall apart, as rivals battled for power – littering Córdoba's streets with the corpses of dozens of great scholars when Berbers rampaged through it in 1013. These magnificent cities existed for less than a century. Many of their best features were looted and carted off to new buildings in Granada or Seville.

As had happened under the Romans and Visigoths, Iberia fragmented as soon as strong central control began to fail. In this case, it split into some thirty *taifas* – statelets led by factions, or parties, whose leaders became known (for various reasons), as the 'party kings'. They are best known for two things: first, the endless warring between them; and second, the sensuous poetry with which they celebrated wine, sex and song. One of the most famous poems recalls youthful night-time trysts beside a river.

> She would pour out wine for me in her bewitching glances
> And in the cup at times, at times in her kisses

The tunes of her lute thrilled me, as if
I heard in those chords the clash of sword-blades.
Then she let her robe fall, her splendid form seeming
To be a bud unfolding from a cluster of blossoms.

One *taifa* ruler summed up his lifestyle like this: 'At night I indulge in amusements and frolics / At noon I rule with a proud mien in my court.'

As they squabbled and became easy prey for the Christian kingdoms to their north, some *taifa* rulers looked to North Africa for help. Indeed, just as Christians viewed the *Reconquista* as a crusade, so Muslims found religious justification for going to defend Al-Andalus – a place sometimes referred to as Dar Djihad, the land of Jihad.

A pattern began to establish itself as those invited to defend Muslim Spain from Christian encroachment then took it over. The first great shock came after the former Visigothic capital of Toledo was lost by the Muslims for ever in 1085. A group of strict Berber warriors, the Almoravids, were called in, crossing the Mediterranean in 1086. 'I would rather die a camel-driver in Africa, than a swineherd in Castile,' Seville's powerful *taifa* ruler, the talented poet-emir Al Mutamid ibn Abbad (who had taken control of Córdoba as well), proclaimed when the decision was taken. He came to regret that. Within a few years, the Almoravids had taken his lands and banished him to captivity, and death, in Morocco. The charms of Al-Andalus, however, appear to have turned the fearsome Almoravids soft. They were ousted in 1173 by a second wave of Berber arrivals, the Almohads, another strict religious group who had grabbed power in Morocco and moved the capital to Seville. These Berbers were poorly connected to the distant intellectual and cultural heartlands of Islam and were more intolerant than their predecessors. The Almohads' purist founder, Ibn Tumart, had urged his supporters in Morocco to eradicate the Almoravids and their comparatively tepid version of Islam. 'Kill them wherever you may find them ... those who refuse to return to the fold will be your enemies until death.' As a result, the glory of Al-Andalus waned. It was soon too late, in any case, to rebuild what once existed. As Muslim Spain fell apart, Christian Spain found fresh opportunities to continue its long-drawn-out assault on Al-Andalus – the Reconquest.

4
Reconquista – Three Spains

On 23 May 844, an armoured, cape-wearing knight on a brilliant white horse rode onto a battlefield known as the Field of Slaughter, just to the south of the River Ebro near Clavijo, in the La Rioja region of northern Spain. On his cape, the knight wore a red cross with a sharpened end that turned it into a sword. This was really one of the apostles, Saint James, returned from the dead to lead the Christian army (which had refused to pay a tribute of 100 virgins to Muslim raiders) to victory. Saint, battle and alleged tribute are all mythical, but Spaniards believed this story for centuries, which is why St James is known as Santiago Matamoros, 'James the Moor-Slayer'. It is also why he is Spain's patron saint.

Statues and paintings of the saint delivering a mortal sword blow as his horse rears over a prostrate Muslim warrior can be found in churches along the ancient and hallowed pilgrimage route to Santiago de Compostela in Galicia. That is where St James's body miraculously appeared eight centuries after he had died in the Holy Land. It supposedly floated into an Atlantic *ría*, or fjord, on a stone raft and was dragged ashore by oxen. An alternative theory sees the site where his tomb was allegedly found as the grave of a charismatic, mystical fourth-century Galician bishop called Priscillian, who was executed for heresy. Under torture during his trial in Trier, Germany, Priscillian had allegedly admitted to encouraging nudity at his outdoor, night-time meetings.

His head was chopped off, making him the first Christian heretic ever to be executed, and his remains shipped home to Galicia.

The legend of Santiago the Moorslayer captures an essential truth about the Spain that emerged as Al-Andalus went into decline: its identity was shaped by conquest, expansion and opposition to Islam. Of the three, the latter proved the most potent and long-lasting. One of the small Christian kingdoms to emerge at this time, Castile, gained its name from the castles, or *castillos*, planted on hilltops as it expanded southwards.

The term *Reconquista* is contentious, since it gives the idea of a continuous crusade rather than a spaced-out, on-off series of land grabs by competing Christian kings and nobles over eight centuries, in which people of both faiths occasionally switched sides. The heroic El Cid, protagonist of a famous twelfth-century epic poem (and of a 1961 Hollywood blockbuster starring Charlton Heston as Rodrigo Díaz, whose nickname 'El Cid' comes from the Arabic for 'the master') is the best example of a sword-for-hire. He fought on both sides before establishing his own mini-statelet based on Muslim Valencia.

Whatever the mix of motives, the facts are clear. Al-Andalus shrank as it was harassed by a set of Christian kingdoms. The term *Reconquista* ('re'-conquering rather than conquering) allowed later generations to unify a hotchpotch of events that happened over eight centuries. It is also a reminder, however, that the Christian kingdoms always had a 'natural' enemy and an area of potential expansion in which warfare could be justified as crusade.

So who were these 'crusaders' who took 781 years (at least thirty generations, advancing at an average of one kilometre a year) to complete this *Reconquista*? The two unifying factors are that they were people of the north, and mostly – but not entirely – Christian. Beyond that, it is difficult to find unity. The first we hear of them is in 718 (or, perhaps, 722 – the exact date is not clear), when Pelayo won his first victory at Covadonga, allegedly with help from the

↑ The Christian *Reconquista* advanced at an average of one kilometre a year over eight centuries as Christian and Muslim Spaniards (illustrated here at Belmez, Andalucia, in the Cantigas de Santa Maria manuscript of Alfonso X) vied for control of Iberia's many kingdoms.

Virgin Mary – a statue of whom would be found in a nearby cave. The battle became fetishized as the founding event of 'reconquered' Spain, and generations of Spanish girls have since been baptized with the name Covadonga. Historians disagree. 'Spain wasn't born in 722,' observed Juan Pablo Fusi. In fact, he points out, the term '*español*' – or 'Spaniard' – only really began to be used towards the end of the eleventh century.

Given the size and power of Al-Andalus up to then, this is hardly surprising. The disjointed nature of the *Reconquista* reflects the fact that Christian Spain was itself divided, as statelets formed in the north and fused, morphed or spawned new entities on their borders. Romanization had not wiped out the different ethnic groupings of northern Spain, whose lives were relatively untouched by the sophisticated and culturally porous Mediterranean. In the far north-west were Asturians and Galicians. At the western fringe of the Pyrenees there were Basques, and to their east – in the Spanish Marches that marked the border between Charlemagne's territories in France and the Muslim invaders in the eighth and ninth centuries – were the Occitans and Catalans. The latter pushed south to Barcelona early in the ninth century, where powerful counts ruled for several centuries.

The small Asturian entity that spread west and south eventually morphed into the Kingdom of León. It came to occupy a large and densely populated area bordered by the River Duero to the south. By 910, the capital was León itself, and attempts were being made to follow Visigothic law while Mozarabic Christians from Al-Andalus were invited to migrate north. The latter brought with them a new hybrid style of 'repopulation' architecture which produced Arab-inspired horseshoe arches and doorways in ninth- to eleventh-century churches in the Duero basin.

To begin with, the priorities on this frontier were mostly defensive. Al-Andalus was rich, powerful and given to constant, successful raiding. Its estimated population of 3 million at the turn of the millennium was six times larger than the Christian north. Just preparing defence against the regular assaults by the likes of Almanzor was a large enough task. Dynastic inheritance, marital alliance and war saw Christian kingdoms form and reform in different patterns before a gradual settling down. The kingdom of León eventually had three main Christian rivals along its frontiers: the kingdom of Pamplona (later Navarre), which stretched into (and often over) the Pyrenees; the kingdom of Portugal, to the south of the Duero; and the independent county of Castile, to its east. In the meantime, the Catalans pushed further south, while between them and Castile lay the landlocked kingdom of Aragón.

The glory years of the caliphate brought few opportunities for Christian expansion. In fact, it was the Muslims (by now a majority of the Iberian population) who gifted the key moment of the *Reconquista* to their northern enemies in the first half of the eleventh century when central control of the caliphate broke down. The subsequent infighting allowed for significant Christian land grabs, and border *taifa* states often sought alliances with the Christians as they fought one another.

By this time, Iberia's principal Christian kingdoms were consolidating. In the hundred years that followed from 1135, the four main players of the next few centuries took control of almost everything else. Portugal was constituted, and the kingdom of Pamplona became Navarre. The royal families of Aragón and Barcelona married, creating the ambitious Crown of Aragón. Castile and León, meanwhile, united with Galicia to create another formidable kingdom referred to simply as 'Castilla', or Castile.

A rare moment of cooperation on the battlefield at Las Navas de Tolosa in 1212 (known in Arab history as the Battle of Al-Uqab), showed that, if these kingdoms united, they could defeat even the warlike Almohads. Their great victory was part-financed by a loan from one the most prominent members of a flourishing community of Jews in Christian Spain, Joseph ben Salomon ibn Shoshan. In the following years, the frontier was rolled back as the different kingdoms pushed south. Valencia and the Balearic Islands were added to the Crown of Aragón by Jaime I, though they were deemed separate kingdoms, like the principality of Catalonia that emerged from the lands ruled over by the counts of Barcelona. Ferdinand III of Castile, meanwhile, took the once glorious city of Córdoba in 1236. The cathedral bells from Santiago were recovered and sent back to Galicia.

When Seville was also taken in 1248, Al-Andalus was reduced to the kingdom of Granada – and Christian Spain was now mostly divided between the two great powers of Castile and Aragón. The third major kingdom on the peninsula, Portugal, had split from Galicia in 1095 and also now completed its southern conquest (and settled its borders) by driving the Moors out of the Algarve in 1249. Granada was now treated as a vassal state and obliged to buy peace by paying tribute.

It is no coincidence that, at around the same time as Seville was captured, Spanish chroniclers – normally used to writing up the heroic deeds of individual monarchs – began to write histories of a place they called Spain, which they traced back to the Christian Visigoths. Rodrigo had thrown this away, they said, but it could now return to its previous glory.

That took a long time. This was partly because the conquered lands had to be digested and 're-Christianized' (though Muslims could stay and were known as *mudéjares* – the mirror image of the Mozarabic Christians to the south). The isolated old Christian communities that had survived centuries of Muslim rule were out of touch with the rest of the Catholic world, which had mostly adopted the Roman rite. A papal dispensation allowed them to maintain their peculiar liturgy, the Hispano-Mozarabic rite, which is still used today by small groups based in Toledo. Conservatives, from Archbishop Francisco Jiménez de Cisneros in the sixteenth century to Pope John Paul II in the late twentieth century, have encouraged its continuation, since this boosts a narrative implying that Spain's Muslim period was a hiccup in its otherwise Christian history.

Enemies must, of course, be demonized, and the Spanish Muslims were painted as obsessive despoilers of Christian virgins. This did not stop Christian kings from appreciating the magnificence of what had fallen into their hands. Ferdinand III, for example, rebuilt the Alcázar palace complex in Seville using Muslim artisans to produce the greatest example of so-called *mudéjar* architecture in Spain, which blended Muslim and Gothic (and, later, Renaissance)

↑ Early *Reconquista* Christians adorned the Romanesque churches of the Pyrenees with precious murals like this seven-eyed Apocalyptic Lamb, painted around 1123 in Sant Climent church, Taüll, Catalonia.

styles. One of its most famous spaces, the Patio de Las Doncellas (The Courtyard of the Maidens), was named to relay the myth of an annual tribute of 100 Christian virgins demanded by Muslim rulers.

In Zaragoza, likewise, Aragonese monarchs treasured the eleventh-century Aljafería Palace, which is now home to the regional parliament of Aragón.

Most importantly of all, however, the always porous frontier across which Muslims and Christians had traded and raided for centuries allowed for the import of cultural riches. Toledo was awash with ancient manuscripts of the kind that had filled the magnificent libraries of Córdoba, many of which had been smuggled north before or after the city was twice sacked by Berbers in the four years after 1009. This was partly because Toledo had surrendered without a fight to Alfonso VI, King of León, Castile and Galicia in 1086, who declared himself 'the king of the two religions'. As a result, little was destroyed, Muslims could hold on to their property, and much of the Arab-speaking population – including Christians and Jews – stayed.

Toledo had been one of the most cultured *taifa* states. Even more learned, however, were the *taifa* rulers from Zaragoza. The last of them, Sayf al-Dawla, known as 'The Sword of the Dynasty' (or Zafadola to Spaniards), exchanged his remaining lands for property in or near Toledo when he surrendered to Alfonso VII in 1140. Like El Cid, he blurred the divide between religions by spending the rest of his life fighting for Alfonso and against other Muslims. More importantly, however, his library almost certainly travelled with him to Toledo. Obtaining fresh texts may have been relatively simple, too, since major Muslim cities like Marrakesh (capital of the Almoravid empire, which had included Al-Andalus) were much closer than, say, Paris or Genoa.

These manuscripts now helped a culturally backward Christian Europe recover lost classical texts and gain access to the thinking, science, medicine, astronomy and agriculture of more advanced eastern cultures. Arabic learning was often based on Greek texts that had disappeared from Western Europe or were only conserved in potted versions like those of Isidore of Seville. It was these texts and the improvements on them by Arabic, Persian and Indian scholars that learned Christians began to thirst for. A tradition of translating emerged, never centralized but later known as the 'School of Translators' of Toledo, in order to make all this knowledge available in Latin. The 'school' had two separate bursts of activity in the twelfth and thirteenth centuries. Often, it brought together teams of Arab-speaking Mozarabs or Jews with educated clerics who could write in Latin or Old Castilian.

Translators appeared from around Europe, drawn to the intellectual riches. At least four came from Britain. They included a Michael Scot (also a talented sorcerer, since science and sorcery went together, as did astronomy and astrology), Alfred the Englishman, John of Toledo and Daniel of Morley. The latter had abandoned the intellectual tedium of Paris on hearing 'that the doctrine of the Arabs ... was all the fashion in Toledo'.

The most famous translator was the Italian Gerard of Cremona, who had been seeking out mathematical and scientific works by Ptolemy and, according to his students, 'made his way to Toledo, where, seeing an abundance of books in Arabic on every subject and, pitying the poverty he had experienced among the Latins concerning these subjects, out of his desire to translate, he thoroughly learnt the Arabic language'. He was then able to pick his subjects 'in the manner of a prudent man who, walking through green meadows, weaves a crown from flowers – not from all of them, but from the more beautiful – he read through the writings of the Arabs, from which he did not cease until the end of his life to transmit to Latin, as if to a beloved heir, in as plain and intelligible way as was possible'. Gerard's translation of Galen's lost works on medicine and of further medical work by the great Arab polymath Avicenna were the most influential of his eighty-seven translations (confusingly, there may have been a later scholar who shared Gerard's name exactly, which might account for such abundance). Some were still being used to train doctors in the eighteenth century.

Among the previously undiscovered scholars whose translated works now sparked a Twelfth-Century Renaissance in Europe (laying the foundations of the later Italian and European Renaissances) were several from Al-Andalus. In fact, two of the greatest philosophers in Islam and Judaism, Averroes and Maimonides respectively, were born in Córdoba just a dozen years apart in the early twelfth century. Influenced by Aristotle, both struggled with the problem of integrating human intellect and experience with religious belief. How do faith and reason fit together? Averroes' answer was brilliantly simple – if God gave us intellect, then reason was a gift from him. Maimonides, who wrote in both Arabic and Hebrew, addressed the same question in his famous *Guide for the Perplexed*. His answer was more subtle, but also squared the circle by rejecting 'mystery, superstition, and any elements inconsistent with truths of reason', according to scholar Jonathon Jacobs.

Averroes, Maimonides and Gerard of Cremona were contemporaries, separated by just 140 miles of Spanish countryside. Since the translation phenomenon was already in full sway, it is perhaps natural that Averroes' own *Commentaries* on Aristotle were soon available in Latin. As a result, he had greater impact in the west than the east. In fact, both he and Maimonides (who fled Al-Andalus but continued to write in Arabic) lead inexorably to Thomas Aquinas – while Roger Bacon and Copernicus also owed part of their learning to the Toledo translations.

Jews played a key part in the translating process, not least because they were more likely to speak all the languages involved. They had not been welcome in Almohad-run Al-Andalus, and some of their elites moved north, sparking a Jewish golden age that had the cultural and economic powerhouse of Toledo as its principal city.

Although Spain's Jews sometimes claimed descent from the tribe of Judah expelled by Nebuchadnezzar six centuries before Christ, they did not in fact arrive in force until the first or second century AD, when Hispania was Roman. Intermarriage eventually made them ethnically indistinguishable from other Hispano-Romans. Initially, they had flourished, too, in Al-Andalus. The 2,500 inhabitants of Lucena (Eli hossana, אלי הושענא, in Hebrew) near Córdoba, were exclusively Jewish in the eleventh and twelfth centuries. In 2006, after mechanical diggers started work on a ring-road, bones appeared from the largest Jewish cemetery of that period found in Europe, with more than 346 graves.

The idea of an idyllic medieval Spain where the different religions always lived in perfect harmony, does not, however, survive close scrutiny. Occasional waves of religious fanaticism brought death, suffering or exile. In Islamic Spain, a first major pogrom claimed up to 4,000 lives in Granada in 1066 (including the Muslim king's Jewish vizier Joseph ibn Naghrela). Almost a century later, in 1148, Maimonides was amongst those to flee the fundamentalist Almohads. He found refuge in Almería, feigned conversion to Islam and ended up in more tolerant Cairo. His departure did not change a fact that Spaniards rarely dwell on: Iberia, and especially Christian Spain, was becoming the European capital of Judaism. By the end of the fourteenth century, indeed, Spain had the world's largest Jewish community. Numbers are hard to determine, but Castile may have had 250,000 Jews, or one for every fifteen Christians, while another 40,000 or so lived in Aragón. Seville was considered to have the world's largest Jewish quarter, with 35,000 people and twenty-three synagogues. They enjoyed the protection of Christian monarchs until, that is, a young couple called Isabella and Ferdinand revolutionized Spanish history by bringing together the crowns of Castile and Aragón at the end of the fifteenth century.

5
Isabella and Ferdinand

On 13 December 1474, a twenty-three-year-old woman with green-blue eyes and auburn hair processed along the chilly streets of Segovia, preceded by a red-faced aristocrat carrying an upside-down sword. The young woman was Isabella of Castile, half-sister to the recently deceased King Enrique IV, and the sword was a threat which symbolized her right to impart justice and use violence against her enemies. Isabella was claiming the crown in what was really a kind of coup.

The legitimate heiress was actually Isabella's twelve-year-old niece, Juana La Beltraneja – the deceased king's only child. Enrique had made this explicit, despite gossip about whether she was really his daughter or not. The deceased king had suffered a condition known as acromegaly, a late-developing form of gigantism that gave him outsized limbs and unusually thick facial features. It also provoked rumours that he was impotent. According to the visiting German doctor Hieronymus Münzer, Enrique and his wife Juana of Portugal made the Christian medieval world's first recorded attempt at artificial insemination, with the king masturbated by his doctors and his sperm delivered down a small gold tube into the queen's vagina. This did not work, and when the queen later became pregnant, gossips claimed the king's favourite, Beltrán de la Cueva, had been sent into her bed.

The relevance of this story does not reside in the truth or falsity of Enrique's inability to father children, but in Isabella's own determination to paint him, via her chroniclers, as impotent. This was done both to bolster her usurper's claim to the crown and as a metaphor for his style of rule – marked by a dislike of pomp as well as an appreciation of Jews and, especially, Muslims. Isabella did not intend to be like him.

Castile had no great tradition of queens regnant, and even those who backed her claim expected Isabella's husband Ferdinand – heir to the neighbouring, if lesser, lands of the Crown of Aragón – to rule. Part of the crowd looked on sullenly during her procession around Segovia, which took place while her husband (who had been visiting his father's kingdoms) was still away in Zaragoza. 'It seemed to them a terrible thing for a woman to show off the attributes that belong to her husband,' one of his chroniclers reported. Even Ferdinand was surprised. 'Tell me whether in the past there has been a precedent of a queen who has ordered that she be preceded by the symbol of punishment of their vassals,' he exclaimed. 'I do not know of any woman who has ever usurped this manly attribute.'

On 2 January 1475, Ferdinand finally reached Segovia, having confided that 'he was confident of overcoming the situation with patience and that he was sure of triumphing by assiduously satisfying the demands of conjugal love'. That love was marked by his wife's jealous passion (and Ferdinand's illegitimate children). His confidence was well placed. A deal was struck, which was flexible enough to save face, allowed for later adjustments and wrested power from the nobles who had chipped away at royal rule over the previous century. In fact, these two young monarchs formed a remarkable partnership that made Isabella the first great female monarch of Europe.

Isabella and Ferdinand were bullish, energetic and young. The headstrong couple had married against Enrique's wishes, ignoring a treaty that gave a veto to both him and Castile's most powerful Grandes, or grandees, as Spain's senior aristocrats were known.

↑ Isabella of Castile by John of Flanders, *c.*1500–1504. Europe's first great queen regnant turned Castile into the motor of Spain in the fifteenth century, and left it as master of history's first globe-spanning empire. She also set up the Inquisition, expelled the Jews and forced Muslims to convert.

↑ Ferdinand II of Aragón, king of Spain's other major kingdom, married Isabella of Castile in 1469 to create a unique partnership of equals as the first joint monarchs of (almost) all Spain. Portrait by Michiel Sittow.

They had hoped to marry her off to a distant prince, with candidates including the future Richard III of England and a half-blind, elderly French count deemed 'ugly by the extreme thinness of his legs'. Instead, seventeen-year-old Ferdinand sneaked into Castile for the wedding disguised as a page-boy. His wife was still just eighteen.

A successful power-sharing agreement, based on mutual trust, saw them dominate the next four decades of Spanish history. Previous monarchs had handed power to so-called *validos* or *privados* – nobles who ruled for them, gifting parcels of royal wealth to buy the loyalty of fellow aristocrats. As a result, great magnates with private armies could challenge or defy monarchs. Castile's kings were ceremonially austere with no great ritual coronations, baptisms or funerals (Enrique IV's corpse had been carted off on a wooden board).

Isabella and Ferdinand's rule would instead be dependent on the direct leadership of a couple who, by working together, doubled their executive capacity. They also led in person. One of their first measures was to call up the Santa Hermandad, a militia that usually provided troops in times of war, to act as an internal police force. It helped stamp out the banditry that had flourished under weaker monarchs, while also acting as a repressive force that brought royal power ever closer to people's daily lives.

When Ferdinand's eighty-year-old father, Juan the Great of Aragón, died in 1479, the couple (with Ferdinand now aged twenty-seven and Isabella twenty-eight) became the first joint rulers of something that, at least geographically, looks much like modern Spain. In fact, this was the temporary union of two monarchies – Castile and Aragón – through marriage. The internal laws and the monarchs' power-sharing arrangements differed from one kingdom to another. These remained separate entities. Muddling things further, the Crown of Aragón was itself a union of the four semi-autonomous kingdoms or principalities of Catalonia, Valencia, Majorca and landlocked Aragón itself. In the north, meanwhile, the independent state of Navarre remained a third force in Christian Spain. To the south, the Nasrid dynasty held on to Spain's last Muslim kingdom, based on Granada.

As a young woman deemed unlikely to govern, Isabella had not been prepared to rule, yet hers was the larger kingdom in this partnership. Castile's population of 4 million was several times greater than that of Aragón. The wool and wealth from its 5 million merino sheep made it 'the Australia of the Middle Ages' (as one historian says) and turned the *meseta* into a centre of power whose international fairs in towns like Medina del Campo attracted traders from across Europe. Indeed, in a turnaround from the past (and in contrast to the future), *meseta* cities were now richer and more sophisticated than those on the coasts or the valleys. The Crown of Aragón, meanwhile, had a glorious medieval history of empire and conquest in the Mediterranean, seizing territories in Italy and as far away as Athens. It was, however, perennially at war with France – which drained its resources – and often suffered internal rifts between the crown and its four component kingdoms. The royal family still held territory in Italy, and Ferdinand had been made king of Sicily when he was sixteen, though this was administered for him by others.

In a Castile that was used to obeying local magnates rather than monarchs, the young couple had to work hard to impose their personal authority. Isabella, for example, took herself to notoriously lawless Seville and meted out such harsh punishments that the Bishop of Cádiz pleaded with her to tone down the 'terror and horror' that was provoking such 'despair and sin'. She ignored him. Monarchs did not succeed by being nice. After the chaos caused by warring between grandees and the insecurity of previous decades, people also appeared to want tighter rules that made them safer. A cowed populace was, anyway, more likely to obey. The crown was to be 'impotent' no more.

All this made Isabella and Ferdinand mould-breakers in European forms of monarchy. They wanted semi-absolutist powers in order

THE IBERIAN PENINSULA BEFORE THE CONQUEST OF GRANADA IN 1492
KINGDOM OF FRANCE
CANTABRIAN SEA
Former Kingdom of Galicia
Principality of Asturias
Señorío of Vizcaya
Former Kingdom of Castile
KINGDOM OF NAVARRE
KINGDOM OF CASTILE
Kingdom of Aragón
Principality of Catalonia
KINGDOM OF PORTUGAL
Former Kingdom of León
Former Kindom of Toledo
CROWN OF ARAGÓN
Kingdom of Valencia
Kingdom of Mallorca
Former Kingdom of Murcia
Former Kingdom of Córdoba
Former Kingdom of Jaén
Former Kingdom of Seville
KINGDOM OF GRANADA
MEDITERRANEAN SEA
THE MAGHREB
N
0
200
KM

to rule with minimum interference from untrustworthy and greedy grandees who had seen themselves as near equals with a right to share in governing the country. Instead, Isabella and Ferdinand increasingly hired lawyers, priests and bureaucrats educated at universities in Salamanca and elsewhere to run their administration.

Unity was crucially important to them, too. They were not concerned, however, about unifying Spain into a single nation. What they sought was religious conformity. That could not be achieved while Iberia was still home to a Muslim kingdom.

6
Fall of Granada

Isabella had grown up in the small but prosperous *meseta* town of Arévalo, a place dense with legends about Spain's heroic past. Hercules was said to have gazed at the stars from here and a nearby palace was reputed to have housed Visigothic kings. Castile's poets and historians described the latter as manly, moral and magnanimous kings and predicted that God was awaiting the right moment to return the country to glory. All it needed was the right monarch, who would not only save Spain but go on to reconquer Jerusalem and reverse Christendom's wider decline.

Added to this heady mix were the songs and stories of chivalry told out loud at dinner or other times, which Isabella loved. The magical worlds of Lancelot and Merlin, meanwhile, sat on her shelves, along with knightly tales of derring-do which would be condemned by a male contemporary as 'based on lust, love and boasting ... causing weak-breasted women to fall into libidinous errors and commit sins they would not otherwise commit'. The strait-laced Isabella was unlikely to fall in that direction, but the Spanish idea of chivalry was intimately bound up with its interminable crusade against the Moors. Little had been achieved in the *Reconquista* over the previous two centuries beyond demanding tribute payments from the Nasrid dynasty rulers of Granada. War, however, kept nobles busy, generated booty and, if it was against Muslims, was righteous. After they had defeated internal opponents who had gathered around Isabella's niece Juana la Beltraneja and her Portuguese backers, the young monarchs needed to keep the troublesome grandees busy to stop them fighting each other or rising against the crown. War against Granada could do that. It was time, in other words, to revive the *Reconquista*.

In fact, it was the nobles who started the final phase of the Reconquest. In February 1482, the Marquess of Cádiz made an independent raid deep into Muslim territory, grabbing the town of Alhama, which lay just 56 kilometres from Granada. When that needed defending, it was his traditional local rival – the Duke of Medina Sidonia – who arrived to help, while Isabella and Ferdinand decided to leverage the victory into a long-term campaign. Fortune came to their aid, as family squabbles amongst Granada's ruling Nasrid dynasty weakened the Muslim response.

Crucial to their future success were recent advances in the science of gunpowder and artillery, making these weapons far more potent. Cannons, indeed, could finally breach the heavy stone walls of castles and towns that had proved unassailable for centuries. Ferdinand led the fighting while Isabella acted as quartermaster general, making sure her army was well fed and equipped with up to 180 cannons. Often, just the sight of these ensured the surrender of a thick-walled Muslim town (whose people were given generous terms if they gave up without a fight). A particularly vicious siege of Málaga – whose defence was hardened by a group of religiously motivated North African fighters, the *gomeres* – ended in August 1487, and by 1491 Granada itself was being strangled.

Volunteers had arrived from across Europe as news of the successful crusade spread and Christian Spain's reputation grew. The English aristocrat Edward Woodville, known as Lord Scales,

→ The Muslim kingdom of Granada, run by King Boabdil from the Alhambra palace complex in Granada, was the last to fall to the Christian armies in 1492.

and brother-in-law to England's King Edward IV, appeared with over a hundred archers and foot soldiers. When a rock knocked out two of Woodville's teeth, Ferdinand had to console him about his disfigured face, saying that a crusader's wounds were necessarily 'more beautiful than deformed'.

On 2 January 1492, after secret negotiations, the last Muslim king of Granada, Boabdil, left the walled palace complex of the Alhambra, the snowy peaks of the Sierra Nevada rising up behind him. The highest point, the Mulhacen, is named after one of his predecessors as king, Muley Hasan. A scripted ceremony saw him hand over the city keys before heading to lands in the nearby Alpujarra highlands – the steep, south-facing foothills of the Sierra Nevada – that had been given to him as recompense. Legend has it that Boabdil looked back at the city and wept at a spot that became known as the Pass of the Moor's Sigh. The nineteenth-century American romantic writer Washington Irving recorded a version in which Boabdil's mother Fatima scolded him. 'You do well to weep as a woman over what you could not defend as a man,' she said. Celebratory masses were held as far away as London and Rome, marking the arrival of Spain as a new and respected power in Europe.

Christian Spain already had a large population of *mudéjar* Muslims, known popularly as Moors, Mohammedans or Saracens. With the fall of Granada, this increased enormously in size – even if part of the population, and much of the nobility, left for North Africa.

The initial surrender agreement was designed to prevent trouble, with Muslims keeping their own laws and religion. For a ruler as obsessed with religious purity as Isabella, that was always going to be a problem. For the time being, however, this new territory of Castile needed to be slowly digested. Christian settlers were encouraged to move there but proved to a rough bunch who were mostly 'men of war or adventurers and many were wholly given up to vice'.

Skilled, diplomatic administrators from both church and state were appointed to keep the peace and prevent any offence that might stir rebellion – while Isabella and Ferdinand slipped away and did not return to stay for many years.

→ German traveller Christoph Weiditz drew pictures of the Muslim Morisco inhabitants of Christian Spain at the beginning of the sixteenth century.

97

Allso gandt die morischgen weiber für sich an zu sechen auf der gassen In granada.

Also gand die Edlen frawen moisgen
aůff der gassen Jr granadasegizlin
gnant darffa hůn

7
Seeking Asia, Finding America

The world-transforming year of 1492 had only just begun, and Spain was to be its fulcrum. Amongst the witnesses to the surrender of Granada was a Genovese navigator called Christopher Columbus, who had been trying to peddle a plan to sail to Asia by crossing the 'Ocean Sea', as the Atlantic was then known. He assumed that nothing separated the two continents of Europe and Asia in that direction. He was by no means alone, though some believed that mysterious islands known variously as the Isle of the Seven Cities, St Brendan, Antillia or Brazil (where Basque chronicler Lope García de Salazar insisted, in 1470, that King Arthur was buried) were in the way. Following the calculations of the tenth-century Arab cosmographer al-Farghani, or 'Alfraganus', and mixing in his own observations while sailing to the Azores, the Canary Islands and Iceland, Columbus believed Japan was just 2,400 nautical miles away. He was wrong, but his mistake was transformative for Spain and the rest of the world.

For years, Columbus had been pestering the Castilian crown (and the Portuguese, French and English) to back this expedition into the unknown. Committees pored over his plans and deemed success either improbable or impossible. He was riding disconsolately away from Granada and his latest rebuff when a royal messenger galloped up behind him. Queen Isabella had changed her mind.

With his request for three boats and eighty-eight crewmen, Columbus's expedition was cheap. If it went wrong, as many expected, the cost and the men could easily be written off. With his gallantry, fearlessness and genuine religious fervour, he was also the kind of romantic adventurer who appealed to Isabella. He was also openly flirtatious, and a later letter praises her as the woman who holds 'the keys' to his desire as well as offering 'the scent' and 'taste' of his goodwill. More importantly, and like other monarchs, Isabella and Ferdinand were aware of the impact of what became known as the fifteenth century's 'great bullion famine' – a shortage of precious metals in Europe that had peaked three decades earlier – making it a propitious time to propose ventures that promised gold.

Columbus sailed with two lightweight caravels, the *Pinta* and *Niña*, and a sturdier, 60-foot carrack, or *nao*, the *Santa María*, on 3 August 1492 from the southern Atlantic port of Palos, beside Huelva. He stopped off at the Canary Island of La Gomera and then headed west on 6 September, lying to his men about the distances covered daily so they would not mutiny when they realized how far from home they had travelled. This did not assuage a growing fear that they might never find land or return to it. On the night of 11 October Columbus thought he could see a tiny glimmer of light in the distance 'like a wax candle rising and falling', but it had disappeared by the time Isabella's overseer, Rodrigo Sánchez de Segovia, looked for it from the deck of the *Santa María*. Overnight, the nimble *Pinta* raced ahead, and the following day its lookout, Rodrigo de Triana, spotted land.

Columbus rowed ashore to what he assumed was an island off mainland Asia, planting the flag of Castile on a small outpost of the Bahamas – probably San Salvador (Watling Island). Convinced that he had found Asia, Columbus called the good-natured, semi-naked people he met 'Indians'. In fact, they were Taínos – indigenous folk from Caribbean islands and the coast of Florida. 'Indians' stuck, however, as a word to describe the indigenous inhabitants of the

Americas, and the Caribbean islands eventually became known as the West Indies.

The Italian adventurer reported that they possessed 'handsome bodies and fine features'. Their yellowish-brown skin reminded his sailors of the native Guanche peoples of the Canary Islands (some of them only recently conquered). If it weren't for their thick, straight black hair, he reported, they were 'so fair that if they wore clothes and stayed out of the sun and wind they would almost be as white as people in Spain'. Some wore small items of gold jewellery, none had ever seen a sword before (these 'they held by the sharp edge, cutting themselves') and they appeared not to worship any god. The promise, then, was of gaining gold for Castile and souls for Christ – the greatest possible treasures for his patron Isabella. There could be no real danger from a people who hurled themselves to the ground at the sound of gunpowder and, later, proved terrified of large fighting dogs and horses.

Columbus sailed further into the Caribbean, discovering more islands and peoples. On reaching Cuba, he was convinced that locals had told him the 'Great Khan' (a legendary Asian prince, for whom he carried letters from the Spanish monarchs) was just ten days sailing way. After finding numerous islands, grounding and wrecking the *Santa Maria* and setting up camp alongside a friendly village on an island he named La Española (Hispaniola, now home to the Dominican Republic and Haiti), Columbus left thirty-nine men behind in a wooden fort at a place he called Natividad. He sailed for home on 4 January 1493 with the two remaining vessels, which became separated in the rough Atlantic weather. An Englishman known as Tallarte de Lajes and Irishman Guillermo Ires were among those left behind (and were killed, along with all the others, before Columbus returned with a much larger fleet eleven months later).

Columbus reached Lisbon on 4 March, having been so convinced that his vessel, the *Niña*, would sink that he wrote a message explaining his discoveries, sealed it inside a wax tablet and tossed it overboard in a wooden barrel. 'That everlasting God who has handed your Highnesses so many victories, has now given you the greatest victory ever delivered to any monarch until now,' he wrote to Isabella from Lisbon. He promised her numerous slaves, 'as much gold as you need' and 'a multitude of peoples so concentrated together who, with very little effort, can be converted to our Holy Faith'. Columbus's capacity for exaggeration was immense, and he still thought he had discovered the outlying islands of Asia, but his letter was prescient.

We do not know what the seven surviving Taínos who accompanied Columbus back to Spain thought. They were displayed as part of a colourful spectacle – including turkeys and numerous, multi-coloured parrots – that processed across Spain to Barcelona, where Isabella and Ferdinand were staying with their court. 'He showed the monarchs the gold and other things that he had brought from the other world; and they and those with them were amazed to see that all of it, except the gold, was as new to them as the land it came from,' the Spaniard Francisco López de Gamarra wrote sixty years later. 'What they most stared at were the men, who wore gold rings in their ears and noses, and were neither white, nor black, nor brown, but rather jaundiced-looking or like the colour of stewed quince. Six of the Indians were baptised.' Isabella and Ferdinand were the godparents. Without knowing it (since Columbus still insisted that they came from Asia), Spain had now opened its doors to the Americas, adding a new aspect to its accidental role as a global meeting place and bringing about an encounter between the previously invisible 'west' with the European north, the African south and the Muslim east. The world, in other words, was getting to know itself through Spain.

The Spanish monarchs urged Columbus to go straight back with a larger fleet, and he eventually made three more trips, spending seven out of the next eleven years exploring. He became increasingly despondent at his failure to find gold and lost in mystical and existential dreams about what his journeys really meant. When he encountered the Paria peninsula of modern-day Venezuela he failed to follow up on his instinct that this might be 'a very large continent which has hitherto remained unknown' rather than just another large island. That instinct was driven by the terrible outpouring of the River Orinoco, which produced

> a deafening roar, like the noise of an enormous wave crashing against rocks ... and currents going from east to west with all the mighty fury of the Guadalquivir in full flood ... To this day, I can feel the fear spreading through my veins that I felt with the thought that, with such force, we were in danger of capsizing.

Columbus was a terrible administrator who constantly fell out with people. Eventually, the task of overseeing the exploration and colonization of these new Castilian lands was taken out of his hands and given to others. Columbus returned to Spain in 1504, an embittered man, dying two years later at around the age of fifty-four.

First, however, a carve-up of the new worlds being discovered by both Castilian Spanish and Portuguese navigators was agreed at the Spanish town of Tordesillas on 7 June 1494. Columbus had overestimated the distance between Spain and the Caribbean, telling Isabella and Ferdinand that it was 750 leagues away. As a result, the dividing line was placed 370 leagues west of Cape Verde, in Africa. In theory, this was so that Portuguese vessels could sail into the Atlantic from Africa to pick up winds and currents that pushed them home.

In fact, the Caribbean was much closer and, unknown to the signatories, to its south lay a continent whose eastward bulge spread across to the Portuguese side of the dividing line. Part of South America, in other words, belonged to Portugal, and this eventually gave birth to modern-day Brazil. The 1479 Treaty of Alcaçovas, by which Isabella's possession of the Castilian crown had been settled, had also conceded Portugal exclusive rights over exploration and commerce south of the Canary Islands – effectively blocking most of Africa and the eastern route to Asia off from Spain.

The first African slave known in the Americas sailed into La Española with the fleet of Nicolas de Ovando in 1501. His name is recorded on the ship's log as 'Juan', and he arrived with his silversmith owner, Juan de Córdoba. Little more is known about him, except that he was not alone. At least one other unnamed black slave and three freed slaves journeyed in the same fleet, with others probably not deemed worthy of registering.

The first black African to disembark in what is today the United States did not arrive at Jamestown in 1619, as American schoolchildren are taught, but was the central African-born freed slave Juan Garrido. He arrived in the Spanish Caribbean in 1502 or 1503 and was, in effect, just another conquistador. He accompanied Juan Ponce de León to explore Florida in 1513, by which time there were several hundred enslaved people and freedmen from Africa on Spain's Caribbean islands. Garrido claimed to be the first man to successfully grow wheat on the new continent when, later on, he set up an estate in Mexico. 'I was present at all the invasions and conquests and pacifications that were carried out,' he wrote in a letter. Yet another African slave, Moroccan-born Esteban Dorantes, was, by accident, part of a small group that wandered far into the American West. He was one of four men to survive an expedition to Florida in 1527, eventually wandering across Texas and into California (and persuading the indigenous peoples they met that they were healers) before finding their way back to a Spanish settlement ten years later.

Vigorous debate about whether the local Taíno people could be enslaved, saw Isabella decide that they were innocents who had yet to be told about God rather than infidels who deserved slavery. Indeed, she ordered that the slaves sent by Columbus returned home. As her newest subjects, they had 'to be treated in the same way as our subjects and our vassals', she declared in 1501. Columbus and other settlers disagreed but had to obey. Instead, the local peoples were trapped into the so-called *encomienda* system, by which they 'owed' labour to a Spanish settler. This system provoked the ire of Dominican monks and an early debate about 'human rights' – from which black Africans were excluded.

On 21 December 1511, the newly arrived Dominican friar Antonio Montesinos called the people of Santo Domingo into church and harangued them angrily.

> You are living and may die in mortal sin because of the cruelty and tyranny with which you deal with these innocent people ... Are they not human? ... Do they not have rational souls? Are you not bound to love them as you love yourselves? Do you not understand this? Do you not feel this?

Far more dangerous to the Taínos was smallpox, against which they had no defence. Epidemics broke out in Cuba and Hispaniola in 1519, decimating the population. The following year it spread to Mexico, possibly killing Moctezuma's successor as Aztec emperor, Cuitláhuac, and other kings whose bodies filled with pustules that 'spread everywhere, on one's face, on one's head, on one's breast'. Smallpox not only left indigenous people bed-bound, dying and unable to care for themselves, but also unable to fight, depressed and in awe of the Europeans who had greater immunity to the disease they had brought with them. As a result, the population of Hispaniola halved, and even Friar Bartolomé De Las Casas – the most famous of the churchmen who campaigned for indigenous people to be treated as equals – soon called for African slaves to be imported in order to replace the missing labour. The status of black Africans as 'enslaveable' infidels – based on an assumed contact with Islam – had been decreed by the Vatican in papal bulls issued earlier in the century to the Portuguese as they set about conquering parts of North Africa in what was seen as a Christian crusade. These bulls did not discriminate between Berber and other Muslims in the north, and sub-Saharan black Africans, perhaps because Islam had already reached the gold-rich empire of Mali. 'We grant that you and your successors as Kings of Portugal ... will have in perpetuity, the right to invade, conquer, seize, subject and reduce into perpetual slavery the Saracens, pagans and other infidels and enemies of Christ, whoever they are and wherever their kingdoms are,' one papal bull stated. Another referred specifically to 'Guineans [West Africans] and other negroes, captured by force or bought ... with legitimate contracts'.

More than 10 million Africans would be enslaved and shipped to the Americas over the next five centuries, with many dying along the way and all subjected to degrading inhuman treatment and violence. Spain started this trade in human beings and was among the last to end it, with the final shipment reaching Cuba illegally in 1867. By that time, 900,000 Africans had been transported to Cuba alone. That is eight slaves for every square kilometre of land on the island.

In the late fifteenth century, as Spain began this process of dramatic and often brutal demographic change on another continent, it also started to question its own ethnic and religious mix. Jews and Muslims had long formed a significant part of that. A violent transformation, however, was coming.

8
Purity

The German traveller Nicholas von Popplau crossed Castile, Valencia and Catalonia on horseback in 1484 and was shocked to find so many Muslims and Jews living peacefully in Spain. 'Some condemn the King of Poland because he allows various religions to live in his lands, while the lands of Spain are inhabited by baptised and converted Jews and also by infidel Moors,' he said. 'The queen is the protector of the Jews.' Technically, he was right. Non-Christians lived under royal protection, which could be withdrawn at any time. In European terms, Spain was the outlier. Muslims were almost entirely absent from the rest of western Christendom. Jews had been expelled from much of the rest of the continent, leaving England in 1290, while France had five different expulsions before 1394.

Christian Spain had followed a different path. In the first half of the thirteenth century, the conqueror of Seville – Ferdinand III 'the Saint' – had termed himself 'king of the three religions'. The script on his tomb in Seville is in four languages: Spanish, Latin, Arabic and Hebrew. The Hebrew text declares him ruler of Sepharad, the Jewish name for the Iberian Peninsula. In fact, that inscription would have been commissioned by his learned, polyglot and polymath son, Alfonso X, the Wise – perhaps the greatest admirer of Islamic art and knowledge in Christian Spain.

A Renaissance man before such people existed, the

philosopher-king Alfonso (who ruled Castile from 1252 to 1284) was 'the most intellectually impassioned of all medieval rulers and the most creatively inspired', according to his biographer Simon Doubleday. His interests, and publications, ranged from chess and music to laws, astronomy and astrology. He could read everything from Castilian and Catalan to Latin, Arabic and Hebrew. A massive compendium of law codes, the Siete Partidas (or Seven Parts), included 2,700 essays which shaped civil law as far away, in time and distance, as the United States. In Washington, a carved relief of the aquiline-nosed Spanish king overlooks the gallery doors to the House chamber, along with that of an earlier Spaniard – the Jewish philosopher Maimonides. In Spain, one of Alfonso's most durable inventions was the Mesta, an association that oversaw the abundant herds of merino sheep that brought wealth to Castile for centuries and left behind it the *cañadas reales*, or royal cattle tracks, along which animals can still be herded towards the warmer south during autumn, and to the cooler north in the spring.

This remarkable monarch's Alfonsine Tables revolutionized astronomy. Copernicus's personal copy, which he used three centuries later at the University in Krakow, still survives. Another copy, dated to 1492 and held in Florence, has notes scribbled on it by Galileo Galilei. Alfonso's cycle of 419 devotional Songs of Holy Mary, or Cantigas de Santa María, are still performed today. They were written, along with much *trovador* music of the period, in the Galician-Portuguese of western Iberia. His gorgeously illuminated manuscripts reveal many secrets, from the instruments of his court to the mixed array, and dress sense, of Muslim and Christian musicians he employed.

The joint presence of Christianity, Judaism and Islam made fifteenth-century Spain almost unique in Western Europe. Yet this tolerance was never as consistent or harmonious as it is frequently depicted. Outbursts of inter-religious violence occurred alongside the phenomena of everyday *convivencia* and mutual cultural enrichment. Minorities might be tolerated, but they were not equal. Separate laws, taxes, places of worship, dress codes and neighbourhoods all marked the separation.

There were pogroms, too. These were especially brutal at the end of the fourteenth century, when attacks were provoked by rabble-rousing populist preachers like Friar Vicente Ferrer. This messianic and influential future saint, known as the 'angel of the Apocalypse', deemed Spain's Jews to be 'tailed beasts who menstruate like women'. Unsurprisingly, many opted for conversion and safety. Three-quarters of those in Aragón, for example, changed religion. Converts were looked down upon both by those who remained Jews and by their newfound fellow Christians. 'Many Jews in Spain left the faith of Moses, and especially in Seville, where most abandoned their self-respect,' wrote one contemporary Jewish critic. In cities across both Castile and Aragón – and very pronouncedly in Seville – a large new social group known as the *conversos*, or 'new Christians', emerged.

From the very start, *conversos* were the subject of slander, suspicion and deep envy, especially since some were highly cultured and quickly became successful (several were bishops), while groups occupied entire city neighbourhoods. With their conversion, they automatically enjoyed the same rights as 'old Christians', who suddenly found themselves with new competitors for jobs, patronage and clients. Often, too, they maintained social and family ties – and some cultural customs – with those Jews who bravely held on to their faith. Civil strife between the 'new Christians' and 'old Christians' in cities like Toledo and Córdoba had been one of the most destabilizing parts of the outbreaks of lawless chaos during the reigns of Isabella's father, Juan II, and her brother, Enrique IV. Previous monarchs, however, had investigated claims that the *conversos* were secret Jews and concluded that this was a lie.

Isabella and Ferdinand decided otherwise, believing anti-Semitic churchmen like the Dominican prior Tomás de Torquemada. A novel 'royal' Inquisition, headquartered inside the monarchs' administration, was set up to hunt down *conversos* who were fake, or just bad, Christians. With royal control binding together the formidable powers of church and state, this was a qualitative leap from earlier, tamer, church-organized inquisitions in Western Europe.

The Spanish Inquisition, as it became known, was not just unfair, but hypocritical and defined by culture or race as much as by religion. Few Spaniards were properly observant Christians, since the quality of priests was so poor that nobody taught them how to officiate. 'Given that the old ones are such bad Christians, the new ones are [also] bad,' wrote the chronicler Fernando del Pulgar. 'To burn them all because of this would be the cruellest of things.' But burn they did, starting in Seville in 1481, when half a dozen of the richest and most important people in the city were incinerated in the Plaza de Tablada. The Inquisition's terms – including anonymous denunciation and a system of torture or punishment that often made it wiser to admit guilt and pay a penalty than argue innocence – turned suspicion into false reality.

Confession brought fines and humiliation at public auto-da-fé ceremonies but allowed one to live on as a '*reconciliado*' who had done penance. In Seville, up to 500 *reconciliados* walked miserably through the streets together in rag-like gowns and tall, conical *sanbenito* hats. Those who fled were declared guilty and their possessions handed over to the royal treasury. Civil authorities carried out executions by fire or garotte. Even the dead were sometimes dug up and burned, if they were posthumously accused of heresy and no relative dared defend them. 'One should not neglect those deemed to have died as Jewish heretics, who should be exhumed so they can be burned and so that the tax collectors can deal with their goods,' instructed Torquemada, who became Inquisitor General in 1483. As a result, families paid fines for relatives who had died up to seventy years before.

↑ A later imagining of the founder of the royal Spanish Inquisition, Tomás de Torquemada, allegedly urging Isabella and Ferdinand to expel all Spain's Jews – which they did, in 1492.

The contemporary *converso* chronicler Alfonso de Palencia estimated that half of Seville's new Christians – some 16,000 people or one-sixth of the population – passed through the Inquisition's hands in the early years. Seville was just the start, as accusations about contacts between alleged heretics in different towns and cities inevitably spread across the country. As a result, the monarchs built a nationwide network of inquisitors that included Ferdinand's kingdoms. The Inquisition thus became one of the first fully 'Spanish' institutions to unite the two monarchs' kingdoms.

In fact, the Inquisition was not nearly as bad as we assume. Centuries of Protestant propaganda magnified its size to grotesque proportions. Witch hunts of women in Protestant Europe, for example, were far more lethal. The number of Inquisition victims dwindled over time, and a recent Vatican study shows that fewer than 2 per cent of the 125,000 people tried were executed. Although the institution survived until the nineteenth century, the total number of executions may have been around 1,500 over four centuries, or four a year.

That does not make the Inquisition any less sinister, or terrifying for fifteenth- and sixteenth-century *conversos*. Long-lasting fear, in any case, is instilled in the early stage of any campaign of terror, and the Inquisition's frightening reputation was very much alive in Spain four centuries later.

The Inquisition also provoked a growing obsession with race. Proof of that came with the contemporaneous spread of 'purity of blood' rules. These banned *conversos* from elite institutions or monastic orders solely due to their Jewish blood. A university college in Salamanca produced the first ban in 1482, and the Jeronymite order excluded *conversos* in 1493. In 1501, Isabella herself banned the children and grandchildren of Seville's *reconciliados* from holding public offices.

For the Jews themselves, the Inquisition was just a warning. In 1477, Isabella stated that Spain's Jews were 'mine', following the royal tradition of protection. In Seville, she warned anyone wishing to harm them that: 'I take under my safekeeping, protection and royal defence the said Jews in the said *aljamas* [their neighbourhoods] and each one of them, their persons and goods are assured by me.' Just six years later, however, they were expelled from the bishoprics of Seville, Cádiz and Córdoba. Some 5,000 people had to leave their homes, mostly going to Toledo or northern Castile. Inquisitors had argued that their mere presence encouraged *conversos* to 'judaize', by observing old family cultural traditions or, worse, Jewish religious rituals. It was an advance warning.

In 1492, all the Jews were expelled from Spain completely. Inquisitors claimed that they led *conversos* astray by their mere presence. A trumped-up case of the ritual assassination of a Christian child – a standard trope – had seen a Jewish cobbler called Yuce

Franco and three *conversos* burned at the stake by the Inquisition the previous year (though the crime, with no corpse, had allegedly happened fifteen years previously). The first expulsion order was written by the chief inquisitor himself, Tomás de Torquemada, and covered only his bishopric of Girona in Catalonia. It was dated 20 March 1492.

Eleven days later, Isabella and Ferdinand signed a nationwide expulsion order, repeating Torquemada's words.

> Great damage is done to Christians by the contact, conversations and activities that they share with the Jews, who always try – by whatever means they can find – to subvert and snatch faithful Christians away from our holy Catholic faith ... When some grave and horrific crime is committed by some members of a group, it is sufficient reason to dissolve and annihilate that group ... after much deliberation, we have agreed to order all Jews and Jewesses to leave our lands and never come back.

The Jewish population of Spain had already fallen to 90,000 people. More now converted to Christianity, including the eighty-year-old *rab mayor*, or royal appointed leader of Castile's Jews, Abraham Seneor, and his family. Those who refused to give up their religion had until July to 'sell, barter or transfer all their movable and immoveable goods' and then 'take their possessions and wealth out by sea or land, as long as they do not take gold, silver, coins or other things banned by the laws of our kingdoms'.

Portugal, Navarre, Naples, Egypt, the kingdom of Fez and the Ottoman empire were the favoured destinations. Goods had to be sold at cut price, and many people were robbed on their route to exile. Further expulsions soon followed from Navarre, Portugal and Naples, and hardship drove many Jews back to Spain as converts. Portugal's King João was especially harsh, taking some 2,000 children captive and sending them to populate São Tomé – off the west coast of Africa, and known as 'the Snakes Islands' – where many died.

Most, however, were expelled to Fez, where the treatment was even worse. 'The Moors appeared and stripped them naked to their bare skin. They threw themselves upon the women with force, and killed the men, and slit them open up the middle, looking for gold in their abdomens, because they knew that they swallowed it,' claimed a Christian writer who dealt with some returnees.

Around half of Spain's Jews left definitively, while the rest converted. What was once the world's largest Jewish community had been destroyed. Those who did best went to the Ottoman empire, where large communities of Sephardic Jews thrived over the next few centuries. Just as with the Inquisition, the expulsion of the Jews was one of the few executive actions to cover all the kingdoms of Isabella and Ferdinand's Spain.

While Castile now expelled its Jews, its Muslim population had suddenly exploded with the annexation of Granada. There were already some 25,000 *mudéjares* living across Castile (which had a population of 4 million). They were valued for their building skills, as carpenters, plasterers, bricklayers and ceramicists. Like the Jews, they were organized in their own communities, followed their own religious laws and had their own internal justice system. Their 150 local *aljama* communities were almost always small, occupying a handful of streets that formed *morerías* – Moorish quarters – in towns and cities. Only Hornachos, in Extremadura, was almost entirely *mudéjar*, with its 2,500 Muslims settled on land belonging to the religious military knights of the Order of Santiago, which protected them. Many no longer spoke Arabic, and they were sufficiently similar to their Christian neighbours for rules to be introduced making them wear blue half-moon symbols indicating that they were Muslims. Their *alcalde mayor*, head of Castile's *mudéjares*, was chosen by Isabella herself.

Muslims were far more populous in Ferdinand's kingdoms,

where the grumpy German traveller Popplau claimed that 'cities are occupied more by *conversos* and Saracens than by Christians'. There were 75,000 Muslims in the kingdoms of the Crown of Aragón, which had an estimated population of under 1 million people. They provided much of the labour on the grand country estates of the nobles, especially in Valencia.

The proportion of Muslims in Christian Spain changed dramatically after the conquest of Granada. Now there were up to 400,000, accounting for one in twenty people in Spain. Isabella and Ferdinand were sufficiently aware of the problems of incorporating so many new *mudéjares* into Castile that the surrender treaty with Granada was deliberately gracious. 'When things have reached such an honourable and beneficial end it is right to finish them off by whatever means,' said one Christian observer, who nevertheless believed that the peace treaty known as the *capitulaciones* would not last. 'Now that the monarchs have Granada, which is what they wanted, they can apply cunning to the remaining task and, the Moors being as they are, make them leave the city without breaking the agreements.'

In fact, the new *mudéjares* maintained their property, religion and laws. They were excepted from wearing the distinguishing blue moon marks (though their distinctive dress codes mostly made that unnecessary). They could trade with both Castile and North Africa, enlarging the markets for their artisans, silk-producers and fruit farmers considerably. Granada's elaborate city water system – so much more advanced than in Christian cities – was to be respected, with Christian newcomers not allowed to dirty it by washing clothes. Most importantly, Isabella and Ferdinand pledged that the endowments and other income of the mosques would be maintained 'now and for ever'. Finally, a crucial phrase in the document stated that: 'No Moor or Mooress will be forced to become Christian.'

Within a decade, however, Granada's Muslim population had halved to around 150,000, while some 40,000 Christian settlers

– many of them ruffians with nothing to lose – were lured with tax breaks, land and houses.

Isabella and Ferdinand's peripatetic court mostly stayed away in the years after the conquest, but in 1499 they took up residence in the Alhambra, which they adored, and this became their principal base. From their hilltop palaces and gardens, the Christian monarchs looked down on a thoroughly Muslim city. They brought a new inquisitor for Granada, Francisco Jiménez de Cisneros, who arrived at the end of 1499. His men scoured the Albaicín neighbourhood on the hill facing the Alhambra, looking to forcibly baptize the children of *elches* – as Christian converts to Islam within Al-Andalus had been known. This was an extreme and provocative take on the *capitulaciones* which contrasted with the tolerant spirit of the emollient archbishop, Hernando de Talavera, and the elderly Count of Tendilla, who had jointly governed Granada since 1492. The Inquisition, however, could override them.

Cisneros had been in the city for only a month when his men provoked a rebellion in the Albaicín neighbourhood in December 1499 by forcibly baptizing *elches*' children without parental permission. That sparked three days of rioting and the murder of some of Cisneros' agents. Ferdinand was furious. 'He [Cisneros] has never seen, and does not understand, the Moors,' the king said, demanding 'brains, not stringency'. Forced conversion, he added, was wrong. This had long been royal policy, with that learned Castilian monarch Alfonso X 'the Wise' pointing out in his thirteenth-century law book, the *Siete Partidas*, that 'Christians work to lead Moors towards our faith and convert them through good words and reasoned preaching, not by force or bribery.'

Cisneros himself fled the city but – to most people's surprise – his bullying tactics worked. Soon, up to 300 people a day were being baptized, with mosques turned into churches as entire congregations declared themselves Christian. By February 1500, 9,100 people had been converted and 20,000 more followed over the next few months as the church claimed entire towns and villages. This was conversion by fear, and mostly insincere. 'They embraced the faith and took baptism, but without their heart or only in a ceremonial fashion,' said the chronicler Andrés Bernáldez of this large new social group, who became known as Moriscos. Cisneros did not care and nor, eventually, did the monarchs. 'My vote, and that of the queen, is that these Moors be baptized and if they are not real Christians, their children will be, and so will their grandchildren,' Ferdinand declared.

In September 1501, Isabella expelled those in Granada who refused 'voluntary' baptism. 'They must leave our kingdoms, because there is no reason why there should be any infidels in them,' she wrote. In February 1502 this was extended to the centuries-old *mudéjar* communities across Castile. Isabella would 'no longer permit in these kingdoms of ours people who follow such reprobate laws'. She also made it virtually impossible for people to leave, since they had to do this from ports in Vizcaya, northern Spain, and could only go to Muslim countries that Spain was not at war with – basically meaning Egypt. Conversion was the only way out, and Castile's old *mudéjares* were also baptized en masse. Thousands of books, Korans and precious scrolls were publicly burned on the grounds that, in Isabella's words, 'by the grace of our Lord, the Moors in our kingdom have converted to our holy Catholic faith'.

This was a sham, as even she knew. Islam's *taqiya* rule allowed people to feign conversion if they had no other option. Ferdinand did not dare carry out the same policy in Aragón, where Muslim agricultural workers were key to prosperity. Forced conversion arrived there a quarter of a century later, in 1526, after his death. Trouble was being stored up, but by the time Isabella died in November 1504 after ruling Castile for thirty years, her part of Spain was nominally entirely Christian. Just as the door to the west, and the Americas, was being opened, she had closed the other doors that connected Spain to Africa and to the Arab world.

Isabella's death brought the separation of the two great kingdoms of Spain, and Ferdinand initially retired to Aragón. The crown of Castile was inherited by a rebellious daughter, Juana, who history deemed 'the Mad' perhaps, conveniently, to explain why men always ruled in her name. The first of these was her husband, Philip the Handsome, who was already Lord of the Netherlands and Duke of Burgundy. The contrast with her mother only made Isabella's hold on power as a woman even more exceptional.

When Philip died just two years after he had started to rule in Juana the Mad's name, control of Castile fell back into Ferdinand's hands. In the final years of his life, he managed a surprise conquest of the still independent northern kingdom of Navarre. The last piece of the puzzle of modern Spain was thus put in place, with Navarre incorporated just in time for it to be handed on to his heirs. Ferdinand lived until the relatively old (for the times) age of sixty-three, and his death may have been provoked by over-consumption of the emerald-green blister beetle known as *Lytta vesicatoria*, or Spanish Fly, in an attempt to maintain a sex life and have children with his much younger second wife, Germana de Foix.

Ferdinand's death, in 1516, marked the end of a remarkable forty-year period in which he and Isabella transformed Spain, making it one of Europe's major powers. To some Spaniards his passing marks the end of a golden age before the country's monarchy was 'tainted' by foreign blood. Isabella, especially, became a touchstone for future reactionaries, with the fascist Falange and dictator Francisco Franco both borrowing her symbol of a bundle of arrows in the twentieth century.

In fact, Ferdinand's death pushed Spain even further to the forefront of the western world's history, since the heir to his crowns – his grandson Charles – was destined to be far more powerful than even his remarkable grandparents.

9
Empire

Never in the history of post-Roman Europe has one man inherited so much. Charles I of Spain, also known by his principal title as 'The Holy Roman Emperor Charles V', was the grandson of Isabella of Castile and Ferdinand of Aragón. When Ferdinand died in 1516, Charles took over the crowns of both Aragón and Castile (while his mother Juana remained hidden away in the castle at Tordesillas until her death, aged seventy-five, in 1555). The other side of the family tree was just as grandiose, since his deceased father was Philip of Burgundy, who had been heir to the lands of his own parents: the head of the Habsburg dynasty and Holy Roman Emperor Maximilian I and his wife, Mary of Burgundy. The joint possessions of all four grandparents fell into Charles's young lap before he turned twenty.

Suddenly, Spain was part of a personal empire made up of a sprawling collection of territories stretching across Europe and the Americas. It was run by a man who, following Maximilian's death in 1519, also ensured for himself the title of Holy Roman Emperor (in effect, giving him sway over a swathe of land that stretched from the Mediterranean to the Baltic and North Sea, including modern Germany, Austria, eastern France, the Low Countries and northern Italy).

Charles was the first monarch of all Spain. That did not, however, turn it into a single country. It simply meant that the different crowns within it – of Castile, Aragón and Navarre – shared the same king, as did Ferdinand's lands in Naples and Sicily. Some see Charles's accession as the moment Spain came into existence as a single nation. In fact, it was the beginning of a process whose end lay centuries ahead.

Nor, indeed, was he a particularly Spanish king. Charles had never been to Spain before, spoke French as his first language, and then Dutch, with Castilian Spanish as only his third language. He saw himself, first and foremost, as Burgundian. Indeed, he was proclaimed King of Spain while in Brussels in 1516 and did not travel to his Spanish lands until the following year. He also introduced the unfortunate, jutting 'Habsburg jaw' – a form of genetic disorder in which the lower jaw outgrows its upper half. An entire line of Spanish Habsburg monarchs would bear this remarkable facial feature for the next 200 years.

Charles's vast personal empire had no formal seat. Instead, he travelled continually. In his forty years as king, he spent more than half his time abroad. His main interest was always to conserve or augment the power of the wider Habsburg dynasty. Spain played an important role in that life-long enterprise, though it was sometimes seen as little more than a stable money-making machine to finance his battles elsewhere.

He initially wounded Castilian pride (and power) by importing Flemish administrators. The reputed Spanish historian Manuel Fernández Alvarez claimed he also had an affair with his step-grandmother Germana de Foix (who also spoke French) and they had a child, though supporting evidence is slim. Then he left to pick up his imperial crown, partially paid for – in an extravagant round of bribery of German princes – with Spanish money. This provoked rebellion between 1520 and 1521 from a violent movement in Castile known as the *comuneros*, who wanted to turn things back to Isabella's time. The rebels were easily squashed, but they had a point. From now on, Spain's resources were frittered

away on maintaining an almost impossibly stretched European empire against which France, in particular, fought almost permanently, since it was now surrounded by Habsburg lands. Charles responded wisely to the rebellion. He handed control of Castilian affairs back to Spaniards and spent seven continuous years in his Spanish kingdoms between 1522 and 1529.

Charles was an orthodox Catholic who, after his mercenary troops shocked the continent by running riot in Rome in 1527, had the papacy (which was also a secular power, with considerable territories of its own) in his pocket. Among other things, that allowed him to stymie Henry VIII's efforts at divorcing Charles's Spanish aunt, Catherine of Aragón, in order to marry Anne Boleyn. Henry's solution was dramatic. He split with Rome, and the Anglican church was founded in response to Spanish pride and power.

Charles's own marriage to his well-educated and capable cousin Isabella of Portugal in 1526 was famously romantic. She persuaded him to spend more time in Spain and ruled as regent when he was away. Legend has it that a smitten Charles ordered rare Persian plant seeds for her, thereby introducing the red carnation that eventually became a Spanish symbol and now adorns the patios and balconies of southern cities like Córdoba.

France was only one of his enemies. In Germany, Charles tussled with the new Protestant kingdoms that had begun to follow Martin Luther's teachings. As Europe's most powerful monarch, he was also expected to lead the defence of Christendom against the ever-expanding Ottoman empire of Suleyman the Magnificent. The Ottomans conquered Hungary in 1526, and only Charles's arrival with a large army in Vienna in 1532 brought their advance into

← Charles V was Spain's first Habsburg monarch. He inherited swathes of land around Europe from his four grandparents, including Isabella and Ferdinand, though Spanish was not his mother tongue. Portrait by Bernard van Orley, *c.*1515–16.

mainland Europe to halt (though he had no need to fight the Turks, since the size of his army frightened them off). They continued to do battle, however, over the eastern Mediterranean Sea.

Constant warring with either France, the new Protestant kingdoms or the Ottomans was expensive. Charles frequently took loans from bankers like the fabulously wealthy German Catholic merchant family of the Fuggers. Payments on these loans meant that Castile itself did not benefit as much as it should have from the astonishing new wealth it had found across the Atlantic and was shipping back to Europe in the form of gold and silver.

10
Conquistadors

The speed with which Spain's conquistadors swept through South America was breathtaking. Perhaps only the brutality was more remarkable. Initially, they concentrated on exploring and occupying the Caribbean. There was much to discover. The presence of the vast American continent itself, its northern and southern halves connected by the long sliver of land that now stretches from Panama to Mexico, was not 'discovered' until 1498.

In 1513, Vasco Núñez de Balboa crossed to the far side of the 80-kilometre-wide stretch of jungle that joined North and South America in modern Panama to find the eastern edge of the Pacific Ocean and a future route to Asia. Florida was discovered by the conquistador Juan Ponce de León the same year, and parts of it remained under Spanish control for most of the next three centuries.

The conquistadors were often led by *hidalgos* – a largely empty title that literally meant 'the son of something' (or, rather, that they were sons of 'a somebody'). The title was applied to all Basques from the regions of Vizcaya or Guipúzcoa and to minor Castilian gentry of little wealth but exaggerated grandeur who were sent to the rugged New World to seek their fortunes.

Two million square kilometres of land and 50 million people were claimed by 10,000 Spaniards over just four decades as the ancient civilizations of Aztecs, Incas and others were invaded and occupied. Hernan Cortés took three years to conquer Mexico

(1519–22), and Francisco Pizarro overran Peru in a little over two years (1533–5). Much further south, the future capitals of Argentina and Chile, Buenos Aires and Santiago, had both been founded by 1541. Some previously modest *hidalgos* became fabulously rich and powerful as a result.

Cortés was perhaps the most remarkable – and cruellest – of these conquistadors. He reasoned that only terror would give him victory and indulged in 'a pattern of slaughter, mass mutilation and systematic enslavement of thousands of women and children', according to a recent historian of the conquistadors, Fernando Cervantes. After taking the fortress town of Tepeaca, for example, his men enslaved the women and children, branding their cheeks with the letter G (for *guerra*, or war). Some of the warriors had been torn apart by fighting dogs, while Cortés allowed his cannibalistic local allies to eat others.

As this disturbing scene suggests, Cortés and the other conquistadors did not achieve all this on their own. In fact, some major victories saw them cleverly backing one side of an existing dispute before imposing themselves on the victors. Indigenous allies (Cortés boasted 200,000 of them), mercenaries and contract explorers like the Florentine Amerigo Vespucci also helped. The latter's map-making German admirer Martin Waldseemüller named the new continent 'America' after him. By 1522, the Portuguese explorer Ferdinand Magellan and the Basque Juan Sebastian Elcano had discovered the route around the southern point of the continent, and their expedition became the first to circumnavigate the world. Magellan died in the Philippines without completing the full journey, but Elcano kept sailing and led the remaining crew members home.

For Spaniards, the new continent had all the attractions of a gold rush, and gold and other precious metals were usually the focus of their ambition. Spain's own widespread poverty meant that many had nothing to lose. When a friar called Bartolomé

↑ Conquistador Hernán Cortés conquered Mexico in just three years between 1519 and 1522, by allying himself with the Aztec empire's enemies and using terror or enslavement to instill fear.

De Las Casas sought out poor volunteers to settle lands there (with state loans and tax breaks), he quickly recruited 3,000 and turned down another 6,000 because he did not want to leave landowners without labour. Some 150,000 young Spanish men and women had arrived in America by 1550, intending 'to serve God and his majesty, but also to get rich', in the words of one. Friar De Las Casas,

PHILIP II's EMPIRE

AT THE END OF THE SIXTEENTH CENTURY

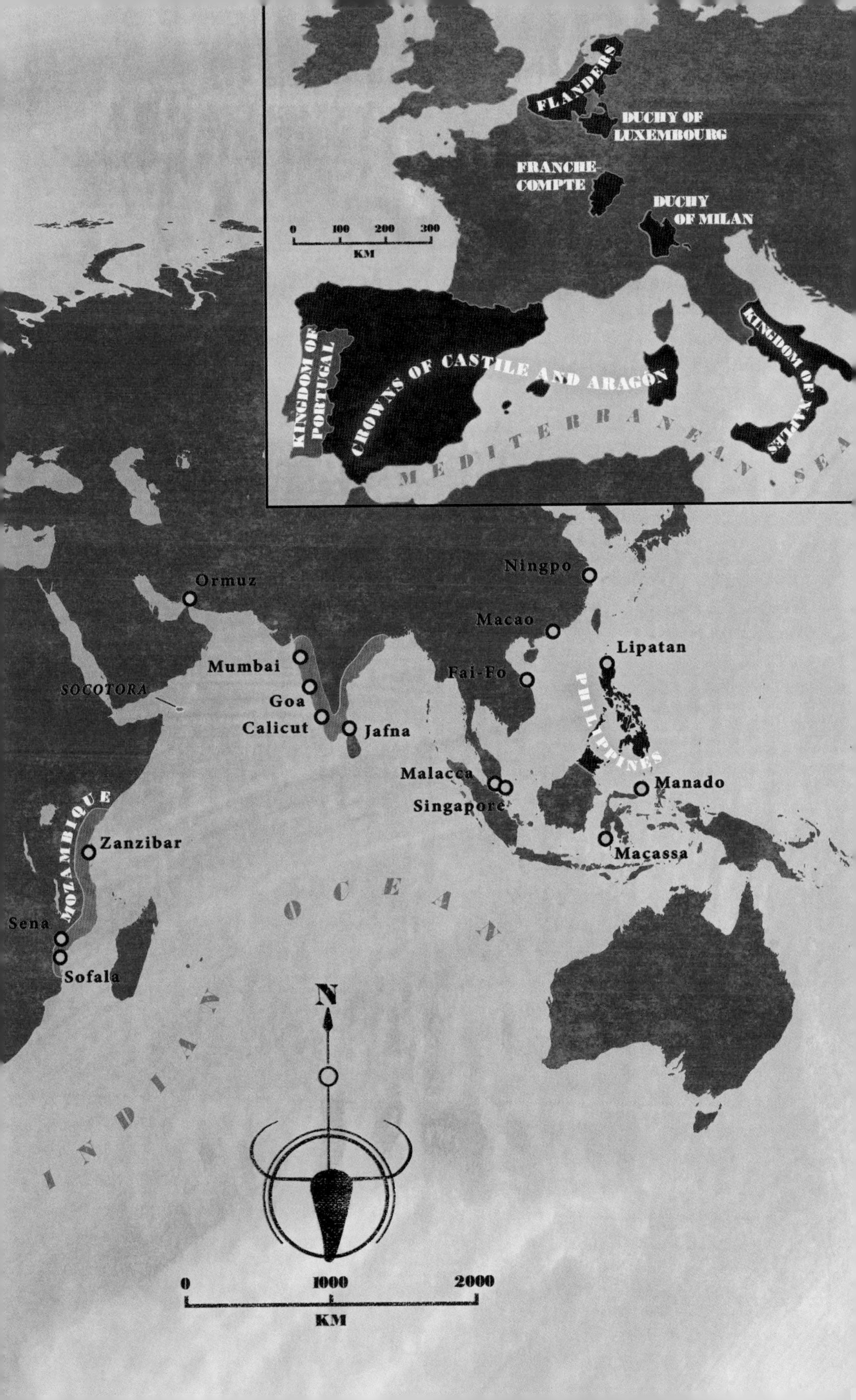

FLANDERS
DUCHY OF LUXEMBOURG
FRANCHE-COMPTE
DUCHY OF MILAN
0 100 200 300
KM
KINGDOM OF PORTUGAL
CROWNS OF CASTILE AND ARAGÓN
KINGDOM OF NAPLES
MEDITERRANEAN SEA
Ningpo
Ormuz
Macao
Lipatan
Mumbai
Fai-Fo
SOCOTORA
Goa
Calicut
Jafna
PHILIPPINES
Malacca
Singapore
Manado
MOZAMBIQUE
Zanzibar
Macassa
INDIAN OCEAN
Sena
Sofala
N
0 1000 2000
KM

in his *Brevísima relación de la destrucción de Las Indias*, was just one of several witnesses who warned of the terrible cost in human lives. War, disease, displacement and neglect saw the indigenous population reduced by 80 per cent over three centuries.

Columbus had initially gone looking for gold, but the precious metal that allowed Spain to set up a lucrative, extractive economy was silver. Mines in Potosí, in the Bolivian Andes, and at Zacatecas, Mexico, eventually provided it in abundance. Conquest and trade were royal monopolies controlled from Castile, which set up a Council of the Indies in 1524 and based its administration in Seville, from where ships were given permits to sail and had to present accounts on their return. By the mid-sixteenth century, after Spaniard Bartolomé de Medina had invented (with guidance from a mysterious German known as known as Master Lorenzo) the 'patio process' – using mercury amalgamation rather than laborious smelting to extract silver from ore – bullion fleets began delivering some 2 to 8 million ducats of silver to Castile every year for an entire century.

As bullion crossed the ocean, Charles spoke joyously of Mexico as a new 'gold-bearing world' within his domains. He also made money off slaves, selling the Augsburg-based Welser company a permit to ship 4,000 Africans for a 20,000 ducat fee.

Seville became the effective capital of this new empire, transforming the city utterly as it filled with merchants, bankers, sailors and slaves. 'You are no city. You are a universe,' the poet Fernando de Herrera proclaimed later in the century after the opening of the Casa de Contratación in 1503 made it the administrative base of colonial trade. No Spaniard could sail without its permission, and navigators received training there, with Amerigo Vespucci in charge as *piloto mayor* (master navigator) until his death in 1512 and Sebastian Cabot holding the role of chief examiner. The taxes it collected varied from 10 to 40 per cent, with precious metals paying 20 per cent. It oversaw the *Flota de las Indias* –

the fleets that periodically set out together to cross the ocean.

The occupation of much of South America during Charles's long rule was one of the most remarkable and deadly land grabs in history. When a gout-racked Charles abdicated in a series of formal ceremonies between 1555 and 1556, he had reigned over Spain for forty years and could boast of controlling vast swathes of land on two continents. He now wisely split his kingdoms between his brother Ferdinand, who received the German-Austrian lands, and his son Philip II, who received the lands in Spain, Italy, the Netherlands and America. He then retired to the monastery at Yuste, in Extremadura, where he died in September 1558. He had done Spain two great favours: first, by giving it an empire of its own; and second, by separating it from the rest of his own personal empire in Europe. That meant, in theory, that Spain was sitting quite literally on a mine of silver (and, to a lesser extent, gold) in South America, and that it could now spend its proceeds on itself – unless its monarchs had other plans.

If Charles V's most remarkable gift to his son lay on the far side of the Atlantic, Philip II was still obliged to share part of the territory in America. The dividing line agreed on by Isabella and Ferdinand at Tordesillas left a large chunk of the American continent in Portuguese hands. Between the two countries, however, they now ruled not just all of the colonized Americas but much of the Atlantic Ocean.

Philip was himself the grandson of a Portuguese monarch, his maternal grandfather Manuel I. In fact, when two Portuguese kings died in quick succession in eighteen months, he successfully claimed that crown too, in January 1580. Generous hand-outs of money and the might of his armies helped persuade doubters and see off a challenger, a distant Portuguese cousin called Antonio, at the Battle of Alcántara. Philip was ruler by September that year, becoming the first monarch of all Iberia. He was quick to reassure the Portuguese, however, that this did not mean their country had ceased to exist or been absorbed into Spain. 'Though Aragón and Castile have a single ruler,' he explained. 'They are not united, but as separate as they were when they had different rulers.'

With this triumph, Philip added Brazil to his already massive personal empire along with a string of Portuguese forts, trading 'factories' and minor colonies following the sailing routes along the West and East African coasts, all the way to India and the Spice Islands, as parts of today's Indonesia were known. Portugal's intrepid navigators had rounded the cape of Africa in 1488 and then pushed east. The Treaty of Tordesillas obliged Spaniards to travel in the opposition direction, and the two great exploring nations eventually bumped into each other in the Pacific Ocean at the Philippines, which were named after Philip.

By 1581, then, the entire Iberian Peninsula was in Philip's power, as was South America, the Caribbean, part of what is now the United States and most of the major maritime routes connecting all habitable continents. Between them, Spain and Portugal claimed '*mare clausum*', or 'closed sea', jurisdiction (via the Treaties of Alcaçovas in 1479 and Tordesillas in 1494) over all the world's major oceans except the North Atlantic. This monopoly on navigation covered some 87 per cent of the world's oceans and was impossible to police. To put it another way, however, if you sailed the seven seas, only one did not theoretically 'belong' to Philip. This was, then, the first global empire on which the sun did not set, 'which, to say truly, is a beam of glory,' as England's Lord High Chancellor Sir Francis Bacon observed.

Just as the Aragonese crown had used viceroys to administer kingdoms like Sicily, so the South American lands were divided into two viceroyalties based in Mexico City and Lima, Peru. Trade was not all one way, with European goods and livestock transported to the Americas. Indeed, a drawn-out process of 'Colombian exchange' saw fauna, flora and diseases leap continents. Potatoes, tomatoes, maize and tobacco travelled east. Wheat, rice, pigs and horses went in the opposite direction. Measles and smallpox did more damage in the Americas than the Black Death had caused in Europe, while another pox – syphilis – may have reached Europe in Columbus's returning ships. Even the arrival of large quantities of silver had an impact far beyond Spain, fuelling inflation in Europe and boosting trade with a silver-hungry China.

While navigators found that the circular currents and winds of the Atlantic allowed them to sail back to Spain, the Pacific proved much harder to navigate. They were incapable of making return trips from Asia to America until an Augustinian friar called Andrés de Urdaneta solved the problem in 1565 by finding the Kuroshio current, which put him on the circular current back across the ocean to the coast of Mexico. The so-called Manila galleons began making round trips to the Americas, with goods that were often bought from Chinese merchants who had exported them to the Philippines and which were then transhipped to Europe. The elaborately embroidered *mantón de Manila* – a shawl originally worn by high-class colonial women and later swirled by flamenco dancers – would become a symbol of this extraordinary global trade.

Ironically, the fact that Spaniards were now emigrating meant they also began to appreciate the fact that – although their homeland was divided into separate kingdoms – they had much in common. 'Even spirits who are most opposed in the homeland become reconciled when they are outside it, and learn to appreciate one another,' remarked one expatriate who missed the 'skies, rivers, fields, friends, family and other pleasures' of home. Empire, in other words, helped unite Spain, not least because so many Spaniards could share in the project of despoiling it.

11
Slavery that Bears with it a Crown

Philip II was already well prepared by the time his father passed him the throne. He was twenty-eight years old, had governed Spain during his father's long absences and had been king consort of England after marrying Mary I two years before her death. He was also an authentically Spanish monarch, born and raised there, and he did not leave the country for the four decades that remained of his rule after 1559. He was conscientious and successful to the point of masochism, seeing monarchy as a 'form of slavery that bears with it a crown'. Joy was not his thing.

Philip was unfortunate in his family life. Two wives – Maria Manuela and England's Queen Mary – died before he ascended to the throne. His English experience, where he helped Mary turn back the tide of Protestant Reformation begun by Henry VIII, was not happy. In fact, according to the historian Eamon Duffy, the couple unleashed 'the most intense religious persecution of its kind anywhere in 16th century Europe' and Philip would boast that 'many heretics had been burned' during his time in England. More than 450 Protestants were killed, including the Archbishop of Canterbury, Thomas Cranmer, who was executed in 1556. This was the spirit he brought with him to the Spanish throne.

His third marriage, to the young Isabel of Valois, ended in double tragedy. His dim but ambitious son Carlos (born to Maria Manuela) both fell in love with her and began plotting against his

↑ Philip II married England's Queen Mary and, after her death, inherited the vast Spanish part of his father's empire. He extended it further, while obsessing over the minutiae of government. Portrait attributed to Sofonisba Anguissola, 1573.

father. Philip arrested him personally, and the young man was locked in a tower, where he soon died, aged twenty-three, in July 1568. Isabel, who did not return the prince's love but nevertheless tried to protect him, died that same year, giving birth to a stillborn child. Philip had been strict with Carlos but did not deserve

the reputation he gained for cruelly driving two young lovers to their death – the version Giuseppe Verdi told three centuries later in his opera *Don Carlo*. Only a fourth marriage, to Ana of Austria, produced a stable male heir in Philip III, even if he wasn't much to his father's liking.

During Philip II's reign, Spain's itinerant court – which had long wandered from city to city trailed by hundreds of pack animals – finally came to a halt in 1561 at Madrid, a small Castilian city with good water, a decent castle (the now disappeared Alcázar), fine hunting and plenty of space for development. Fifty kilometres away, on the slopes of the often snow-capped Guadarrama mountains, he also built a magnificent, if austere, royal mausoleum and monastery of perfect proportions at El Escorial, described twenty-five years after his death by Welsh traveller James Howell as 'the eighth wonder of the world'. It was just one of some one hundred buildings whose construction the detail-obsessed monarch intervened in directly. At the vast El Escorial complex, he sat in a small room perusing documents, ruling an empire and procrastinating. Ever since Isabella and Ferdinand's time, a growing band of bureaucrats had accompanied the court. They helped churchmen and nobles to run a number of royal councils overseeing everything from the Americas to the Inquisition. Philip added to this with councils for Portugal, Italy and Flanders, but insisted on taking major decisions himself, and often 'so slowly that even a cripple could keep up with them', according to one adviser.

The lands his father left him in Holland proved a poisoned chalice, since he had to spend large sums fighting the seven Calvinist provinces that split off and waged a savage war of independence, which they had effectively won by 1581. Externally, England became an added threat, along with the old enemies of France and the Ottomans.

← Philip II built himself a magnificent, austere palace at El Escorial, near Madrid, where the bones of former Spanish monarchs are still kept.

Funding wars outside Iberia remained a huge drain on resources, and, since Spain still consisted of several entities, rather than one single nation, the kingdoms contributed unequally. Castile carried most of the burden, while the kingdoms of the Crown of Aragón (including Catalonia, Aragón and Valencia) gave less and did so reluctantly.

Castile, where taxes were continually hiked, could not possibly fund these endless wars on its own, so Philip turned to two other sources: South America and foreign bankers. Philip nevertheless failed to balance the books and declared 'bankruptcy' (by defaulting on loans) four times during his forty-two-year rule.

This overspending was made worse by his determination to help protect those bits of the Holy Roman Empire that his father had handed to other parts of the Habsburg family. Warring with France was brought to an end (for the time being) at the start of his reign with the Treaty of Le Cateau-Cambrésis in 1559, which maintained Habsburg domination of Italy. His struggles against the Ottomans took place mostly at sea, with the successful defence of Malta, a resounding victory off the coast of Greece at Lepanto in 1571 and the capture, but subsequent loss, of Tunis.

England's support for the rebellious Dutch Protestants – who were now led by the first William of Orange – very nearly produced the first foreign invasion of Britain since 1066. The ransacking of Spanish settlements and bullion fleets by privateers like Francis Drake was also threatening Philip's income, so he responded by assembling the 'great' or 'invincible' Armada. Its departure had to be delayed a year after Drake 'singed the king of Spain's beard' by raiding Cádiz and various Portuguese outposts, but in 1588 it finally set sail.

Poor coordination, bad weather and – less importantly – some plucky fighting by English boats brought disaster to the imperial fleet. In fact, only some 35 of the 127 vessels in the Armada sank and these were often transport vessels rather than fighting ships.

↑ As the Christian world's greatest power, it was Spain's task to lead the defence of Europe against the expanding Muslim empire of the Ottoman Turks, with the great 1571 sea battle at Lepanto, in the Gulf of Patras, providing a crucial victory.

Just three out of twenty galleons were lost. The Spanish Armada's failure, however, had helped ensure the continued success of the Dutch rebellion and the drain on resources that this produced. Rather than sink the Armada, indeed, the whole affair sank the Spanish economy.

An ambitious English counterattack the following year seems to have been a far bigger disaster for Philip's enemies, with perhaps only 102 of the 180 vessels led by Sir Francis Drake ('*el pirata Drake*' to Spaniards) and John Norris in a raid on Spain and Portugal returning to port. The men of this defeated force suffered even more. Only 3,700 of the 27,600 troops made it home in time to claim their wages, according to historian Luis Gorrochategui (though other historians accuse him of exaggerating, and see the overall troop numbers as below 13,500). Drake and Norris did their best to hide the scale of the disaster from Queen Elizabeth. Nor did they mention that a woman called María Pita had taken command of the defence of La Coruña after her husband, an army captain, was killed. She is said to have helped drive the English out of the city's old town to the cry of 'Those with honour, follow me!' María Pita's entry in Spain's *National Biographical Dictionary* places her under a single category, 'heroine' and says that tradition credits her with 'attacking and knocking down the English flag-bearer, provoking a fresh response from the defenders and the expulsion of the attackers'. She was just the first in a series of women who, whenever Spain was under attack during the next two centuries, would prove their valour, building an image of bold and indomitable Spanish women who were far superior to any foreign enemy who dared attack their country.

12
Ecstasy

Teresa of Ávila was never clear about whether it was a cherub or a seraph who drove the fiery golden lance in to her as she slept, but she recalled enjoying it very much. 'He appeared to me to be thrusting it at times into my heart, and to pierce my very entrails; when he drew it out, he seemed to draw them out also, and to leave me all on fire with a great love of God,' the Catholic Church's greatest female theologian wrote. 'The pain was so great, that it made me moan; and yet so surpassing was the sweetness of this excessive pain, that I could not wish to be rid of it.'

With her emphasis on asceticism, self-mortification and ecstasy, this Carmelite nun of noble origins born in 1515 provided a spiritually intense and intellectually adventurous contrast to the corrupt, lazy and self-satisfied churchmen who had driven away the likes of Martin Luther and split the western Christian church. That made her, too, a perfect warrior in the spiritual battle against Protestantism. The writings which saw her inducted into the club of great theologian saints in 1970, as the first female Doctor of the Church, together with her work as a reformer of convents and founder of the Discalced Carmelites order, all make Teresa a heroine of the Counter-Reformation.

While attempts to impose religious purity on the Dutch were a costly and bloody failure, an Inquisition crackdown against Protestants at home under Philip II had prepared Spain for its role as

↑ The mystic Saint Teresa of Ávila, painted here by Peter Paul Rubens, was a bulwark of the Counter-Reformation, and perhaps the most important female writer in the history of the Roman Catholic Church.

the main bastion of the Counter-Reformation. Roman Catholicism also remained the crucial cultural bond amongst the not-yet-united Spanish kingdoms, where Catalans, Basques, Galicians and others all spoke their own languages.

If religion was what bound Spain together, it was also its most important cultural export. Missionaries were not just sent to South America, where conquest could be justified as a holy endeavour, but also to China, Japan, India and other parts of Asia. Philip's Indies, meanwhile, were kept 'pure' by the banning of Jews, Protestants and

Muslims from crossing the Atlantic. At home, powerful new religious orders emerged that would help export Roman Catholicism around the world. Ignatius of Loyola, a Basque nobleman and warrior, founded the Jesuit order, which realized that schooling, and education as a whole, were crucial to building the machinery by which Catholicism could both retain its hold on Spain and become a truly universal faith.

There remained, however, one anomaly. Almost one in fifteen Spaniards, belonged to a group – the Moriscos – whose devotion to Christianity was either dubious or nonexistent. The pretence, on both sides, that the Morisco population of Granada had been properly – rather than forcibly and falsely – converted to Christianity came to a head with a serious revolt in 1568. It was a bloody and hard-fought conflict that took three years to put down. Philip was harsh on losers, banishing the 100,000 Moriscos of Granada, which lost a quarter of its population, to other parts of Castile.

Near the end of his forty-three-year reign, Philip complained that, while God had laden him with kingdoms, his heir Philip III was 'a son incapable of ruling them'. This comment said more about the dour father than his son, who continued many of his father's policies when he inherited his crowns in 1598.

In fact, Philip III finished off a process that had started under Isabella and Ferdinand, when he definitively expelled the Moriscos in the years between 1609 and 1614.

The final expulsion was done piecemeal, as the Moriscos were forced out, consecutively, from Valencia, Aragón and, finally, Castile. Some 267,000 people left Spain. Few could trace their lineage back to anyone not born and bred on Spanish soil. Their departure left Valencia, especially, without much of its rural workforce and saw lands that had been cultivated for centuries abandoned. As with the Jews, however, it is possible that many returned secretly and with the connivance of neighbours and lords.

The expulsion of the Moriscos damaged Spain's economy, but Philip III's peacemaking elsewhere (with a 1609 ceasefire calling off the war in Flanders and the Dutch Provinces for sixteen years) reduced considerably Spain's outgoings for the moment. Silver continued to pour in from Latin America, even though bullion fleets were increasingly harassed by English or Dutch pirates, privateers and buccaneers. This was still not enough to pay off the debts inherited from his father, so he cheated – debasing Spanish coinage.

In fact, the series of financial crises over previous decades had already driven governments to debase coinage constantly. In 1599, the year after Philip III took over, *vellón* coins began being made out of pure copper (rather than silver) and four years later were sent back to the mints and restamped to double their value. If its financial problems were ignored, however, Spain seemed to be living through a period of remarkable stability. A mellow Pax Hispánica ruled until Philip III's death in 1621, and that helped the rise of what became known as the Golden Age of Spanish culture.

13
A Golden Age

Sometime in the first years of the seventeenth century, a wiry and eccentric knight errant set out from a town in La Mancha. His name was Don Quixote and he was, of course, a fictional character and protagonist of what is hailed as the first modern novel in the western tradition. Quixote was not a real knight. He was a dreamer who belonged to that impoverished class of lesser gentry, the *hidalgos*. Miguel de Cervantes, the author of this tale, informs us that Quixote has been driven mad by books. More exactly, he has read too many tales of knightly derring-do in so-called chivalric romances – the pulp fiction of the time – and feels a need to model his behaviour on the heroes of those stories. Unfortunately, Quixote does not live in the Middle Ages, and his mindset is badly out of tune with the times. That makes him a figure of mirth, as he tilts at windmills, imagines flocks of sheep are hostile armies and convinces himself that his flea-ridden old nag Rocinante is really a sturdy charger.

Don Quixote is funny and tragic. His nostalgia for the simple rules of chivalry reflects a slow decline of Spanish glory that set in as it moved into the seventeenth century. If we were to date the first timid sign that decline might set in after more than a century and a half of expansion, we might choose 1574, when Spain lost the North African city of Tunis to the Ottomans. Cervantes himself had helped occupy Tunis the previous year. He had fled

↑ Miguel de Cervantes is credited with inventing the modern novel in 1605 by publishing the first part of *Don Quixote of La Mancha,* which is also an ironic commentary on the end of romantic medieval chivalry.

Madrid and joined the army in 1569 after wounding a man in a duel and then lost the use of his left hand at the famous Lepanto sea battle against the Ottomans in 1571. This was the largest sea battle ever fought, with 400 ships involved, almost all powered by oarsmen and not much different to the old Roman triremes. Just as the stand-off at Vienna marked the limits of the Ottomans' overland progress, so Lepanto showed that they could be stopped at sea. In retrospect, however, it was also a high point of Spanish glory in the Mediterranean.

If the loss of Tunis was a blow for Spain, worse soon came for Cervantes. In 1575, his boat was captured by Berber corsairs off Barcelona. He spent five years in captivity in Algiers before his ransom was paid (after four failed escapes), and he returned to Madrid, eventually working as a tax inspector. For any contemporary, the nobility of the cause Cervantes had fought for as a soldier was obvious, since to fight Ottomans was to partake in holy war. The same could not be said of scrapping with the French in Italy, when the pope might back the other side, or even to battle recalcitrant Dutch Protestants. That, however, is what Spanish soldiers spent much of their time doing from now onwards.

With so much tax money and bullion going through the royal coffers – most of it destined to be spent on wars or loans – even a meagre percentage spent on cultural patronage would have helped fuel a moment of splendour. As cities like Madrid grew in importance, so did the demand for entertainment, culture, intellectual spirituality and the self-glorification of portrait painting. While seventeenth-century Spain battled to maintain its political power in Europe, artistic life flourished. 'It is the century of splendour and decadence, of both a new dawn and decline,' the historian Antonio Domínguez Ortiz says.

The so-called Spanish Golden Age has no well-defined temporal frontiers. Some trace it as far back as that extraordinary year of 1492, when the humanist scholar Antonio de Nebrija produced *Gramática castellana*, the first book of Spanish grammar and the first for a modern European language. He published three decades before a first Italian grammar was produced, while English had to wait a century. Nebrija's grammar, soon followed by a dictionary, was also part of an attempt to establish the predominance of Castilian Spanish over the Peninsula's other languages. In his dedication to Queen Isabella he explained, presciently, that language was 'the instrument of empire' and a tool for assimilating conquered peoples. Just as importantly, however, his extensive and wide-ranging works reflected an increasingly self-confident, stable and wealthy society where culture could be cultivated without fear of massive societal disruption from war, rebellion or the breakdown of law and order.

By the early seventeenth century, the need for entertainment was fulfilled by the commercial plays, or comedies, churned out by the likes of Lope de Vega (with 500 plays, 3,000 sonnets and a smattering of epic poems, novels and novellas) and Pedro Calderón de la Barca (who wrote 120 comedies, plus 100 other works, often on religious themes). Their 'cloak-and-sword' intrigues often took a poke at the same old-fashioned, stiff morality of the aristocracy and the dreams of chivalry that Cervantes lampooned in El Quijote. At their best, these playwrights rivalled their English contemporary, William Shakespeare, who died within two weeks of Cervantes in the spring of 1616.

Cervantes remade the novel when he published the first part of *Don Quixote* in 1605 (though some see the twelfth-century Andalusian writer Abubakr ibn Tufayl as Spain's first great novelist, with his *Robinson Crusoe*-like tale of a feral desert island boy, *The History of Hayy Ibn Yaqzan*). The second part of *Don Quixote* came ten years later, shortly before he died, and the two parts are still being read and retranslated today. A genre known as picaresque, meanwhile, introduced a series of loveable rogues, cheats and liars – the *Buscón* of Francisco de Quevedo or the anonymous *Lazarillo de Tormes* – to the admittedly small reading public. Successful frauds have intrigued Spaniards ever since.

Don Quixote has been borrowed to support many theories about the human condition, and to Spaniards themselves he also came to mean many things over time. The nineteenth-century philosopher Miguel de Unamuno, for example, saw him as representing the wilder, creative side of Spanishness and called for the country to renovate itself by taking back 'the tomb of the Knight of Madness from the hands of the *hidalgos* of Reason'.

Although *Quixote* is fantasy, there is social realism and biting critique in its portrayals of Spanish society, as there also are in the picaresque genre. In fact, it is this realism (along with its irony and the deliberate, witty 'intertextual' play with other books) that marked it as new and different. It also, however, reflected a sad truth about the 'golden age' and the 'glorious empire': that its people were getting poorer, as benefits flowed abroad or were pocketed by a few, while inflation made the poor even poorer. In that sense, Latin American gold and silver did little to prevent growing misery amongst the peasants and city poor who made up most of Spain's population. The city of Cáceres, in Extremadura, registered 26 per cent of its population as 'poor' in 1557. Four decades, and many bullion fleets, later, that had risen to 45 per cent. 'The picaresque world of petty thieves, vagabonds, prostitutes and tricksters was something more than just a product of the literary imagination: it was a faithful reflection of the real problems that Spain was facing in that era of crisis,' explains historian Henry Kamen.

Among the new poor were often members of a newly arrived group, the gypsies. Cervantes's novella *La Gitanilla*, *The Little Gypsy Girl*, which is included in his *Exemplary Novels* collection, gives us an early glimpse of a people who would later fascinate romantic travellers to Spain. Cervantes is sometimes sympathetic, but mostly reflects early prejudices against gypsies and establishes outrageous tropes that survive today. They worked as entertainers, he tells us, but were 'born as thieves' and liked kidnapping Christian children (a trope shared with Jews). The first of these is demonstrably true, as Cervantes knew, while the prejudices probably reflect the bitterness generated in his own family as it became embroiled in a dispute over money and its own gypsy blood.

Although their name reflects a popular belief that they were 'Egyptians', Europe's gypsies were originally a nomadic people of Indian stock. They had reached Spain by 1425, when the first of a series of self-styled nobles (in this case, Counts Juan and Thomas of 'Lower Egypt') began asking permission to enter the country with groups of around 100 followers in order to visit holy sites. Just five decades later, at the Corpus Christi celebrations in 1479, an acrobat, dancer and horse-rider called María Cabrera arrived with a gypsy troupe to entertain guests at the palace of Diego Hurtado de Mendoza, Duke of Infantado, in Guadalajara. If her dancing entranced the duke, her horse-riding abilities apparently left him speechless after she asked to join the very masculine game of *cañas*, in which two sides played at war on swift Spanish ponies and armed with bamboo canes. Their romance produced an illegitimate priest son called Manuel who, in turn, had an illicit relationship with Cervantes's aunt and was the father of her quarter-gypsy daughter Martina. As a result, the Cervantes and Mendoza families became engaged in legal warfare over money for the child's upkeep (which was mostly used to maintain the lifestyle of various members of the writer's family). The heroine of *La Gitanilla* – La Preciosa – is really a snatched baby called Constanza Meneces, but she still proudly declares: 'There is no such thing as a stupid gypsy man or a foolish gypsy woman. Since it is only by being sharp and ready that they can earn a livelihood, they polish their wits at every step.'

By Cervantes's time Spanish authorities had passed numerous laws to either expel gypsies or force them to settle and conform, with Isabella and Ferdinand starting the process by ordering them to find 'proper' jobs in 1499. Discrimination persisted across the centuries. In the worst anti-gypsy measure of all, the so-called Gran Redada, or Great Round-up, Spain's entire gypsy population of up to 12,000 people were arrested overnight on 30 July 1749, after the pope had first passed a law preventing them seeking refuge in churches. They remained locked up or were used as forced labour for up to sixteen years. Many more 'anti-gypsy' pieces of legislation were passed (upwards of 230, according to one count), seeking to eradicate the community entirely or force them to become settled town-dwellers, as most eventually did. As the gypsy writers

Silvia Agüero and Nicolás Jiménez point out, expulsion or extermination would have robbed Spain of everything from the themes of work by playwright Federico García Lorca, painter Salvador Dalí or composer Manuel de Falla, to the infinitely rich world of flamenco music and dance, its many great artists and the wonderful, Oscar-nominated 1963 flamenco film *Los Tarantos*. Around one in seventy Spaniards are now thought to be gypsies, or of gypsy origin, though this is never officially measured – making them an often invisible, ignored or looked-down-upon minority.

It was in visual art, however, that Spain shone brightest, with El Greco producing his bizarrely elongated portraits in Toledo (almost certainly by choice, rather than due to a supposed astigmatism), while the likes of Diego Velázquez, Francisco de Zurbarán and Bartolomé Murillo painted kings, aristocrats and the new class of merchants made wealthy by American trade. Churches throughout Spain were adorned with saints, biblical scenes and expressions of religious mysticism.

Given the wealth that flowed through its port, it is not surprising that Seville became the centre of much of this. The city's embrace of Baroque, and the works of Murillo, are best viewed in the chapel at the Hospital de La Caridad, tucked behind the dazzling white Maestranza bullring. The hospital's great patron, and prior, was a wealthy merchant called Miguel de Mañara – who went down in history as the model for that infamous Spanish philanderer and trickster Don Juan. Mañara's tomb certainly suggests that this son of a flashy, *nouveau riche* merchant from Corsica who had made his fortune in Peru felt a need to repent for his early life: 'Here lie the bones and ashes of the worst man the world has ever known,' the inscription reads.

→ As home to the administration of trade with the Americas, Seville became one of the wealthiest cities in Spain – and one of its main slave cities. In the eighteenth century, it would build one of the country's first permanent bullrings.

In fact, the libertine Don Juan Tenorio was the invention of playwright Tirso de Molina, who had written his *El Burlador de Sevilla* (translated as either the Trickster, Playboy or Seducer of Seville) earlier in the century. That 'compound of cruelty and lust', as Jane Austen called him, espoused the common belief that you could behave as badly as you wanted during your life without ending up in Hell, as long as you squeezed in a formal act of contrition before death.

Mañara's worst vice, in reality, was an addiction to that American import known as chocolate, but he seems to have suffered from a sort of colonial guilt. Inherited wealth and the showiness of his family sat uncomfortably on him, especially after Seville was overrun mid-century by the plague and rioting. Personal tragedy also struck with the early death of his adored wife Jerónima. Mañara turned to his *sevillano* friend Murillo for a dozen of the biblical scenes of mercy and charity crammed onto the chapel's walls which provide a narrative of goodness to contrast with his family's less reputable past. The dark, cruel paintings here by another Seville artist, Juan Valdés Leal, with their putrefying corpses of finely dressed bishops, also accuse a city drowning in wealth from the Indies of being obsessed with transient mundane brilliance and forgetting the inevitability of death or judgement. The busy paintings and elaborate, golden altarpieces of saints, virgins and tubby, winged cherubs in the chapel are a reminder that Baroque art sought to overpower the senses and provoke awe at the divinity of God. 'One pants for breath,' wrote W. Somerset Maughan after a visit to the 'hothouse' chapel.

The Spain of this period, indeed, became quintessentially and exaggeratedly Baroque as the Jesuits pushed church-builders to embrace the style in, for example, the cathedral at Granada or the cathedral towers in Santiago de Compostela. Several generations of the 'ultra Baroque' Churriguera family, meanwhile, filled Madrid and Salamanca with wedding cake altars and elaborately

↑ Juan Valdés Leal's paintings in the Baroque chapel of the Hospital de la Caridad in Seville are a reminder that wealth and prestige are no use in the afterlife.

carved church façades. Once more, however, Spain did not provide the impulse, but brilliantly synthesized the Baroque forms that were blown in from both southern and northern Europe.

14
He Has Ravished Me

In late August 1623, a relatively unknown twenty-five-year-old artist travelled through the summer heat from Seville to Madrid carrying a finished painting of city water-sellers and an introduction to a chaplain at the royal court, Juan de Fonseca. It took Diego Velázquez a single day to stun the court – since Fonseca immediately bought the picture, had Velázquez paint his own portrait quickly and then showed it off to incredulous friends at the royal Alcázar. A few days later, the eighteen-year-old king Philip IV sat for him. He would never allow himself to be painted by anyone else in his life, with the sole exception of Rubens. Velázquez painted the young monarch in all his long-chinned, Habsburg pallidness – 'puffy, adenoidal, so pale the blue veins are visible beneath the clammy white temples', says art critic Laura Cumming. Yet Philip came alive in this picture and later portraits where Velázquez performs his stunning trick of producing a truthful image with paint strokes that his first biographer described as 'unintelligible close-up. But a miracle from a distance.'

What was it about Velázquez that made him the first of several Spanish painters to be considered the world's greatest artist (like Goya the following century, or Picasso two centuries after that)? 'He has astonished me; he has ravished me,' swooned modernist Édouard Manet after he saw the Velázquez works that French and

British collectors had plundered from Spain during the Peninsular War. Cumming points to his humanity:

> If the art of Velázquez teaches us anything at all it is the depth and complexity of our fellow human beings. Respect for the servants and the dwarves, the jesters and the bodyguards, the old woman frying eggs and the young boy with his melon, for the princess and the palace weavers, for the seller of water and the seller of books: that is what his art transmits.

↑ In his famous picture *Las Meninas*, Diego de Velázquez shows himself standing at the easel, with King Philip IV and his wife Mariana watching (and reflected in a mirror) while he paints their daughter *infanta* Margaret and her ladies-in-waiting.

His famous portrait of Philip IV's daughter Margaret Teresa and her retainers, *Las Meninas*, is memorable for the self-portrayal of the moustachioed Velázquez himself, looking on intently from behind his easel. The king and queen, meanwhile, are cleverly reflected in a wall mirror while their daughter wears a scandalously wide Baroque *guardainfante* dress-skirt. More remarkable, however, are the figures of Maribárbola and Nicolás Pertusato, the daughter's two dwarf attendants, who look on with an intelligent gaze or play with the dog in the foreground and are every bit as present as the rest. Velázquez painted a similarly grand portrait of Don Diego de Acedo, keeper of the royal seal, who appears as a learned, book-perusing scholar first and, only on a second take, as a man literally dwarfed by the same volume.

Most evocative of all, however, is the portrait of his assistant, the talented Juan de Pareja. Pareja is black, a slave assistant freed by Velázquez during a trip to Rome in 1650, where he painted the portrait. Pareja, who stayed working with Velázquez for another decade, walked around the Eternal City with it while Romans marvelled at the likeness. If anything, his portrait is an expression of a triple normality. Velázquez shows Juan de Pareja as, if not an equal, then certainly as self-confident and visually alert as any painter (and wearing a dazzling white collar that was prohibited to either him or Cervantes in Madrid, where strict sumptuary rules prevailed). The colour of his skin only begs a question about where exactly in Africa his forebears came from. There is no attempt to portray 'otherness'.

Slavery of black Africans was not strange to Spaniards. After Lisbon, indeed, Barcelona and Valencia had become the biggest slave ports in Europe in the years after the transatlantic trade began. Seville was also selling around 1,400 slaves a year early in the seventeenth century, and secondary markets existed in Burgos, Málaga and Valladolid. Spain quite possibly had Europe's largest African population, with visitors observing that Seville was like a

↑ Velázquez's assistant, the freed slave Juan de Pareja, was a highly talented painter who held himself with pride and confidence.

chessboard 'filled with black and white piece, because there are so many slaves'. Cádiz's slave population was nearly 15 per cent by the end of the seventeenth century, while Seville's had been 7.4 per cent in the middle of the previous century. Lucena, the small and once famously Jewish town near Córdoba baptized an average of ten slave children a year between 1539 and 1699. Black Africans probably accounted for 10 per cent of the populations of cities like Málaga, Córdoba, Huelva and Las Palmas. Freed black slaves were also a common, if largely uncountable, presence. Pareja's comfortable dignity suggests that, at least in Velázquez's eyes, there is nothing to comment on here except that the subject is himself an artist. He had spent years painting studio copies, priming canvasses and preparing pigments – and may have authored paintings that were later mistaken as Velázquez originals. Pareja himself would later insist that he was an old Christian, since Ethiopia embraced Christianity long before Spain. An early eighteenth-century litigant of African origin in Seville also successfully claimed purity of blood (meaning that he had no Moorish or Jewish ancestry and could in this case join a Capuchin order) precisely because of his African ancestry.

The astonishing figures for the mixed population of mid-seventeenth century Andalusia also present an historical conundrum. Seville is a city of religious processions, where the Klu Klux Klan lookalike *nazarenos* from *hermandades*, or brotherhoods, solemnly march images of saints around the streets during Easter Week. A black brotherhood, known as the Hermandad de Los Negritos, was founded in 1393 – meaning there were already a good number of slave converts who had most likely been captured from amongst the Muslims in Granada. In 1622, the dramatic and bloodied statue of Christ on the Cross that is still processed by the brotherhood every year was sculpted by Andrés de Ocampo. Until the mid-nineteenth century, it only had black members. Now they are a minority. Where did Andalusia's black Africans go? One suggestion is that they disappeared from registers because Spaniards were not racist and that, since freed slaves were Christians, and Christians were equal, they were simply absorbed into the population. Alternatively, Spaniards were so racist that they did not want to recognize any African blood, and this truth was eventually erased by mixed marriage. It is also possible that many slaves were lighter-skinned North Africans who did not look very different to southern Spaniards. Other theories suggest that most were either shipped to the Americas or were prevented from having families.

In the seventeenth century, at the king's silver mines at Guadalcanal, southern Spain, hundreds of strong, young, enslaved men and women were used to carry out the most arduous tasks. One young girl of royal stock who was snatched off an African beach in 1686, the nun Sister Teresa Chikaba, became a saint after her death, but was reportedly treated like a slave at her convent in Salamanca.

The glories of the Golden Age hide another much glummer truth about seventeenth-century Spain. Elsewhere in Europe, the first stirrings of scientific investigation were helping to push Christians towards a more secular set of values. All this, in the words of the French historian Joseph Perez, was happening 'without Spain's help, and against Spain's will'. Without the creative tension between competing Christian creeds that drove change elsewhere, it did not seem necessary. On a wider scale, power was shifting away from the Mediterranean towards Europe's north and west as it also began looking across the Atlantic for prosperity and inspiration.

In Spain, debt, population decline, high taxes and better imported goods were all seen as proof that the country was losing ground to European contemporaries even as culture bloomed. For 125 years it had enjoyed an impressive succession of monarchs in Isabella and Ferdinand, Charles I and Philip II. The five kings who ruled in the seventeenth century, starting with Philip III, were no match. The kings' chins grew longer, and their brains (or interest in governing) grew feebler. With monarchy in decline, many were happy to see *validos* – men who governed for the king while making themselves rich – leading the country once more. The first of these was Philip III's man, the Duke of Lerma, who oversaw the expulsion of the Moriscos but also saw his patron's death celebrated with a rhyme that went 'A king in power, a kingdom oppressed / Or, more exactly, fleeced'.

It was after Philip III's death in 1621, however, that the towering figure of the first part of the century emerged in the form of the Count-Duke of Olivares. He was an all-powerful, authoritarian *valido* who served the young Philip IV and ran Spain for more than two decades, not least because the king was just sixteen when his father died – though he maintained the family tradition of longevity and reigned for the next forty-four years.

The count-duke's most famous portrait, by Diego Velázquez, has him seated on a rearing horse as if he were a monarch and waving a marshal's baton. His arch-rival was Cardinal Richelieu, who governed an increasingly emboldened and ambitious France, and the painting appears to be a direct challenge to the wily Frenchman. Who is the most powerful man in Europe?

The Spanish crown's possessions in Italy and the Low Countries as it entered the new century were too scattered for coherent governance. Common sense dictated that some should be given up. Obdurate Spanish pride, however, meant they must be defended. Rather like Don Quixote, sense only arrived after a battering, and those came repeatedly. In short, the epic contest between Olivares and Richelieu ended badly for the former and marked a watershed as France triumphed and Spain's glory days drew to an end.

The decline that now set in was felt most in Castile. Attempts by Olivares to share out the burden of defending Spanish power by unifying its kingdoms only proved how entrenched the separation between them was. Olivares wanted Castile's laws to become those of Spain and Portugal as a whole – effectively creating a single nation out of Philip IV's Iberian domains. In short, Castile had kept the empire to itself, bled it dry, run up debts and now needed saving – which it wished to do by imposing its laws and traditions on others. For obvious reasons, that failed.

Respect for royal authority had, in any case, always been relative and this scepticism now found intellectual backing. The Jesuit writer Juan de Mariana's *On Kings and Kingship* affirmed, for example, that despotic kings could be murdered – thereby storing up trouble for Jesuits in Spain and across Europe in future centuries. Mariana also researched and wrote a vibrant history of Spain up to the death of Ferdinand in 1516 (later updated to Phillip III's death in 1621), which was still in use in the mid-nineteenth century. A 1613 treatise *On the Defence of the Faith*, by another Jesuit thinker, Francisco Suárez, produced the radical argument that power resided with the people. They ceded this power to a monarch but could oust any king or queen who failed them. This was no small thing, since contemporaries regarded Suárez as the world's greatest living philosopher. He is still deemed to be the father of international law, and was much quoted by Descartes, Schopenhauer and Heidegger. Perhaps the most popular expression of Spanish dislike of untrammelled authority, however, was Lope de Vega's play *Fuenteovejuna*. Here, during Isabella's rule, a whole town rebels against an abusive knight who considers it his feudal right to rape one of the townswomen and is then murdered. No one will later tell the king's judge who committed the crime. 'Fuenteovejuna did it!' is the only answer. The story is based on a real historical event.

In fact, Spaniards had long been rebellious in the face of abusive authority. An oath traditionally attributed to people swearing fealty to the Aragonese kings, for example, declared that 'We, who are as good as you, swear to you, who are no better than us, to accept you as our king and sovereign lord, provided you observe all our liberties and laws – but if not, not.' Castile, meanwhile, let officials in the Americas publicly flout orders they thought were detrimental to the monarch or the public good. All an official had to do was place the law or instruction on his head and ritually declare that '*obedezco pero no cumplo*', or 'I obey but will not implement'. These 'liberties' were heavily constrained, rarely used and later much exaggerated, but still represent early notions of freedom in a country that would later spill much blood over the concept.

The further one drifted from Castile, the more pronounced this rebelliousness became. 'In the Spanish monarchy, where there are many provinces, different nations, diverse languages, dissimilar attitudes and varying climates, great capacity is required in order to preserve and unite,' observed yet another Jesuit philosopher, Baltasar Gracián, in 1640 (Schopenhauer was a fan of Gracián's punchy, aphoristic wit as displayed in the 300 maxims that made up his famous *Art of Worldly Wisdom*). Local *fueros*, or independent rights, self-government and laws, had formed part of Spain's make-up from before Isabella and Ferdinand's time. Attempts by Olivares to impose central authority came to a head in 1640, when fighting broke out between badly behaved troops stationed in northern Catalonia and the local population. Trouble spread to Barcelona in June, the viceroy was murdered, and representatives of the monarchy and Castile were targeted by an angry mob that included the *segadors*, or harvesters, who had gathered in the city for the hiring season. When those in charge of Catalonia's institutions of self-government joined them, this peasants' revolt became a full political and territorial confrontation. In fact, the Catalans decided to secede from Spain completely, swearing allegiance to the French king. Today the Catalan 'national' anthem, adapted from a nineteenth-century folk song, celebrates the *segadors*' revolt and defines Castile and the crown as natural enemies. 'We must not be the prey / Of those proud and arrogant invaders!'

The French pledged to respect Catalan laws, but the soldiers and administrators serving the new child-king Louis XIV behaved as badly as, if not worse than, Philip's officials. By 1652, the Catalans had had enough, and offered their allegiance once more to Philip IV, who promised not to force them into adopting Castilian law. A first attempt to unite Spain as a single country had failed. Peace with France came at a cost. This was paid for by the Catalans, who lost the long-fought-over Catalan-speaking regions of Roussillon and Cerdagne to France for ever.

Portugal, meanwhile, seethed at the continual demands for money and troops. Spain's enemies were also stealing Portugal's lands in Brazil, where the Dutch had captured Recife and Olinda. With Olivares busy putting down the Catalan rebellion on the far side of the peninsula, the Portuguese declared independence under the Duke of Braganza, King João IV, in December 1640. Portugal was for ever lost to Spain.

When parts of Andalusia rebelled as well, Olivares's reputation crumpled and he retired in disgrace in 1643. Worse was still to come as Philip IV started a series of European wars to uphold his family's personal dynasty. They revealed just how far Spanish military power – which had dominated Europe for more than a century – had dwindled. In 1648, at the Treaty of Westphalia, Spain finally had to accept the independence of its Dutch territories (but held on to Flanders, the core of modern Belgium). The dream of a Roman Catholic Europe led from Spain by Habsburg kings was dust. This was a shattering of Spanish identity and of the ideas of honour, glory and Castilian character that underpinned it. Spain's attempts to hold on to the past, indeed, now looked like an episode of *El Quixote*.

When peasants' revolts sparked by hunger, taxes and bread prices broke out in several parts of Andalusia between 1647 and 1652, it seemed that respect for Castile's monarchy, and all it represented, was dwindling even at home. That helps explain why Philip IV went down in Spanish history as '*el Rey pasmado*' – literally a 'dumbstruck' monarch, supposedly crippled by inbred, genetic stupidity. His jutting Habsburg jaw and comically upturned moustache, so well painted by the man whose brilliance he nurtured, Diego de Velázquez, seemed like proof of his incompetence. The poet and satirist Francisco Quevedo put it this way:

What the people most lament
Is that you do not have the will
To make use of your power.

Yet Philip was also a cultural connoisseur, who sparked an aristocratic craze for buying some of the best art in Europe. He was the chief patron of Velázquez and a man whose own collection of paintings remains at the heart of one of the world's greatest galleries, the Prado Museum in Madrid. In an otherwise inglorious reign, 'the greatest achievement of Philip's life was to have employed Velázquez,' says Cumming. We would know more about his collection if much of it had not burned during a blaze that started on Christmas Eve 1734. Flames consumed all four stories of the Alcázar in Madrid, with servants having time to rescue *Las Meninas* (with a singed cheek on the infanta) and some works by Titian, Rubens and Leonardo (plus the royal family's massive Pilgrim Pearl), but much else was lost. Some 500 works of art went up in smoke.

Philip's attempts at maintaining Spanish glory failed but were also an expression of self-confident pride and ambition, however badly misplaced. His final testament, addressed to his son and heir Charles II, proved that Philip had learned crucial lessons. 'I order my son the Prince, his tutors, governors and the Queen, and his successors, to respect and maintain the laws, privileges and *fueros* of each of my kingdoms, and not to change them.' They should not be foolish enough, he meant, to try to unite Spain into a single country, as Olivares had attempted.

When Philip IV died in 1665, Spain had had just five monarchs (counting Isabella and Ferdinand together) in 186 years. It had gained an empire, and the Golden Age had left a remarkable cultural legacy, but Spain was in crisis and desperately needed to change.

15
Inbreeding

Charles II of Spain was just four years old when he inherited his kingdoms. While predecessors had merely displayed inbreeding via their elongated chins, the impact of generations of marriages between close family members finally manifested itself to the full. Charles's family tree was more like a thicket, dense with crossed matches between cousins, second cousins, uncles and nieces. His mother, Mariana of Austria – whose broad hooped skirts occupy so much space in Velázquez's portraits – was her husband's niece. His parents' common ancestry is so intertwined that twelve separate genealogical routes lead back over five generations to Juana the Mad. Charles was a sickly, dim child, who suffered epilepsy and rickets (some theories also give him two X chromosomes, or Klinefelter syndrome). Although he later married, he was unable to have children and was never expected to live long. The young king gained the nickname 'the Bewitched'. What else could explain such misfortune?

Mariana became regent and handed power to her Austrian confessor, Juan Everardo Nithard. He was the first of several people to govern in a confusing period of court rivalries and concern for the future of the monarchy. If the king was impotent, who was his heir? A weakened Spain, meanwhile, was targeted by France, which picked away at its possessions in Flanders.

More ambitiously, Louis XIV – the belligerent, absolutist and long-reigning 'Sun King' of France – saw a chance to place his Bourbon family on the throne of Spain. His wife, after all, was a Spanish *infanta*, Charles's aunt (and Philip IV's daughter) Maria Teresa. Their grandson, Philip of Anjou, was put forward as a contender. The Habsburgs, meanwhile, promoted their own candidate – the Archduke Carlos, son of the Holy Roman Emperor Leopold.

In all this confusion, some positive measures were taken. The impact of a constantly debased coinage was corrected, with a large devaluation that hit living standards but saw taxes and interest rates fall while restoring confidence in the currency. Foreign adventures were kept to a minimum and mostly involved defence against the Sun King. The complex treaties of Nijmegen, signed by nine parties in 1678 and 1679, and the five-way Peace of Ryswick, which marked the end of the European-wide Nine Years War in 1697, brought stability and peace with France. The path was now reasonably clear for a Frenchman to sit on the Spanish throne.

That is exactly what happened. When Charles II died aged thirty-eight in November 1700, he left a will that declared Philip of Anjou as his heir, becoming Philip V of Spain. Habsburg inbreeding had killed off the dynasty that had ruled Spain for almost two centuries.

Philip V was seventeen, bewigged and beautiful, but unable to speak Spanish. He took power with minimal fuss and was welcomed effusively in Madrid and then by the Catalans when he travelled to meet his new Italian bride, Princess Maria Luisa Gabriela Saboya, as she crossed the border from France. They married at a monastery near the Catalan border town of Figueras. The change of dynasties, it seemed at first, would not be traumatic.

Spain and its empire were too succulent a prize, however, for things to stay that way. Trouble was soon sparked by Philip V's grandfather, Louis XIV. He began suggesting that, with Bourbons (or *Borbones*, as the Spanish branch became known) now on the thrones of Spain and France, the countries might eventually fuse into a single kingdom. As if to confirm this, he also occupied Flanders, claiming he was doing so at his grandson's behest. The result was yet another European war, known as the War of Spanish Succession.

A single kingdom that united Spain and France was a far bigger threat to the rest of the continent than even the vast but scattered European empire that had been inherited by Charles I. England, the Dutch Republic and the Holy Roman Empire formed a rival alliance that backed the Habsburg pretender, Archduke Charles of Austria. In 1702 they declared war on Spain and France, and soon brought Portugal into the coalition.

The thirteen-year war that started in 1701 saw the English grab Gibraltar (and never let go) as well as leading an expedition that took Barcelona, provoking civil war in Spain as the kingdoms of the Crown of Aragón (Catalonia, Aragón and Valencia) joined them under the banner of Charles of Austria. The Catalans, especially, had long felt animosity towards France, while a Habsburg king might have been expected to obey Philip IV's wishes that his successors 'maintain the laws, privileges and *fueros* of each of my kingdoms [including Catalonia], and not change them'.

Catalans were not fighting for independence in the current sense and cannot have foreseen how far centralism would become crucial to the Bourbon regime. They certainly hoped, however, to maintain the loosely articulated Spain they were used to. Unfortunately for them, they backed the wrong horse.

The results of the war were reasonable for the Bourbons, great for Britain, bad for Spain and worse for Catalonia. Philip V remained king, though Spain lost its Italian territories of Naples, Sardinia and Milan along with its final possessions in and around Flanders in the several treaties signed at Utrecht between 1713 and 1715. Barcelona surrendered in September 1714, ending the civil war. The Bourbons had won and still occupy the throne today. They were forced, however, to shed all dreams of uniting Spain with France to create a dominant new European superpower.

England's bounty included Gibraltar and the island of Menorca – which still conserves the traditions of distilling gin and installing sash windows. More importantly, the treaties produced a major chink in Spain's commercial monopoly over the Americas with a highly lucrative permit given to the British South Sea Company to trade 4,800 enslaved Africans and send a 500-ton merchant ship to Spanish America every year. Historian G. M. Trevelyan sums up the Utrecht deals as bringing 'the end of danger to Europe from the old French monarchy, and ... a change of no less significance to the world at large – the maritime, commercial and financial supremacy of Great Britain'. 'Perfidious Albion', as Britain became known, was now a muscular rival. In Spain, Utrecht also marked the beginning of a new era as it opened up to new, foreign ideas.

In 1637, René Descartes had arguably ushered in the Enlightenment with his famous 'I think, therefore I am' – '*Cogito ergo sum*'. That other foundational text and keystone of the seventeenth century's Scientific Movement – Isaac Newton's *Principia Mathematica* – was already thirteen years old when Philip V became king. Spain, meanwhile, had remained in thrall to the proudly unscientific mysticism of Santa Teresa and others. Under the Bourbons, however, it found itself connected to the wider network of Enlightenment thinkers.

At the same time, Bourbon rule saw the sprawling and costly continental ambitions of previous centuries replaced by an efficient, all-controlling French-style centralization. Royal absolutism sat at its core. This finally turned Spain into a single, if often fractious, nation. It also brought prosperity.

The process was never going to be easy. Catalan nationalists today see 1714 as a year of tragedy. Much like the British with Dunkirk, they have turned defeat into a symbol of national resistance, with Catalonia's separate 'national' holiday now celebrated on 11 September, the day that Barcelona capitulated.

Defeat brought punishment. Part of the city's Born district was bulldozed to make room for a new fort (the now-disappeared Ciutadella) from which Philip's troops could control the city. In 1716, Catalonia lost its *fuero* charter, just as had happened to Valencia and Aragón when Philip defeated rebels there in 1707. Majorca lost its *fuero* in 1715. Thus ended a long period of partial self-government that had included a thirteenth-century Magna Carta-style bill of rights known as the Usatges, a parliament of clergy, nobles and merchants called les Corts that had gained considerable legislative powers as far back as 1283 (but had only met twice since 1632) and a Barcelona city council known as the Consell de Cent, or Council of One Hundred Men. The historic importance of the Generalitat, the tax-gathering administration that emerged from les Corts in the thirteenth century and eventually became a regional government, and the Consell were reflected in the magnificent fourteenth- and fifteenth-century Gothic palaces they occupied, on either side of the Plaça de Sant Jaume in the heart of Barcelona. They are still there today, though much of the original architecture is hidden behind later additions.

With the suppression of their fueros, the nations of the old Crown of Aragón had effectively ceased to exist. A newly homogenized Spain emerged, with exceptions in the north. The *fueros* of the Basque provinces and Navarre were left intact, since they had been loyal to Philip V – highlighting the Catalan error in backing the wrong pretender. Even today, as a result, the Basque provinces retain more autonomy than anywhere else in the country. Modern Spain, meanwhile, had finally been 'founded' as a single country. 'Enlightened reform ... and the centralized monarchy and bureaucracy of the new Bourbon dynasty definitively brought Spain together to make a nation,' says historian Juan Pablo Fusi.

In fact, Spain was already undergoing a process of profound transformation driven by less visible economic and social forces, in which Castile was losing population and power. Coastal areas boomed – from the green and rainy northern regions of Galicia, Asturias or the Basque Country to southern Andalusia (especially its Atlantic ports, with Cádiz growing tenfold in the 180 years up to 1786) and the Mediterranean coastlines of Catalonia and Valencia.

If the former kingdoms of Aragón showed little sign of resenting the new situation, indeed, it was because they benefitted from this economic boom. Barcelona, for example, tripled in size over the eighteenth century (though Madrid, as the capital, remained almost twice as big). The grand old cities of Castile, meanwhile, increasingly became dusty museums of historic grandeur, populated by churchmen, land-owners, artisans and the urban poor.

A virtuous cycle of rising wealth and investment also saw crops from the Americas begin to spread, with potatoes and maize changing agriculture in the rainy north. From the Jerez vineyards (whose fortified sherry wines attracted English merchants) to the first large iron mills in the north, progress took a quietly relentless path. Shed of Habsburg obligations in other parts of Europe, the empire in Latin America could both develop itself and help fuel Spanish growth.

A modest new bourgeois class of merchants grew in strength, but power structures initially remained cast in stone. Old aristocratic families and the church administered much of the land through *señorios*. In a confusing mix of rights, they enjoyed such extensive control over their people that fifteenth-century peasants in Catalonia convinced themselves that some *señorio* lords enjoyed a *derecho de pernada*, which permitted them to deflower a bride on her wedding day. The peasants demanded the abolition of this right, though it was either inexistent or had long fallen into disuse. Cities, meanwhile, answered directly to the monarchy. Church wealth was such that it owned 15 per cent of the land, and a feeling that monks, priests and nuns lived better than most other people provoked the first signs of a sentiment that would play an important part in later Spanish history – anti-clericalism.

Forms of royal absolutism had been visible in Spain since the times of Isabella, but this now became almost total. Parliaments were mere rubber stamps. Royal councils became advice-giving bodies as one of them – the Council of Castile – was turned into the centre of government. A new class of royal functionary, the *intendente*, was sent to major regional cities to ensure that central government orders were carried out. A permanent, professional army was formed, in imitation of France and Prussia.

The Utrecht treaty, then, was really a blessing for Spain. Philip V even went on to recover much of the land lost in Italy for his family, thereby honouring the Aragonese crown's centuries of history there. The agreement finally signed in 1748 at Aix-la-Chapelle (Aachen in German) meant that any heir had to renounce their Italian kingdoms – basically Naples and Sicily – and give them to someone else in the family before taking the Spanish crown.

That treaty was signed twenty months after Philip V's death in 1746, and with family pride thus restored (and empire-building restricted), Philip's son Ferdinand VI 'the Prudent' was able to concentrate on Spain and the Americas after inheriting the throne in 1746. He was also to able to indulge an obsession with what had been one of his father's great passions – music.

16
Farinelli and the Melancholic Monarchs

The slender, tall and soft-skinned Italian Carlo Broschi had arrived in Spain in August 1737 with a single mission – to cheer up the depressive monarch, Philip V. Best known by his artistic name, 'Farinelli', he was Europe's finest singer and its best-known *castrato*, who had been castrated as a boy in order to conserve his remarkable voice. This combined a dazzling technique with a form of naive, clear expressivity that made him an object of fanatical adoration. Farinelli, in short, was a star.

The Italian had just spent three years singing in London. There, he had been praised as 'a God' but also lampooned as a eunuch and corrupting sexual influence, whose gender ambiguity was a threat to the nation's young. In Spain, Philip V was so thrilled that he immediately offered him a salaried, well-paid position in the court – on the condition that he no longer performed in public. Farinelli accepted, cancelled his return to London, stayed in Madrid for twenty-three years and never sang to a paying public again.

Farinelli had become rich in England, but Philip offered stability and artistic freedom. The Italian spent much of his time with the cultured heir to the crown, Ferdinand VI, and his musical Portuguese wife, Barbara of Braganza. When Ferdinand inherited the crown in 1746 the *castrato* was also placed in charge of the operas and *serenatas* performed at the Coliseum (or 'Royal Theatre') at the Buen Retiro Palace in Madrid, which became 'Europe's premier opera', according to one historian of music. He also oversaw performances at the complex of palaces and gardens known as the Royal Place, 80 kilometres away in Aranjuez.

One part of Farinelli's job remained the same, however, which was to bring joy to yet another melancholic monarch. He performed two arias a day, one with Ferdinand on the harpsichord and one with Barbara of Braganza playing. Occasionally, the Italian *castrato* and the queen sang together, while their favourite leisure moments included river-borne flotillas designed by Farinelli that mixed musical performance with dramatic lighting of ornamental gardens and fireworks.

Ferdinand may have been grateful to have inherited the services of Europe's greatest vocalist, but he was quick to rid himself of another Italian – his stepmother, Elizabeth Farnese, who had kept the increasingly frail Philip V in power. It was she who had forced her husband to return to the throne after abdicating in 1724 (only for his heir – Ferdinand VI's elder brother, King Luis – to die after an eight-month reign). In fact, it had been Elizabeth who brought Farinelli to Spain as part of a lifelong campaign to cheer up her husband, who may have been bipolar and was so heavily dependent on his wife that she was sometimes described as the most powerful person in Spain. She had also done much to drive the family's aggressive policies in Italy, and it was Isabel's son Charles (Ferdinand's half-brother and eventual heir) who became king of both Naples and Sicily when these realms were recovered.

Some observers noted, however, that the new highbrow king – nicknamed 'The Learned' – was as much under the sway of his own wife, Barbara of Braganza, as his sad and sickly father had been ruled by Elizabeth. 'Rather than Ferdinand taking over from Philip, it is a question of Barbara taking over from Elizabeth,' quipped one French observer.

Ferdinand continued the reformist domestic policies of his father, while his wife helped run a pro-Portuguese foreign policy. What

↑ When the cultured but melancholic Habsburg monarchs Philip V and Ferdinand VI were overwhelmed by depression, their vigorous wives – Elizabeth Farnese (opposite, by Louis-Michel Van Loo *c.*1739) and Barbara de Braganza (above, by Jean Ranc *c.*1729) – kept Spain running.

most delighted the monarch, however, were the arts. He agreed with one of his favourite authors, Father Enrique Flórez, that 'arts and letters can achieve as much for a kingdom at home as arms can abroad – at less cost and of greater use'. Ferdinand was another depressive, who occasionally locked himself away and leaned heavily on his wife – even as the asthmatic and gluttonous queen became increasingly obese. When she developed uterine cancer and died in August 1758, the king went into a steep decline, often refusing to get out of bed. The forty-five-year-old monarch went mad and was reportedly administered opium to stop him trying to bite people. He died twelve months after Barbara of Braganza, a crazed, tragic and lonely figure. Farinelli had failed to cheer him up and soon left Spain to return to Italy.

17
Absolutism in the Century of Light

'It is a crime to criticize any act of government, even when it is wrong.' The words attributed to Ferdinand's half-brother and heir, Charles III, after he came to the throne in 1759 show that full-blown royal absolutism had now reached Spain. The next two centuries of Spanish history, indeed, would frequently be overshadowed by the idea of absolute power, in the hands of monarchs or dictators, and by the struggle to share this with ordinary Spaniards. It is an irony that a monarch who spent much of his day hunting and was not given to intellectual pursuits was also the country's royal embodiment of the Enlightenment. What he lacked in intellect, however, Charles made up for in vigour and conviction. Spaniards call the whole eighteenth century the Century of Light, but it only really began to shine fully under the steady and predictable Charles III.

Perennially sunburned from his outdoor activities, the jolly-looking forty-three-year-old had already been a monarch for twenty-four years, as King of Naples and of Sicily (titles that he renounced on becoming King of Spain). His experience gave him a firm idea of how monarchy should work but also an awareness of his own limitations. Choosing good ministers, above all, would be the key to his reign. Since many of these had imbibed Enlightenment values, they would also try to apply them to Spain. In the meantime, he could go hunting.

There were considerable obstacles to progress. Charles's

councillors wanted to modernize Spain but also to leave its power structure untouched. Enlightenment was to be imposed from above, with aristocrats, churchmen and royal servants expected to lead the way. Some members of the first two groups were delighted to do so, but only if that meant no loss of power or property for themselves. As a result, otherwise profound reforms barely changed a basic structure that meant absentee landlords felt no need to modernize. Why bother, when cereals and sheep provided such an easy living?

Spain enjoyed relative internal calm. Progress, however slow, was being made, wealth was being created and there was little to complain about. Some ill-judged reforms went too far. In 1766, Charles's bullish Italian chief minister, the Marquess of Esquilache, demanded a change in the way people dressed. Castilian men, especially in Madrid, wore long cloaks and such wide-brimmed hats that it was impossible to recognize anyone until you were up close and could see their face. Knives, swords and other weapons were easily hidden under these flowing garments. They offered the perfect disguise, in other words, for ruffians and thieves. Esquilache's insistence that hats and coats be smaller (he wanted three-quarter-length capes and tricorn hats) prompted an outbreak of rioting in Madrid which (fuelled also by food shortages) spread to places as far apart as Zaragoza, Valencia and the Basque Country. 'Long Live the King! Death to Esquilache!' they shouted.

The price for this sartorial rebellion was paid, entirely irrationally, by the Jesuit order. The Jesuits were seen as an enemy of absolutism – a counter-power with their own agenda and a grip on both elite education and parts of the imperial administration. The Jesuits had, indeed, accrued vast powers (notably as landowners in Paraguay), but monarchs remembered the way Mariana and Suárez, for example, had argued that they deserved to be ousted if they failed to serve their people. In 1767, the Jesuits were expelled from Spain, following the example set by absolutist France three years earlier.

The Esquilache riots were a sign that it was not only the aristocrats and the church (which still ran its own Inquisition) who could block Enlightenment progress and reform, but that sometimes opposition came from the people themselves. Religious festivals were often semi-pagan celebrations based on superstition, rather than contemplation or faith. Popular belief in the magic powers attached to fiestas, spectacles and processions surrounding, say, Corpus Christi or Easter was frowned on by the new, Frenchified administrative elites. Sensationalist, melodramatic theatre and pop operettas (known as *zarzuelas*), especially, upset the more cultured figures in government, who wanted them made more refined and educational. Their snootiness about the hoi polloi only served to separate the elites from the masses.

A reaction to this reformist zeal soon set in. A new fashion was set by 'vulgar' show-offs, the *majos*, who wore elaborately colourful clothes, decorated with bright embroidery. Even aristocrats began to imitate their jargon and brash, countryfied dress-code as a way of poking fun at the elites, with their po-faced seriousness and power. Bullfighting took off during these years as a popular spectacle – with the first permanent rings built in Seville and Ronda – in part because it annoyed the new sophisticates who considered it as distasteful as bear baiting. The bullfighters' glittering and garish suit of lights further fuelled the fashion for flashy clothes, which a royal order from 1784 aimed at state officials denounced as suitable only for gypsies, bullfighters, butchers and black marketeers. Indeed, a fashion for the sensuous overkill of Andalusia – its dancers, fiestas and gypsies – swept into Spain's capital city, Madrid, as an almost deliberate snub to the reformers.

This was the city that another great Spanish painter, Francisco de Goya, found when he came to Madrid in 1775. The Aragonese artist painted, drew or designed tapestry cartoons (the cardboard models on which the huge tapestries that hung in palaces and monasteries were based) of *majos*, *majas*, bulls and bullfighters

↑ Francisco de Goya liked to depict Spaniards playing in traditional dress, while a political fashion war set flamboyantly dressed *majos* against those who favoured colder, more sophisticated clothes from France.

as well as the popular fiestas of the city. Shockingly, at least for the Inquisition, one of his *majas* was nude. His noble patrons delighted in them all as a purely Spanish phenomenon.

The bullfighting hero of the time was a young matador from the southern town of Ronda called Pedro Romero, who arrived in Madrid in the same year as Goya and later sat for a portrait with a scarlet-lined cape slung across his shoulders. Legend has it that

Romero's grandfather Francisco had reputedly been the first to fight bulls on foot using a red cape and sword, becoming the first professional *torero*. This oft-repeated story may well be apocryphal, but it is true that bullfighting had once mostly been a mounted affair. The bullfight's origins are unclear, but it not hard to imagine that both the Roman circus and ancient Mediterranean bull-worshipping mythology lie somewhere in the mix of traditions that inspired it. The bull's long-standing mythical status in Spain is spectacularly represented by the four massive granite Guisando Bulls that are lined up together in a field near El Tiemblo, in the province of Ávila. Like some of the 400 other stone animal sculptures scattered across the *meseta*, they date back to four centuries before Christ. A form of bullfighting was certainly in existence by the fifteenth century. That is when Queen Isabella found the spectacle so upsetting that she demanded the points of the beast's horns be covered so that they did less damage (she didn't seem worried about the bull itself).

The church was a problem for the enlightened elite. In 1776, Pablo de Olavide, one of the country's most energetic and successful reformers, was arrested by the Inquisition. There had been no attempt to close the institution down, and some reformers had even hoped that its power might be harnessed as an absolutist tool to reform popular, superstitious religion.

Olavide was a brilliant young man from the colonies, born in Peru, who embraced Enlightenment thought and was sent to help reform Seville, where he modernized its university. He also set up a series of forty-two new towns, villages and hamlets in the interior of Andalusia along the Sierra Morena mountains, with sufficient land given to colonizers (some of them German) to allow them to farm efficiently and apply new agricultural methods. He was a fierce critic of the enemies of progress, including absentee landlords and ignorant clerics. He was arrested, accused of impiety, materialism and heresy and sentenced to eight years' confinement in a monastery. The Inquisition stymied his projects, warning off others.

↑ Bullfighting became another symbol of Spanishness in the late eighteenth century as matadors turned professional and began fighting on foot with colourful capes.

Spain nevertheless became a place that was easier, and freer, to move around. Roman roads had been left to crumble, and sixteenth-century visitors from Northern Europe had found the roads so bad that four-wheel carriages were abandoned at the border. A total of 1,100 kilometres of roads, and 322 bridges were built in the eleven years after 1777, along with canals and new ports. A twice-weekly postal service between Madrid and Barcelona ran from 1763. Internal customs borders largely disappeared (except at the frontiers of the Basque provinces), and the monopoly on trade with the Americas held by Cádiz and Seville was ended in 1765. Coastal cities from the old Crown of Aragón, like Barcelona and Alicante, now found themselves on a much longer list of ports able to access markets previously only open to them via

Castile. A decade later, the trade was opened up to all ports. Royal factories producing glass, porcelain, tapestries and cloth were set up along with a national lottery (in 1763) that still famously shares out the world's biggest prize bonanza 'El Gordo' (The Fat One) every Christmas.

Education boomed, in universities and schools. Historians and economists appeared at universities while the royal academies (of art, the Spanish language, history, jurisprudence and other subjects) founded in the first half of the century began to gain weight. They provided Spain with both an intellectual backbone and a first narrative of itself as a place of great regional variety and complexity.

The new Enlightenment leaders exported their ideas to the empire as well. In simple terms, they tried to turn the economy of Spanish America away from its over-reliance on the extraction of silver and gold towards the production of valuable and exportable new farm products, including sugar, tobacco and cacao. As agriculture spread, the amount of land actually occupied (rather than controlled) by Spain on the continent almost doubled in the fifty years up to 1790. Vast cattle ranches appeared in the flatlands of Venezuela and the pampas of Argentina, while sugar plantations spread rapidly across Cuba and Puerto Rico from the 1760s onwards. The latter needed cheap labour, and the trade in slaves from Africa exploded.

This meant that the population of the continent finally returned to the same size as when the Spaniards arrived. Missionaries and colonists pushed north and east from Mexico, spreading out across a large part of what later became the United States between the Mississippi and the Pacific. San Francisco, San José and Los Angeles were all 'founded' in the five years after 1776. In fact, since a secret 1762 treaty saw France cede to Spain sovereignty over what later became the Louisiana Purchase, it controlled more than half of the future United States (not including Alaska) for the next thirty-eight years.

The new reforms unsettled colonial society and provoked rebellions, most famously an indigenous revolt in Peru lead by Tupac Amaru in 1781. The white (or mostly white) descendants of settlers, or *creoles*, who were used to ruling the colonies, found their easy, privileged lives disturbed. It was one thing to supervise, and live off, a simple extractive economy, and quite another to be forced to act like dynamic entrepreneurs in a world of science and reason. It was rather as if a feudal system was being overturned. They could have chosen to rebel, of course, but – unlike their North American counterparts – they were in a weak position. A fragmented and hierarchical society, in which recently arrived, impoverished Spaniards still felt themselves above the American-born white *creoles*, who in turn felt superior to the indigenous people and black freemen or slaves who made up most of the population, meant the wealthier classes had no appetite for rebellion.

Indeed, trouble in the colonies came mainly from Britain, the Dutch Republic and other nations. In fact, it was now absolutely clear that Spain's main enemy was Britain – specifically its sea power – and its chief ally in the attempt to quell British expansion was now France.

The old Bourbon 'family pacts' between Spain and France that had started with the arrival of Philip V were renewed in 1761. They helped provoke the world's first truly global conflict – the Seven Years War, which started in 1756 and saw Britain temporarily take both Havana, in Cuba, and Manila, in the Philippines. In the final peace, signed in Paris in 1763, Spain regained both, with Menorca returned two decades later. The American War of Independence between 1775 and 1783 provided another opportunity to get back at England, as both Spain and France supported the rebels. Both at home and in the empire, however, the authoritarian monarchy which had been ruling Spain would soon face a completely new kind of threat.

18
Revolution

On 14 July 1789, an angry mob attacked the fort, prison and armoury that represented royal power in the centre of Paris – the Bastille – sending shock waves across Europe. Establishment Spain, whether enlightened, or not, was terrified by the French revolution and its cry of 'liberté, égalité, fraternité'. In fact, there was little to fear. Spain's reforms had not gone far enough for a bourgeois class, of the kind that played such a crucial role in the French uprising, to have emerged.

Spain, however, could not ignore what was happening on its frontier. Charles IV had inherited the Spanish crown from his father the previous year and desperately wanted to help his distant cousin Louis XVI. Yet nothing could stop the advance of revolution, and Louis lost his head to the guillotine on 21 January 1793.

Initially, Charles had been expected to continue with the reforms initiated by his father, and he kept the same secretary of state – the Count of Floridablanca – who had just produced an extensive and detailed reform programme covering everything from reforestation to foreign affairs.

Eventually, however, he turned to a vain and arrogant young man called Manuel Godoy, who happened to be one of his wife's favourites. The 'manly-looking' Godoy was appointed secretary of state at the age of just twenty-five. Rumours spread that Godoy, who had been a private in the royal bodyguard just five years earlier,

↑ Manuel Godoy was a lowly soldier in the royal bodyguard who became, as secretary of state to Charles IV, the most powerful man in Spain by the age of twenty-five. He is infamous for his scandalous womanizing and for allowing Napoleon Bonaparte to send his troops into Spain, thereby sparking the Peninsular War. Painting by Francisco de Goya, *c.*1801.

was the queen's lover. Such gossip was normal for the time and swirled, particularly, around Charles IV's wife María Luisa. It also reflected an established code of behaviour known as the *cortejo*, by which married women of status took and paraded young male companions or lovers. These were preferably drawn from the ranks of the army or the clergy.

In fact, Godoy had been chosen because, as a young and very minor aristocrat, he owed his position almost entirely to the king. Spain's new strongman lived scandalously, and rumours spread that the best way to ensure his favour was to take your 'wives and daughters' to him. Some men did. The monarch, meanwhile, was, according to historian Charles Esdaile, 'a man of limited intelligence whose chief passions were hunting, collecting clocks and watches and playing practical jokes on his courtiers'.

Godoy initially continued with the top-down reformism that was typical of Enlightened Absolutism. A limited raid on the church's land served to provoke its opposition. A bullfighting ban in 1805 brought the wrath of what the elites – and the foppish *petimetre* youth who imitated French dress and manners in a battle of styles with the *majos* – called the *populacho*, the common populace.

Charles IV initially joined an alliance against revolutionary France, which reacted by occupying parts of the Basque Country and Catalonia in 1794. Spain now found itself squeezed between two powerful and belligerent forces. On its border were French revolutionaries. Threatening it everywhere else were English seafarers and the expanding military muscle of Britain. It found itself with little option but to ally with France again in 1796, when the regime known as the Directory decided to challenge the growing might of Britain. It was not, however, an alliance of equals.

This situation came to a head in 1805, when a joint French and Spanish fleet commanded by one of Napoleon's admirals, Pierre Villeneuve, sailed out of Cádiz to confront a force led by Admiral Horatio Nelson off the Cape of Trafalgar. It was a humiliating defeat (with Spain losing ten of fifteen vessels, France losing twelve of eighteen and Nelson's fleet surviving intact) but there was still no way for a weak Spain to escape the French grasp – even though some of the vessels needed to protect Spanish commerce with the Americas now lay at the bottom of the sea.

In 1807, Napoleon announced that he was punishing the Portuguese for their alliance with Britain by dispossessing the Braganza dynasty. To make that threat reality, he would send an army to Portugal which, naturally, had to cross Spain. Godoy promptly offered help to the French. In fact, an agreement with Charles IV and Godoy promised huge personal bounties. Godoy was to be gifted southern Portugal, while the monarch would gain the grandiose title of Emperor of the Two Americas.

Napoleon's troops entered Spain on 18 October 1807. Some marched through to Lisbon, backed by Spanish troops, and arrived just in time to see the king, the government and much of the country's wealth (including the royal treasury and half its coinage) disappearing in a fleet of thirty-six ships protected by the British navy. Either way, Portugal had been captured, and this seemed like a joint Spanish-French triumph.

By early 1808, however, French troops in Spain increasingly looked like an occupying force and, amid growing mutual suspicion, the situation became increasingly fraught. In March 1808, Charles IV tried to leave Madrid but was stopped by angry, riotous rebels in Aranjuez who demanded to know what was happening. Had the French army effectively invaded and taken control of Spain? Godoy, meanwhile, hid. Within days some 10,000 French troops entered Madrid under the command of Marshal Murat and camped in the surrounding countryside. The rebels decided that Charles IV and Godoy could not be trusted and pledged allegiance to his son Ferdinand VII. Charles responded by abdicating in favour of his heir.

That, however, was only the beginning. Bonaparte persuaded both father and son to travel to the French Basque town of Bayonne in April 1808. Once there, they were informed that the best solution was for Ferdinand to return the crown to his father and for the latter to abdicate in favour of Napoleon. That is what they did early in May 1808, and Napoleon installed his own brother, Joseph Bonaparte, on the throne of Spain.

The Spanish royal family and its ministers had been bamboozled. So, too, had the people. Spain was now an occupied country, with an unwanted foreign monarch. It was not something that Spaniards were prepared to put up with. A country that had only been properly formed less than a century earlier finally found a cause that united people of almost all classes and from all its regions – hatred of the French occupier.

19
Dos de Mayo

The muttering against the French had begun long before ordinary Spaniards rose en masse against them. In places like Burgos and Carabanchel, outside Madrid, stealthy, violent attacks on them had already been carried out by people who shouted 'Death to the French!' and then disappeared into the night.

On 2 May 1808, Madrid exploded into rebellion. A crowd gathered in front of the royal palace as a rumour spread that more members of the royal family were being taken away. The mob fell on one of Murat's aides-de-camp, sparking an ugly and unequal battle that pitted men and women armed with little more than billhooks, daggers and flowerpots against the columns of French troops that immediately flooded the city. Two Spanish captains, Luis Daoíz and Pedro Velarde, tried to put up a fight at the Monteleón artillery barracks, helped by a young woman called Manuela Malasaña. All three were killed. By the time order was re-established late that night, some 200 people lay dead in the streets of Madrid, and hundreds more were injured.

A further 300 people were executed immediately afterwards, some for nothing more than possessing a knife. Priests were not

→ On 2 May 1808, the people of Madrid fought an unequal battle against Napoleon Bonaparte's occupying troops amidst concern over the disappearance of the royal family. Goya immortalized their battle.

called to hear their confession. Francisco de Goya recorded the scene in his vast painting *The Third of May*, or *the Executions on the Principe Pio Hill* (now home to the Plaza de España, at the end of Gran Vía). In Goya's version, bloodied bodies pile up as a group of terrified people, including a priest, prepare to be shot. More await their turn, including at least one woman.

The fighting in Madrid sparked a nationwide mutiny against the French. Rumours spread that the occupiers had tried to kill the entire population of Madrid, whose heroic resistance against well-armed soldiers contrasted with the collaborationist *afrancesados* or 'the Frenchified', who had willingly handed the machinery of government (and their own services) over to the new French rulers. In another famous picture, *Second of May 1808 in Madrid*, Goya depicts *madrileños* of both sexes armed with little more than daggers and sticks being trampled underfoot and hacked to pieces by the Mamluk (Egyptian) cavalry units of Murat. Calls were made for the rest of the country to follow their example.

In fact, the French had only occupied parts of Spain – controlling the cities on the route from the border near San Sebastian through to Burgos, Madrid and Toledo, along with a section of Catalonia from the border to Barcelona. Much of the Spanish army was stationed in areas that the French did not control.

The situation remained confusing, however, and it was only on 20 May that it was officially announced that Ferdinand, in whose name the people were turning against the French, had abdicated. By 25 May 1808, a network of '*juntas provinciales*' – provincial governments – had been set up to oust the French and bring back Ferdinand VII, who was now known as *el Deseado*, or 'the Desired One'.

The next six years were dominated by a war that destroyed the country economically but unified it politically and socially. Joseph Bonaparte's 'reign' became almost entirely a military affair, in which France devoted large amounts of money and manpower to fighting

↑ On 3 May 1808, a long queue of *madrileños* awaited execution, but their action the previous day had sparked Spain's War of Independence, known to the British (and Wellington) as the Peninsular War. It was also the start of Goya's obsession with war.

the Spanish rebels and their allies from Britain and Portugal.

The French were arrogant occupiers. Napoleon deemed that Spain had what historian Raymond Carr called 'the worst army in Europe'. Convinced of the moral superiority of their revolution and looking down on the church, French soldiers behaved badly wherever they went. The slightest resistance was answered with terror, not least because French generals knew help was often far away, and that fear was their best weapon. Their men were expected to live off the land, which meant plundering the areas they occupied for food. All this was done in the conviction that they were actually liberating the Spanish from the clutches of the Inquisition, the nobility and centuries of oppression.

The war drew in the British, who launched an Iberian campaign – the Peninsular War – designed to wrest Portugal from Napoleon's hands and support the Spanish fight for freedom. A general called Arthur Wellesley – soon to be made Duke of Wellington – made his name here. The first battles, however, were fought by Spaniards against what was meant to be the strongest army in Europe, which had won previously stunning victories across the continent.

20
War and Independence

With the revolt against the French, the old regime collapsed. One by one, cities that had not yet been occupied declared themselves in rebellion, with local elites taking charge of the individual *juntas*. It was the first time that power had emerged from the Spanish people, rather than being distributed by hereditary monarchs or nobles. On 6 June 1808, a French column found its way barred at the prosperous wine town of Valdepeñas, in La Mancha. At the head of the crowd blocking them, with a cudgel in her hand, was Juana Galán (known as 'La Galana'), who is credited with helping lead a local uprising that cut the principal route between La Mancha and Andalusia. A thousand French troops tried to march through the town and were met by Juana, by men armed with agricultural tools and by women who poured boiling cauldrons of water or oil from their windows. The French responded by burning down part of the town, and La Galana reputedly spent the rest of the war fighting in a local guerrilla group.

Just like María Pita leading the resistance to Drake's men in La Coruña, a number of legendary women would emerge in the fight against the French – with some accomplishments undoubtedly embellished through constant retelling. During the defence of Zaragoza that same year, the twenty-two-year-old wife of an artilleryman, Augustina Zaragoza, later known as Agustina de Aragón, grabbed the *botefeux* from an injured artilleryman and fired the

crucial shot that held the invaders back. This act, recounted in her own official military records, made her a national heroine. She was instantly recruited into the artillery and was later captured by the French but escaped and served throughout the war, taking part in various battles and rising through the ranks to become a lieutenant. She married a doctor twelve years younger as her second husband and was named in Byron's *Childe Harold*.

> YE who shall marvel when you hear her tale,
> Oh! had you known her softer hours!
> Beheld her smile in danger's Gorgon face,
> Then the closed ranks and lead in glory's fearful chase.

Yet another woman, known only as La Fraila, is credited with blowing up a detachment of French soldiers quartered in the hermitage she looked after outside Valdepeñas. In revenge for the death of her son, she set light to their powder store, killing herself as well. Priests also took up arms to defend Zaragoza and other places as Spaniards of all types engaged in a genuine and popular national war of independence.

Spain's army was as numerous as that of the invaders, but poorly organized, badly led and short of both cavalry horses and pack animals. It nevertheless achieved a few famous early victories. On the same day that the people of Valdepeñas were pouring boiling water on French troops, a column was stopped at Bruch with the help of local Catalan militias. A jittery French commander was convinced he was under attack by a much bigger force, since the Catalan *somatén* militia was largely hidden inside some woods and two young drummer boys in the folds of the Montserrat mountain produced rolling echoes that sounded like hundreds of drums were leading the Catalans into battle.

← Artillery volunteer Agustina de Aragón, from Zaragoza, was just one of several heroic women who fought in the War of Independence. Painting by Juan Gálvez, c.1810.

Far more significantly, the Spanish army won a resounding battle at Bailén in Andalusia on 22 July. This was Napoleon's first ever major defeat and, rather than proving that the Spanish army was in excellent shape, it showed that his generals were not always as brilliant as was supposed. By then, the fighters from Valdepeñas and other places had dispersed into the most novel and effective military phenomena of the time – guerrilla groups. These intercepted much of the mail between French troops in Andalusia and their senior commanders in Castile. One such letter allegedly included instructions to General Dupont about the tactics he should use at Bailén, allowing the Spaniards to prepare their victorious attack more effectively.

Guerrilla bands had by now formed across French-occupied Spain. Some were little more than groups of brigands, but their ability to pop up almost anywhere made them a constant and tiring threat. They were bold and brutal, spreading chaos and sending French military planners into disarray. How, after all, do you fight an enemy that continually disappears, but that you feel is constantly around you and which has the backing of the people wherever you are?

The new king, Napoleon's brother Joseph, found himself in trouble almost immediately. He had only just arrived in Madrid when, with rebellions breaking out and an army defeated at Bailén, he moved his forces back north to a line along the River Ebro. The war, however, soon entered a new phase as Napoleon flooded Spain with troops. Wellington was in Cork, Ireland, with an army that he was meant to ship across the Atlantic Ocean to Venezuela. It was sent, instead, to Portugal, where another insurrection against the French was breaking out.

Napoleon himself, now with 300,000 troops, crossed into Spain in November 1808, determined to impose himself. His soldiers smashed their way back towards Madrid, taking Burgos and destroying one of Spain's three land armies at Espinosa de los Monteros. French troops also fought south through Catalonia and most of Aragón, though Zaragoza (and Agustina de Aragón) held out until February 1809, and the Catalan city of Girona also refused to give up the fight for six months. Valencia was not taken until January 1812. Spanish forces, nevertheless, were destroyed at a series of battles in Uclés, Ciudad Real, Medellín, Ocaña and Alba de Tormes.

Only a few things prevented the French gaining firm control. On the one hand, guerrillas kept on fighting, preventing the occupiers from feeling comfortable almost anywhere. On the other hand, Wellington landed in Portugal in August 1808 and began to harass the French from the west.

His victory at Talavera de la Reina (140 kilometres west of Madrid) in July 1809, commanding English and Spanish troops, was a sign of tactical prowess, but he did not have the strength to make a large dent in the French position. Instead, he withdrew back to the Portuguese border. French troops were sent after him but, since a Portuguese army was by now also fighting alongside Wellington and the British, they failed to make ground. By 1810, nevertheless, the French armies controlled much of Spain, with the exception of Cádiz and the south-east.

The War of Independence (as Spaniards call it), or Peninsular War, was mostly not an affair of huge set-piece battles and resounding victories, but a clever war of attrition which slowly exhausted Napoleon's army. Bonaparte himself called it his 'Spanish ulcer' and, when he decided to invade Russia and overstretched himself in 1812, this duly burst. The cautious Wellington had turned Portugal into a fortress, against which the French could tire themselves out and from which he could set out on fresh campaigns. Napoleon pulled troops out for his march on Russia, leaving the numbers in Spain more evenly balanced. He no longer had reinforcements that he could march across the border whenever needed.

When Wellington struck out from Portugal in the summer

of 1812, he defeated the French at Arapiles (near Salamanca) and marched on to Madrid, where he was greeted with jubilation in the Puerta del Sol on 13 August. He was pushed back to Portugal by French counterattacks, but the widely dispersed enemy army now looked very vulnerable.

The following spring, Wellington set out again and – with the guerrillas constantly harassing them – the French suffered defeat after defeat. The major set-piece battle was at Vitoria, in the Basque Country, on 12 June 1813, when 120,000 allied soldiers sent the French army running back to the frontier. Looking back at the war during his later exile, Napoleon rued his mistakes. 'War in Spain ruined me,' he wrote. 'The Spanish war destroyed my reputation in Europe, increased my embarrassments and provided the best training ground for the English soldiers. I myself trained the English army.'

By the end of the year, Ferdinand VII ('the Desired One') had been restored to the Spanish throne. On 22 March 1814 he returned amid popular joy and a sense of shared pride. Spain's national war of liberation had been won, but had it really united the country?

21
Ferdinand VII – the Desired One

Ferdinand's return provoked nationwide euphoria, but Spain was a country destroyed by the war. Some 300,000 Spaniards had died, while famine and chaos had added perhaps another 200,000 fatalities, with death striking around one in twenty of Spain's roughly 11 million people. The economy was in tatters. Much of the progress of the previous century had been undone, with factories destroyed, cities devastated, and Castile's vast flocks of sheep decimated. Spain also owed thirty times more money than its exchequer received in a year. Was it really worth it?

In fact, a monarchy led by Joseph Bonaparte might have been a great success. His regime had planned reforms that only revolution and bloodshed had won for France. They would have meant creating a two-chamber parliament, abolishing the Inquisition, defanging the excessively powerful landowners and the church while, for the first time, sending most children to school. Bonaparte declared the suppression of two-thirds of Spain's monasteries, but was too busy with war to impose the measure. These radical plans explain why part of the reformist elites backed him. They were viewed, however, as traitors, and the adjective *afrancesado* (Frenchified) became an insult.

Instead, Spaniards had started their own sort of revolution, initiating a politically progressive and daring exercise in constitutional liberalism. The *juntas provinciales* eventually gave way to

CONSTITUCION
politica
DE LA MONARQUIA
Española.
Promulgada en Cadiz
á 19. de Marzo de 1812.

a 'supreme central junta' in 1808 and a parliament that met in Cádiz in September 1810. With some 300 members, one in five of them from the Americas, this parliament declared that national sovereignty lay in its hands and produced one of the most remarkable documents in Spanish history – its first written constitution (excepting Napoleon's own constitution for Spain, published two years earlier in France).

The Cádiz Constitution was finalized on 19 March 1812 (the day of Saint Joseph, which is why the constitution would also gain a female version of his nickname as 'Pepe', becoming La Pepa). Many of the new constitution's measures were as radical as those proposed by the Bonaparte brothers. The Inquisition was to be abolished, as were the old feudal *señorios* of landowners. Everything from farming and industry to commerce and printing were freed from royal or state control. Spain was to become a liberal parliamentary monarchy that guaranteed individual rights and basic political freedoms for its people. Sovereignty resided in the nation, meaning Spaniards on both sides of the Atlantic, rather than in the monarch. 'The Spanish nation is formed by all Spaniards from both hemispheres,' it stated. 'The nation is free and independent and cannot be part of the patrimony of any one family or person.' 'The people' were now 'the honour and glory of the nation'.

This bright new Spain still wanted hereditary kings, but with limited authority and separation of powers between courts and lawmakers (including the monarch). It was a remarkable document that, in the words of historian Juan Pablo Fusi, was 'politically and morally admirable'. Its promoters became known as 'liberals' and were among the first in the world to bear this political moniker.

← In 1812 Spaniards wrote a progressive, liberal constitution which proclaimed that, while they were fighting for the return of King Ferdinand VII, he must share power with the people.

The intellectuals, lawyers, churchmen, aristocrats and others who wrote the 1812 constitution claimed inspiration in the Spain that had existed before foreigners first began to run it, with the arrival of the Habsburgs. That was stretching the facts. The last truly 'Spanish monarchs', those proto-absolutists Isabella and Ferdinand, must have turned in their graves. The influential deputy Agustín Argüelles took this idea of an ancient nation even further, reducing eleven centuries of history to a long-running battle for liberation by declaring that 'Spaniards were in the period of the Goths a free and independent nation'. He added, also, a stirring cry: 'Spaniards, you now have a *patria* [homeland].'

This, then, was the Spain that welcomed back Ferdinand VII, who had spent the war in luxurious exile with his brother Carlos at Charles Talleyrand's Valençay chateau. It was a Spain that had a constitution, but where the rest of the state needed rebuilding.

Ferdinand did not like the Cádiz Constitution, which he immediately abolished. Instead, royal absolutism returned with a vengeance. As a Spanish historian who was born at this moment, Modesto Lafuente, later put it, this was not now 'a free nation that was proud of its rights ... but, instead, a fanatical and enslaved nation that adored its master and, in utter humiliation, kissed the hand that would now enchain it'.

The returning monarch was bright but notoriously harsh, spiteful and heavy-handed. He was also overweight and given to periods of great sloth. Liberals had added hope, progress and ambition to Spain's war of liberation, but now they were the enemy. Some 12,000 families fled into exile, joining the *afrancesado* elites who had backed Bonaparte as Ferdinand augmented the monarchy's direct powers. The Inquisition was re-established, the Jesuits returned, and church tithes were reinstated. Aristocrats regained their estates, and the clock turned back.

A tale of national resistance, however, had been forged. It lives on today as what Raymond Carr called 'a myth of enormous potency, available to radicals and traditionalists alike'. The mob, or *populacho*, had become 'the people' and these, however chaotically, had spoken. They had also been roundly ignored. Spain's next two centuries of history were all about that.

22
Freedom from Spain

Spain's empire had joined the fight for independence from France. Enslaved people had been excluded from the Cádiz Constitution, but full citizens from the empire had gained a voice and power. The return to royal absolutism changed that, provoking an angry response. A continent-wide rebellion now saw Spain shed almost its entire empire at a speed that proved even faster than the original conquest. Within just eleven years, almost all of it had gone.

One reason for the dramatic and sudden success of the independence movements in Latin America was that war had left the metropole in a state of ruin. In order to tame the colonies, Ferdinand VII had to build a large army almost out of nothing. Or, rather, he had to compose one out of a mixture of guerrilla leaders, officers who had risen in the chaotic army that fought the French and the friends who had accompanied him into exile. This army was overstuffed with officers, many of dubious quality. It was a state of affairs, indeed, that remained constant for the next 120 years, providing a publicly financed middle class of officers who were both excessively self-important and often dangerously under-employed.

A tradition was soon established in Spain, of military *pronunciamientos* – coups, or attempted coups that brought constant, dizzying changes in government. These destabilized Spain for much of the rest of the century and encouraged the idea that military men should run the nation. Most *pronunciamientos* were more about individual conviction or ambition than popular will. When, however, a colonel called Rafael del Riego encouraged troops stationed near to Cádiz to rebel on the first day of 1820 rather than embark on ships taking them to fight in America, he struck a chord. Riego had the support of the liberals and found himself popular amongst those who did not wish to fight. Troops about to embark from the north-western ports Ferrol, La Coruña and Vigo (all in Galicia) joined him.

It was nothing like a popular revolution, but in the still chaotic state run by Ferdinand VII there was no one to oppose this tame uprising. Ferdinand's solution was to suddenly declare that the liberals were right and swear allegiance to the same constitution he had abolished eight years earlier. This initiated the so-called Liberal Triennium: a three-year burst of enthusiasm for reform, representative government and freedom of expression that saw hundreds of newspapers, 'patriotic society' clubs and cultural clubs opening up. The Inquisition, an unwanted symbol of exceptionalism used by enemies to paint Spain as the most backward country in Europe, was temporarily suppressed. For a short period, indeed, Spain looked as though it could become one of the most progressive countries in Europe.

Yet just three years later, in 1823, absolutism returned. In France, the monarchy had been restored under Louis XVIII. Spain was invaded by the so-called Hundred Thousand Sons of San Louis, who were tasked with 'freeing' it from the clutches of 'radical' liberals. The Sons of Saint Louis were French, but they represented a coalition of absolutist monarchies around Europe who wanted one of their number on the Spanish throne. They stayed for five years, effectively reinstating (though far less intrusively and with a gradual withdrawal) the French occupation of Spain that began with Bonaparte.

This time, the liberals faced repression and terror. Riego was hung in Madrid's Plaza de la Cebada, and anyone who had supported the

1812 constitution was in trouble. Many of Spain's best brains, and most of its liberal spirits, fled the country again, heading for France or Britain. There were even reports that, in some places, people had shouted '*Muera la libertad y vivan las cadenas!*' – 'Death to freedom, and long live our chains!' Others called for the 'death of the nation' (meaning the liberal version of a country that belongs to its people) or 'death to the *blacks*', as liberals were also known.

Nowhere was Ferdinand VII's return more damaging, however, than in mainland South America. Over the previous century, Enlightenment reforms, when imposed by absolutists, had simply seemed like imperial meddling to the *creole* elites of the empire. The United States had gained independence in 1776, and a slave revolt in Haiti had eventually won freedom from France in 1804, though the ensuing massacres of white French colonialists could not have enthused Spanish America's own creole communities. Even though tension was building between local elites and peninsular Spaniards, there was little popular support for the idea of independence until Napoleon's invasion.

Just as *juntas provinciales* were set up across Spain to lead the rebellion against him, so the colonies formed their own *juntas*. Initially, this was done in Ferdinand VII's name and against Napoleon, with some of them represented at the Cortes of Cádiz that wrote the new constitution. As war dragged on in Spain, however, and contact became more difficult, patience ran out. In 1811 alone, the imperial yoke of a country now belonging to the Bonapartes was shaken off in places as far apart as Caracas (Venezuela), Bogotá (Colombia) and Quito (Ecuador). Buenos Aires (Argentina) and Santiago de Chile started the same process the following year.

Spain was weak, but not everyone wanted to leave the empire. Much of Peru and today's Bolivia, along with Central America and the Caribbean islands remained loyal, as did some parts of the countries that had just declared independence. As a result, loyalist and pro-independence armies clashed across the continent. By 1815, Spain had recovered power in most places – excepting modern-day Argentina, Paraguay and Uruguay. By now, however, Ferdinand VII had returned to the throne. To his absolutist mind, the problem in America was purely military. The rebels simply needed to be squashed, like the liberals at home.

In fact, Spain had just 45,000 troops to cover an entire continent. It also had a king whose belligerence helped to swell the ranks of those demanding independence. Rebellion exploded again in 1816 and was over within eight years. In the south, the rebels were led by José San Martín, who had fought for the restoration of Ferdinand VII (and the constitution of Cádiz) in Spain. In the north, rebellion was led by the charismatic, mercurial, violent and ambitious liberator Simón Bolívar – who eventually 'freed' seven times as much land in the Americas as George Washington. The tenacity and skill of these two very different generals saw Spain evicted from a million square miles of territory during a campaign that required epic marches through jungles or over snow-capped mountains. They were helped by entire 'regiments' formed of experienced Irish and British mercenaries who had been demobilized after the Napoleonic Wars.

Essentially, this was swapping a distant emperor for the largely unenlightened creole elite to which Bolívar and San Martín both belonged. Despite his protestations of equality for all men, or the swaggering style of his sword-wielding lover Manuela Sáenz (who outraged conservatives by dressing like a man and going around with a retinue of fearsome black female servants), Bolívar ultimately failed to produce anything more than a repetition of the worst of Spanish inequality in Latin America. 'Independence is the only thing we have won, at the cost of all else,' he said before his death in 1830.

Mexico and Central America were amongst the last to leave the Spanish Empire and did so only after the end of the Liberal Triennium, when absolutism returned with a vengeance. That left

Peru and modern-day Bolivia, which gained independence after a final defeat for Spain at Ayacucho in 1824. On 6 August 1825, Upper Peru named itself after the liberator himself, as Bolivia. Everything except Puerto Rico, Cuba and the Philippines had gone.

Between 1810 and 1825, then, the empire had all but disappeared. Not only had Spain been ravaged by war, but it had also shed the power that came with possessing almost an entire continent.

Without an empire, Spain was even more broke than before. With the liberals out of power, it was less likely to find a way out of debt. A small clique of reformists – heirs of the old Enlightenment tradition – did their best, but found reactionaries standing in their way. These were mostly to be found in the church, in the lands that still conserved their *fueros* and some self-government, or where the owners of smallholdings and other conservatives feared change.

In Catalonia a group of reactionary clergy and smallholders known as the 'malcontents' rose up in revolt in 1827, demanding, amongst other things, the return of the Inquisition. Liberals, meanwhile, tried to encourage their own popular rebellions – with several attempts in 1831 alone. One of these saw a plotter called José María Torrijos, his British co-conspirator Robert Boyd and forty-six others shot on the beach at Málaga after being caught in a clandestine landing there, having set out from Gibraltar to start an uprising. The liberal artist Antonio Gisbert Pérez painted their execution, depicting a scene that appears like a sombre seaside reenactment of Goya's *Tres de Mayo*. The same year a woman called Mariana Pineda from Granada (who had previously smuggled a friar's outfit into jail so that her cousin could escape the death sentence) was garrotted after a flag embroidered with the words 'Liberty, Equality and Laws' was found in her house.

← Simón Bolívar, the Liberator, turned against Spain and won independence for the northern part of South America after Fernando VII reneged on the 1812 Constitution of Cádiz. Portrait by José Gil de Castro c.1823.

THE DISAPPEARING EMPIRE

LOSSES IN THE AMERICAS

On Ferdinand VII's death in September 1833, the country was still firmly divided between reactionary absolutists and progressive liberals. He had been one of the worst monarchs in Spanish history, but his death complicated things more, since the two sides backed different candidates to succeed him. The next conflict, as a result, was civil war.

23
The Long Civil War

The bloated, balding and gout-ridden Ferdinand VII's final great contribution to sowing conflict had been to marry for a fourth time in 1829. His previous three wives had died in quick succession, and Ferdinand's new wife was his twenty-three-year-old niece, María Cristina. The other marriages (including to a cousin and another niece) either had not produced children or these had died as infants. María Cristina, however, gave birth to a healthy girl, Isabella, just ten months after their wedding. A law was passed immediately to change a requirement for the heir to the crown to be male, following Bourbon tradition.

The heavy-smoking monarch finally had an heiress, but Isabella was just three years old when he died, leaving María Cristina as regent. Ferdinand's fanatically pious brother Carlos – who had been heir until Isabella was born – thus saw his ambition to reign dashed at the last moment. In divided Spain, he became the magnet for reactionaries who supported the ultra-Catholic forces of absolutism. They included, especially, Basques and Navarrese whose independent *fueros* had been threatened by the Cádiz Constitution. They wanted to avoid the same fate as the Catalans, whose *fueros* had been taken away as punishment for opposing Philip V a century before. The rise of this powerful faction that backed Carlos's continued claim to the crown pushed María Cristina into the arms of the liberals and the army. These, then, became the two sides of

Spain's first great civil war, which was known as the First Carlist War (Carlos's supporters were 'Carlists'). They were also a first version of the battle lines of the future, since the fight between liberals (or progressives) and reactionaries (or conservatives) dominated Spain's politics until the late twentieth century. A chaotic one hundred years had begun, when apparently dramatic and abrupt changes often produced no long-term change at all.

Civil war was started in 1833 by Carlos's supporters, who already boasted a force of armed followers, military commanders and the backing of prominent churchmen. It was no mere flash-in-the-pan *pronunciamiento*. The seven-year war, in which a further 150,000 people (out of 13 million) were killed, increased the number of Spaniards to have died as a result of war over three decades to some 650,000.

The Carlists, who wore broad red Basque-style berets, established sometimes shaky control over much of northern Spain. The area they dominated stopped short of Madrid and Valencia, with a few outposts further south. Most of the fighting was in the Basque region, Navarre and the old kingdom of Aragón, where Carlist passions were deepest. The lower clergy did much to keep these inflamed, while the elaborately moustachioed Basque general Tomás de Zumalacárregui proved a talented commander. He, however, was hit in the leg by a stray bullet while watching his troops besiege Bilbao and died of septicaemia on 24 June 1835.

This was a crude and bloody war, which established a tradition of vengeful massacres of captured soldiers. In the part of Spain that was still firmly loyal to the established monarchy, war inevitably brought another period of chaos in which the beginnings of a party system began to emerge in politics, but government itself could do little beyond maintaining an army and quelling attempted uprisings within its own ranks. A partial disentailment (*desamortización*) of monasteries by the government of Juan Álvarez Mendizábal in 1836 allowed lands to be sold off and a war-exhausted exchequer to be restocked, while creating a new pool of wealthy capitalists. Some 4,000 properties were sold, tying their buyers to the cause of Spanish liberalism – but further alienating the church.

In fact, many church buildings had been abandoned, since monks and friars fled to the Carlist zone as anti-clericalism, another feature of the coming century of confrontation, slipped into violence. Seventy-three friars in Madrid were killed after being accused of poisoning the city water supply with cholera. Church buildings were burned down in Barcelona, Valencia and Murcia.

Elections held in 1834 allowed only fifteen out of every 10,000 men to vote. A new, bustling middle and lower middle class, nevertheless began to form debating and cultural clubs, while elections to parliament and town halls saw a separation between '*progresistas*', who wanted deep, rapid and democratic change, and conservative '*moderados*', who mistrusted democracy (while still opposing the radical absolutism of the Carlists). It was only now, in 1834, that the Inquisition was formally abolished – eight years after the hanging of its final victim, the Valencian teacher and supposed heretic Cayetano Ripoll, by its offshoot organization the Council of Faith.

A rough compromise, reached after soldiers of the royal guard rebelled against María Cristina, saw a new constitution passed in 1837. This did not seriously damage royal power but increased the number of eligible voters to one in twenty men.

As *moderados* and liberals argued about the limits of Spain's still feeble freedoms, popular discontent with the regency began to grow. War had placed the military at the centre of politics. Generals like Juan Prim, Baldomero Espartero, Ramón María Narváez, Francisco Serrano and Leopoldo O'Donnell dominated politics from 1840 to 1868. In many ways, in fact, they were more politicians than military officers.

The great hero of the Carlist War was General Espartero, who played a crucial role in the governments between 1837 and 1840.

At the end of that period, however, he led a successful coup against María Cristina's regency. She left the country, while Espartero was hailed in the streets of Madrid as the new regent. Her ten-year-old daughter, Queen Isabella, would have to grow up without her mother for the coming few years.

María Cristina had been meddling and money obsessed. She accumulated offshore funds in Cuba and Paris built up from graft and corrupt business deals. She was also, like her daughter, popularly defined by a sexual appetite deemed unsuitable for her gender – a common way of trying to ridicule Spanish women with rank or power. She had married her lover, Fernando Muñoz, just three months after Ferdinand VII died. Muñoz was not an aristocrat (his parents owned a street stall, or *estanco*) and she was only supposed to be regent while still a widow, so the marriage had to be kept secret – though most of Madrid and all the aristocracy knew about the relationship. While regent, María Cristina had five children with Muñoz. Those in the know pretended to ignore the pregnancies, hidden under voluminous dresses. The final shove, indeed, came after an anonymous pamphlet revealed her married state. It painted her as a slave to her own 'burning, brutal and wrongful passions' and obsessed with a 'common, bald and gross' commoner husband who beat her during her drunken fits of jealousy. 'She has also made sure to hoard gold belonging to all Spaniards so she can live in splendid luxury anywhere in the world if circumstance obliges,' it said.

The couple had indeed become very wealthy. Exile gave them even more opportunities. They were part of a group of Spaniards who became immensely rich in the nineteenth century by illegally trafficking slaves. A gap in the market opened up after Britain banned trafficking in 1807, and it became even more lucrative (and risky) after Spain followed suit in 1820. As the risk involved in a now illegal trade increased (with the British patrolling the Atlantic), so did the profits. Slavery itself, rather than trafficking,

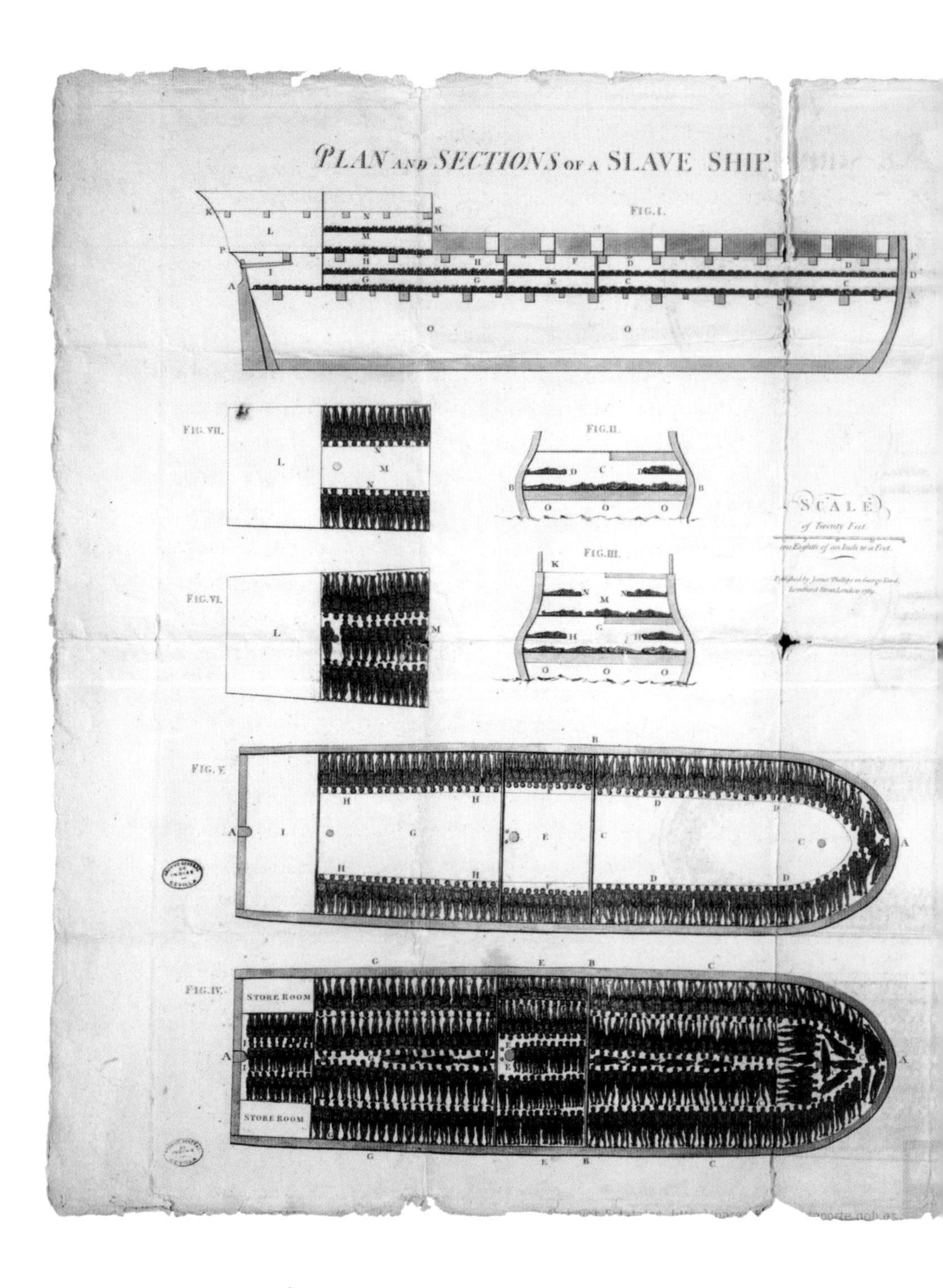
PLAN AND SECTIONS OF A SLAVE SHIP.
FIG. I.
FIG. II.
FIG. III.
FIG. IV.
FIG. V.
FIG. VI.
FIG. VII.
SCALE
of Twenty Feet
STORE ROOM
STORE ROOM

remained legal. Suddenly, more than sixty Spanish slave-trading posts appeared on the West African coast between the River Niger and the Congo.

The former regent made vast sums by trafficking illegally into Cuba (at least half of Cuba's enslaved people, or 400,000 Africans, arrived after the trade in human beings was banned). Even when out of power, she was able to influence or buy off local officials. 'Let's enjoy a feast of blacks,' Muñoz – by now made Duke of Riánsares and Grandee of Spain – said in a letter to their trading partner in Cuba after they had bribed the island's captain general to turn a blind eye. 'Send them if they are good-looking and not too expensive,' he said in a separate letter about female slaves, later complaining that he had been sent one who was 'broken from the waist up'. The royal couple were likely also investors in *La Amistad*, a trafficking vessel that Cuban-born slaves successfully hijacked in 1840. It then sailed to the United States, where they were represented in court by former president John Quincy Adams and won freedom.

Since she was friends with other slave-traders, María Cristina ensured that several received noble titles from her daughter Isabella II or, later, from her grandson Alfonso XII. Perhaps the most infamous was the Marquess de Comillas whose brother-in-law Francisco Bru felt compelled, when a statue of him was raised in Barcelona, to publish a book revealing the source of his wealth. 'He trafficked in human meat. Yes, dear readers, he was a slave-merchant.' Wealthy Spanish families, like the Pastor bankers and Ybarra merchants or the Martínez Pérez de Terán shipbuilders made their first fortunes as nineteenth-century slavers.

← As Britain and other countries banned slave-trading in the nineteenth century, Spaniards continued to ship slaves to Cuba and elsewhere – placing orders for ships to be built that could travel directly from Africa. This English ship design was stored in Spain's state archive.

María Cristina's move into exile was by no means the final jolt in an increasingly unstable political situation, and when the dictatorial Espartero was ousted in 1843, another implacable military man, Ramón María Narváez, became the new power-monger. Queen Isabella II was suddenly, and surprisingly, declared capable of ruling at the age of thirteen and the following year she 'appointed' Narváez as head of the government. He remained the central figure in the ten-year period known as the *Década Moderada*, the decade of the *moderados*. Although they were strong conservatives, they still had to put down an even more reactionary rebellion when a smaller civil war, known as the Second Carlist War or the War of the *Matiners*, broke out (sparked by a refusal to marry the young Isabella to the Carlist pretender to the throne, Carlos Luis de Borbón). This lasted two and a half years and was mostly confined to Catalonia, ending in 1849.

A confused Spain still had to choose its post-absolutist path. Narváez thuggishly put down all revolts, while inventing an elaborately corrupt new system which made stability, rather than freedom, the priority. His conservative *moderados* wanted a constitutional monarchy, with a strong monarch backed by a corruptly elected parliament of elite, and often wealthy, men. This system was consecrated in a new 1845 constitution that remained – with the occasional break or rewrite – the basic model until 1923.

Narváez's solution was pragmatic and cynical. The monarchy was strengthened again, and the Roman Catholic Church returned to its position as the state religion (with certain powers to match). A small *moderados* elite could tussle for power amongst themselves. Fraudulent parliamentary elections (with only 90,000 voters in the whole country) were fixed by a new network of civil governors who rubber-stamped the change of factions, limiting power to them and the monarch. Those same civil governors, appointed to each of the forty-nine provinces set up in 1833 (and still in existence today, though the Canary Islands were later divided in two) became regional strongmen, with a new police force called the Civil Guard at their orders. State efficiency increased dramatically, but such powers were an open invitation for abuse and corruption, which were eagerly grasped. In fact, they created a systemic form of corruption – and a culture – that would hamper attempts at progress into the twenty-first century.

The relative stability created by this corrupt system did at least allow for reforms of taxation that permitted the government to pay the army and itself. With little money left over, however, for roads, education or much else, the peasant population remained illiterate and unable to travel or learn about their country.

The economy grew as industrialization and agricultural techniques slowly advanced, but ultimately this meant that instead of having 12 million mostly poor people in it, Spain now had 18 million. Flight from the countryside began as the textile industry grew in Barcelona and other parts of Catalonia while factories appeared across the country. The industrial revolution, a late arrival in Spain, was finally underway. It marked a far deeper change than anything politics had managed, allowing capitalism to surge and generate the inevitable tensions that came with that development.

The cliques who ruled this growing Spain handed out public contracts or rights to help expand cities, say, or build ports and canals to friends, clients or themselves. Corruption was so rife that the author and politician Donoso Cortés, writing in 1851, claimed that 'not since Creation has the world seen such bare-faced, shameless pillaging'. A country that had been united by war against the French was now being plundered by the elites who ran it.

These elites were tiny, especially in the political sphere. They gifted themselves a new Houses of Parliament building, the Congreso de Los Diputados, in Madrid, where factions of conservative *moderados* battled each other. Isabella II, meanwhile, was wedded at sixteen to her refined but dull twenty-four-year-old double cousin Francisco de Asis, whose parents were María

Cristina's sister and Ferdinand VII's brother. The vivacious and spontaneous queen gained a reputation as sexually voracious, with her constantly changing bed companions also mixed up in politics. As with her mother, indeed, campaigns against her were often based on scurrilous gossip. Popular cartoons showed Francisco wearing a cuckold's horns, and doubts were voiced about the paternity of her twelve pregnancies – which produced ten children, only five of whom survived. Gossip-mongers, meanwhile, also claimed that her husband was homosexual. Since he was small and wiry, and her appetite for food and voluminous skirts made her seem enormous, even later photographs of the couple looked cartoonish. Whether true or false (and the sexual shaming of royal women was by now a malicious tradition) none of the above added to the monarchy's standing.

The pattern of *pronunciamientos* by politically ambitious generals was by no means over, and trouble broke out again as the pendulum swung violently back in July 1854. 'What's happening now?' the great ironic-realist writer Benito Pérez Galdós sighed wearily in a novel about the 1854 Revolution, written half a century later. 'Spain's history carries on as normal. It's a military uprising.' There would be, indeed, at least fifty attempted coups in the period from 1814 to 1981 – only half of them a genuine threat, but still an average of one every three years and with a far greater frequency during the turbulent nineteenth century.

This time, however, there was also genuine popular revolt. The Madrid palaces of the new barons who had made money out of the existing corrupt system were burned (including one belong to Isabella's increasingly wealthy mother María Cristina, who had returned to Madrid), barricades appeared in the streets, and the head of the police was killed. The queen was blamed for the brutality with which the so-called 1854 Revolution was put down, and it was soon clear that the Decade of the Moderates was over. Progressives now had a two-year spell in government (the 'Bieno

↑ Gluttonous Queen Isabella II had at least a dozen pregnancies, amid scurrilous rumours about her sex life and supposedly cuckolded husband. She was driven into exile in 1868, as Spaniards turned against monarchy.

Progresista'), with the queen still in place, before the pendulum fell the other way, and a chaotic period of short-lived governments began. The only real achievement in this time would be the introduction of obligatory, and free, education from the age of six onwards in a law pushed through parliament by a largely unsung hero and government minister, Claudio Moyano. This was not yet put into full practice, but set up a basic model that survived until 1970.

Corruption had not stopped Spain from growing or becoming more joined up. A country which had just 440 kilometres of railroads in 1855 had more than 5,000 by 1866. Growth, as ever, was unevenly distributed, both geographically and between classes. In 1860, a census found that two-thirds of the country still worked in the primary sector, and one-third were seasonal rural day workers, *jornaleros*. In the poorest parts of Andalusia, where the great landowners had their estates, only 10 per cent of people could read or write. Most were too poor and hungry to rebel, but others began to occupy land, burn crops, or simply became *bandoleros*, highwaymen.

Signs of economic strain had started to appear in 1862, with the American Civil War slowing down cotton supplies to Catalonia's textile industry. When banks began to crash in 1866 after investments in railways failed to pay off and crops also failed, discontent spread, and bread riots erupted in several cities.

By now people began to see the monarchy itself as a problem. Isabella's allegedly outrageous sex life and obvious gluttony did not help. Periodic revolts began to be accompanied by shouts of 'Down with the Bourbons!' In June 1866, soldiers from an artillery barracks in Madrid, led by their sergeants, tried to overthrow the monarchy. Sixty-six of the participants were shot, but it was a sign of things to come.

The queen was finally ousted by yet another military rebellion, in September 1868, when the progressive generals Juan Prim and Francisco Serrano led a coup that – after a battle at Alcolea claimed 400 lives – sent Isabella II into exile. Following her mother's example, Isabella had treated Spain as part of her personal patrimony, according to her biographer Isabel Burdiel, and her private life helped turn Spaniards against the monarchy. She had resisted attempts to tear down the edifice of absolutism, which had now lost this latest battle against progress.

The rebellion that ousted the queen was largely greeted with joy and became known as 'La Gloriosa', or 'The Glorious Revolution'. The erratic pendulum of nineteenth-century Spain had swung violently to the opposite extreme once more. Democracy, of a limited kind, was to be given a first chance. Would it work?

24
Democracy, Sort Of

In 1868, Spain lurched into a six-year phase of freedom known as the *Sexenio Revolucionario* or *Sexenio Democrático*. It turned out to be neither revolutionary nor very democratic, but still produced a giant leap forward. Newspapers could publish what they wanted without fear of the censors, and they did. The prolific realist writer Pérez Galdós, sometimes called 'the nineteenth century Cervantes', gave free rein to his hatred of church hypocrisy and the idea that 'non-reason is considered reasonable', selling more novels than ever. Slavery was finally abolished, but the rules did not apply in Puerto Rico until 1873 or in Cuba until 1886.

The new government, in any case, did not want real revolution. Serrano was declared 'regent' and so technically ruled for the absent monarchy (by now Isabella had abdicated in favour of her son, Alfonso XII). The factions behind the revolution struggled to agree a new model for Spain. This was inevitably going to be a compromise, since they included Serrano's liberals, Prim's progressives and a mixed group of so-called 'progressive democrats' (also known as 'federal republicans') whose factions demanded either genuine democracy, republicanism, federalism, or a mix of all three. Eventually, they opted to continue with constitutional monarchy, under a more democratic system that constrained the monarch.

For many people, however, monarchy and freedom were incompatible. Some republicans, also, increasingly embraced federalism as

↑ Isabella II's 1868 abdication brought chaos as candidates jostled for the crown while, according to this satirical drawing from the newly free press, 'lady democracy' fled. The winner was King Amadeo, an Italian prince, who lasted just two years and also abdicated.

a way of recognizing the country's obvious internal diversity. A century and a half had gone by since the suppression of the *fueros* in the old kingdoms of the Aragonese crown, but Spain was still a country in which several nations and their different languages co-existed. Galicians, Catalans and Valencians – for example – mostly spoke their own tongue while rural Basques maintained the remarkable and unique language of Euskara.

Richard Ford, a nineteenth-century British writer who travelled extensively across Spain, had spotted these differences – especially in Catalonia. 'They are neither French nor Spanish but *sui generis* in language, costume and habits,' he explained in his *Handbook for Travellers in Spain*, published in 1845. 'No province of the unamalgamating bundle which forms the conventional monarchy of Spain hangs more loosely to the crown than Catalonia, this classical country of revolt, which is ever ready to fly off.'

As well as federalism, other new political ideas also took off. Working-class movements emerged from 1870 onwards, while atheism, anarchism and collectivism began to form part of public debate.

Voter suffrage was extended to all men over twenty-five in time for elections in 1869, and Spain suddenly had 4 million voters. A middle-ground coalition of progressives and liberals led by Serrano and Prim thus ensured itself an absolute majority of 236 seats. The more purist democrats and federalist republicans became their main opposition on the left, while a handful of conservative *moderados* and Carlists sat on the right.

If Spain, however, was to remain a monarchy, yet nobody wanted Isabella II, who would be king? In a turnabout, it was now the government which chose a monarch, rather than the other way around. After scouring Europe for spare royals, the regime's leader, General Juan Prim, opted for the second son of Italy's King Vittorio Emanuele II, Prince Amadeo. He was a safe bet since neither the British nor Emperor Napoleon III would feel threatened. A rival French candidate, the Duke of Montpensier, was discarded after he killed Queen Isabella's brother-in-law in a duel, while the German Leopoldo Hohenzollern Sigmaringen had a name that was so unpronounceable to Spaniards that they jokingly turned it into '*Olé, olé. Si me eligen*' (Bravo! Bravo! If they choose me).

In November 1870, Amadeo's appointment was put to parliament. The decision was by no means unanimous – with 191 out of 311 votes – while one in five parliamentarians voted for a republic instead. Nor did it produce popular joy. A jeering crowd reportedly gathered for a satirical performance in Madrid's Retiro Park (which had only recently been opened to the public), where the new Italian monarch was proclaimed 'Macaroni the First'.

As Amadeo prepared to travel to Spain on 27 December 1870 and snow fell on Madrid, General Prim left parliament shortly after 7 p.m. His coach pulled up by the doors, and Prim got in with two assistants. As it reached the end of Turco Street and prepared to turn into Alcalá Street, it was ambushed by a group of men carrying guns under their cloaks. Prim was mortally wounded. It was never clear whether angry radical republicans, the Duke of Montpensier or some other rival was to blame. With so many enemies, it was hard to tell. Prim died three days later, just as his Italian royal protégé landed in Cartagena. Amadeo was proclaimed monarch on 2 January 1871 and the new regime instantly began to fall apart.

Civil war broke out again in 1872 as the fundamentalist Carlists bridled against the progressive regime and saw another opportunity to force their alternative candidate for king on Spain – who by now was a grandson of the original Prince Carlos they had backed during the first Carlist War. This Third Carlist War saw the rebels capture much of Catalonia, Navarre and the Basque Country, with 'Save our religion!' as their battle cry. A Carlist promise to the Catalans to reinstate part of their autonomous *fueros* helped keep the war alive until 1876, by which time 50,000 people had been killed and Amadeo had fled. His position had been hopeless from the start. Squeezed between those who wanted a Spaniard as king and those who wished to overthrow the monarchy, he had abdicated in February 1873. It did not help that, initially, he knew so little about Spain that, when told that his carriage was passing in front of the house where Miguel de Cervantes had lived before his death 250 years earlier, he reportedly declared: 'Well, he hasn't been to see me yet, but I'll make sure to visit him.'

With Amadeo's abdication, parliament declared Spain to be a federal republic. This infuriated the Carlists further and worried Europe's other monarchies as they struggled to digest the establishment of the Third Republic in France in 1870. They need not have worried. Internal arguments raged about how this new federal republic, formally Spain's First Republic, would be built.

Some could not wait. A so-called 'cantonal revolt' brought radical local uprisings across Spain, starting in Cartagena, as each area declared itself a semi-independent 'canton' in an as yet unformed federal Spain. Given a chance to express themselves, Spaniards had automatically turned to localism. Many still knew little of their country beyond their own village, town or province, and the narrative of national unity produced by the war of 'independence' six decades earlier now seemed like a short but bright fire that had been quickly doused by Ferdinand VII. The 'cantonal revolt' provoked not just further bloodshed but another coup which brought what, in effect, was a temporary dictatorship under the liberal general, Francisco Serrano. For the opponents of liberty, it was all proof that the *populacho* (meaning the people) could never be trusted, that federalism was shorthand for the break-up of Spain and only authoritarianism (or worse) prevented anarchy. Two radically opposed ideas of Spain had appeared during the Republic, and these 'two Spains' would tear violently at one another for a century, squeezing out the middle ground.

Having reached one extreme, the pendulum of Spanish history was set to swing back radically and suddenly. A seventeen-year-old military cadet at Sandhurst – Isabella II's son, Alfonso de Borbón – would help provoke that turn.

25
The Ladies' Revolution

The British ambassador called it 'the ladies' revolution', since Madrid's great mansions were full of salon conversations about restoring the old Bourbon monarchy. In 1874, the young Alfonso de Borbón, in his so-called Sandhurst Manifesto, declared himself to be Spanish, Catholic and liberal. Only a hereditary constitutional monarchy could provide the combination of peace, political freedom and rule of law that Spain desperately needed, he added.

When General Arsenio Martínez Campos rose in his name on 29 December 1874, it was a bloodless revolt with no real opposition. In fact, this rebellion simply accelerated the political project of the great conservative political thinker and historian Antonio Cánovas del Castillo, who had spent several years arguing for a fresh start under young Alfonso. The new monarch was greeted enthusiastically when he arrived in Barcelona on 9 January 1875. He immediately appointed Cánovas as prime minister, and a new, calmer period of Spanish history began.

Politics became a largely civilian, if still highly corrupt and undemocratic, affair. Generals were sent to war and soon defeated both the Carlists in February 1876 and, two years later, the Cubans they had been fighting since sugar-cane planters and other wealthy islanders had rebelled against imperial rule in 1868. As a result, Alfonso XII became known as 'the Peacemaker'. The army remained, however, in charge of suppressing internal rebellion against Cánovas's regime and was by no means ready to stay out of politics for ever.

A new constitution passed in 1876 also suppressed the separate *fueros* of the three Basque provinces – Vizcaya, Alava and Guipúzcoa – who thus paid, like the Catalans in 1714, for backing the losing side in the Carlist war. Military service, taxes and other 'national' duties that they had previously avoided were now imposed. They retained, however, a curious advantage over other parts of Spain, for while taxes were collected directly elsewhere, the provincial administrations (or *diputaciones*) were charged with raising a specific sum from the whole province every year. A version of this system, the '*concierto económico*', remains in place today.

If sovereignty now resided in the king and parliament, the latter became a playground for two parties – Cánovas's conservatives and the liberals led, initially, by Práxedes Mateo Sagasta – who jointly fixed elections in order to take turns in power. A small rump of democrats, republicans or progressives, meanwhile, were allowed to win around 10 per cent of the seats. This was dubbed the *turno pacífico*, the Peaceful Turn, and was an attempt to imitate the British tradition of alternating government by two parties. Obviously, however, it did this without taking public opinion into account. In short, the monarch occasionally, for whatever reason, named a new prime minister from the opposition, who would call elections and always win.

Debate outside parliament was initially stifled by new censorship laws, while the Roman Catholic Church regained its central role, especially in schools and universities. A deal with the Vatican, meanwhile, took away much of the Carlists' cause for complaint about a weakened church. A small number of university professors like Francisco Giner de Los Ríos, seeing their right to contradict Catholic dogma removed, resigned and set up the Institución de Libre de Enseñanza (the Institute of Free Teaching). It served as a haven where they followed the ideas of German philosopher Karl

Christian Friedrich Krause on tolerance and diversity of thought in academia. Their long-term influence was large, and many of Spain's most important future intellectuals passed through the Institución's doors, but they were outcasts from power. The stultifying atmosphere of intellectual laziness, fake erudition, petty envy and grandiosity amongst Spain's still small middle class was best summed up in the 1884 novel *La Regenta* (rated by some as second only to *Don Quixote* in the Spanish canon), by the realist Leopoldo Alas, who wrote under the pseudonym Clarín. The opening sentence, which describes the thinly disguised northern provincial city of Oviedo (or Vetusta, in the novel), also sums up the state of affairs across Spain: 'The city of heroes was having a nap.'

Rigged elections ensured not just that the chosen party won, but that the loser obtained a reasonable number of seats. This meant that the opposition was not tempted by armed rebellion, since it was guaranteed a later return to government. In fact, detailed and arduous negotiations preceded each election, to ensure the agreed outcome with the names of those to be elected placed into an elaborate grid that became known as the '*encasillado*'. This was so granular that, in a largely rural country, provincial strongmen who could deliver the required outcomes gained huge local power. They were referred to by one of the few words to be imported into Spanish from the Taíno culture of the Caribbean, using a version of a term for tribal chiefs: '*caciques*'.

The *caciques* were local businessmen or landowners who had often become wealthy by buying up church or communal land as this was sold off over the previous decades. After agreement was reached in Madrid on who was to win (and where), civil governors in the provinces negotiated with *caciques* to fix the results. *Caciques* bullied both voters and rival candidates. They used their power as employers, their access to government largesse or straightforward thuggery. If that did not work, they stuffed ballots or faked results. This task was initially made simpler by a decision to remove the vote from 80 per cent of those previously eligible, leaving just 860,000 voters. Even when suffrage was expanded later, however, the system continued to work. Democracy was a sham – but an efficient one.

Everyone knew how this worked. In 1884 the term *caciquismo* entered the dictionary of the Royal Spanish Academy (which is still, today, the arbiter of 'correct' Castilian Spanish). It meant: 'abusive interference in certain affairs by a person or entity, using their power or connections'. By 1897, the celebrated cartoonist Joaquín Moya was able to publish a map of Spain showing the faces of the chief *caciques* in each province. Since many public jobs changed hands with each turn in power, each party built up a clientele dependent on their largesse.

For more than four decades (in twenty elections between 1879 and 1923), this system functioned with pendular predictability. Every two or three years, elections were held. They were always won by whichever of the two main parties was in opposition, and always with an absolute majority (with a short period of relative majorities during the First World War). Senior members of both parties always won seats.

This elaborate fraud stored up discontent for later but brought short- and mid-term advantages. Government programmes could be launched and finished. Violence was limited. By the time Alfonso XII (who had at least two illegitimate and unrecognized children with opera singer Elena Sanz) died of tuberculosis in 1885 at the age of twenty-seven, the system was fully implanted. An informal deal known as the Pardo Pact was struck as he lay on his deathbed to continue it. The historian Claudio Sánchez Albornoz claimed his final words to his wife, the future regent María Cristina of Habsburg, contained two crucial pieces of advice. '*Cristinita, guarda el coño y de Cánovas a Sagasta y de Sagasta a Cánovas*' ('Lock up your vagina, and [in government] go from Cánovas to Sagasta and then from Sagasta back to Cánovas').

María Cristina was pregnant at the time, and the new heir –

↑ Elections were fixed during the 'peaceful turn' at the end of the nineteenth century to ensure that the main two parties took turns to govern, with well-known local political bosses or *caciques* delivering the pre-agreed results in different regions at each election. Illustration by Joaquín Moya *c.*1897.

Alfonso XIII – was not born until the following year, leaving power in the hands of politicians like Cánovas during a sixteen-year regency.

Some progress was made on freedoms. A liberal government, for example, did away with censorship in 1883 and ushered in a period of dynamic journalism. The sphere of political debate was also widened with laws legalizing trades unions and extending voter suffrage to all men over twenty-five.

The guarantee that power would remain in the hands of what one Spanish historian has called 'a single political class' tamed, stifled or corrupted critics. That diminished the chance of yet another *pronunciamiento*, but kept politics in the hands of rural elites and a growing, if still minority, urban middle class. Only a third of Spaniards lived in municipalities of more than 10,000 people in 1900, and most city dwellers were working class. It also required everyone involved to connive in a lie. That, in turn, destroyed any sense of communal nation-building, replacing it with rampant 'work the system to get ahead' individualism. 'Every Spaniard's ideal is to carry a statutory letter with a single provision, brief but imperious: 'This Spaniard is entitled to do whatever he feels like doing,' the writer Ángel Ganivet commented.

The population continued to grow quickly, from 16.6 million to 18.6 million in the last quarter of the nineteenth century, with Madrid and Barcelona now each boasting more than half a million inhabitants. It was a time of grand plans to remodel cities, connect them with trains and provide sewers and running water. The neat plan drawn up by Catalan engineer Ildefonso Cerdà for expanding Barcelona with a large grid of handsome new city blocks, known as the Eixample, was being put into place. One block was reserved for architect Antoni Gaudí's flamboyant and fanciful Sagrada Familia temple project. Since the temple had to be paid for by public subscription, the great architect eventually lived on site and went door to door seeking funds before he wandered, dishevelled and unrecognizable, in front of a Number 30 tram and died in June 1926. Cerdá's city design was widely imitated across Spain. Train lines finally consolidated the idea that remote Madrid was the true centre of Spain, since these often radiated out to provincial cities, making the capital an obvious meeting point of finance and industry as well as politics, administration and the royal court.

With politics tamed by the *turno*, the most significant new movements were created clandestinely. Anarchism, imported from Russia via Italy, grew alongside socialist trade unionism. The anarchists emerged as a formal political organization from the clandestine Spanish Regional Federation of the International Workers' Federation in 1881 after trades unions were legalized. They went underground again at the end of decade, hating hierarchy while favouring direct action and violence.

On the evening of 7 November 1893, well-dressed members of Barcelona's growing and increasingly sophisticated bourgeoisie met at one of their favourite gathering spots on the city's tree-lined Ramblas boulevard, the Gran Teatro del Liceo. The opera house had been built fifty years earlier and was a symbol of the new-found sophistication that accompanied industrial wealth. *William Tell*, by Rossini, was being performed. Up in the gods, a professional smuggler and anarchist called Santiago Salvador settled in and waited for the second act. In a bag, he carried two hollow cast-iron spheres with a diameter of 9.5 centimetres. They were studded with eighteen spikes (or 'pins'), filled with white crystals of mercury difulminate, or *knallquecksilber*, which would explode if they were hit. These were Orsini bombs, of the kind designed in 1850s England by Italian exile Felice Orsini.

At around 11 p.m., during the second act, Salvador stepped up to the edge of the balcony and hurled his bombs into the stalls. The first exploded in row thirteen, killing twenty people. The second bomb fell on a woman who was already dead and it failed to explode. Salvador was caught and garrotted the following year. The garrotte, in which a chain or cord is slowly tightened around the neck, was a favoured form of Spanish execution from the Middle Ages and had been a recurrent subject of Goya's darker works. It was used until 1974.

Salvador had exacted revenge for the execution of an anarchist friend caught trying to kill General Martínez Campos, the officer whose *pronunciamiento* triggered the restoration of the monarchy and who was now captain general of Catalonia. Anarchists, indeed, had made Barcelona their capital, as they turned Spain into the country where their political creed was strongest. Tit-for-tat killings brought another attack during the Corpus procession in Barcelona in 1896, further executions of anarchists and, finally, the assassination of Cánovas himself. He was shot dead on 8 August 1897 by Italian anarchist Michele Angiolillo, at a spa near the Basque town of Mondragón. At the time, Cánovas was enjoying his sixth 'turn' as head of the government.

The Spanish Socialist Workers Party (PSOE), meanwhile, was formed under Pablo Iglesias, and an allied trade union, the General Workers Union (UGT), was founded in 1888. Membership was small, but they eventually became Spain's largest left-wing party and trade union. (They still are.) As industry grew, so inevitably, did trade unionism, which also spread to the rural areas where workers were most exploited, particularly among the large aristocratic estates of Andalusia and Extremadura.

By the time of Cánovas's death, the progress that had transformed Spain's economy had done little to improve the lives of the population as a whole. Primary education was still scattered, and 55 per cent of fifteen- to thirty-year-olds could not read or write, with much higher percentages in the countryside and amongst older Spaniards. There was much, in other words, for Spain's still poorly organized working class to complain about.

Cánovas's death, however, was not the key event of the end of the century. That came the following year, in 1898, when Spain lost its last three major colonies: Puerto Rico, Cuba and the Philippines. A short-lived American–Spanish war was partly stirred up by false news reports published by media magnate Randolph Hearst. His newspapers turned the mysterious, but almost certainly accidental, sinking of the USS *Maine* armoured cruiser in the port at Havana into a Spanish attack, and called for the US to 'Remember the *Maine*! To hell with Spain!' Thomas Edison's film studios in New Jersey also produced fake films of Spanish firing squads killing Cuban rebels. The war ended in humiliating naval defeats for Spain in both Cuba and the Philippines. The two defeats at least brought an end to Spanish wars against independence fighters that had begun in the mid-1890s and had always been costly.

↑ Spanish prime ministers led risky lives. Four were shot dead between 1870 and 1921, with Antonio Cánovas del Castillo killed by an Italian anarchist in 1897, depicted here by V. Ginés.

Together, however, the defeats became known as 'the Disaster'.

Spain's idea of itself suffered dramatically. Five centuries of imperial history had come to an abrupt end and when Spaniards looked around – at France, Britain, Germany or Italy – they saw countries that had galloped ahead of them on the back of the industrial revolution. Even small European nations, like Belgium, Portugal or Holland, still had distant colonies. What, people wondered, was wrong with Spain?

'We have been defeated by the United States because we were ignorant and weak. We were so stupid that we refused to acknowledge their strength and [advances in] science. We need to regenerate ourselves through work and study,' the neuroscientist and Nobel Prize winner Santiago Ramón y Cajal declared, as Spain indulged in a bout of introspective self-flagellation. Intellectuals vied to make their conclusions ever more dramatic. A decade later, the

,000 REWARD.—WHO DESTROYED THE MAINE?—$50,000 REWARD

NEW YORK JOURNAL

AND ADVERTISER. FIRST EDITION.

NO. 5,572. —NEW YORK, THURSDAY, FEBRUARY 17, 1898.—16 PAGES. PRICE ONE CENT

DESTRUCTION OF THE WAR SHIP MAINE WAS THE WORK OF AN ENEMY

$50,000!

$50,000 REWARD! For the Detection of the Perpetrator of the Maine Outrage!

Assistant Secretary Roosevelt Convinced the Explosion of the War Ship Was Not an Accident.

The Journal Offers $50,000 Reward for the Conviction of the Criminals Who Sent 258 American Sailors to Their Death. Naval Officers Unanimous That the Ship Was Destroyed on Purpose.

$50,000!

$50,000 REWARD! For the Detection of the Perpetrator of the Maine Outrage!

POWDER MAGAZINE

NAVAL OFFICERS THINK THE MAINE WAS DESTROYED BY A SPANISH MINE.

Hidden Mine or a Sunken Torpedo Believed to Have Been the Weapon Used Against the American Man-of-War---Officers and Men Tell Thrilling Stories of Being Blown Into the Air Amid a Mass of Shattered Steel and Exploding Shells---Survivors Brought to Key West Scout the Idea of Accident---Spanish Officials Protest Too Much---Our Cabinet Orders a Searching Inquiry---Journal Sends Divers to Havana to Report Upon the Condition of the Wreck. Was the Vessel Anchored Over a Mine?

Assistant Secretary of the Navy Theodore Roosevelt says he is convinced that the destruction of the Maine in Havana Harbor was not an accident.

The Journal offers a reward of $50,000 for exclusive evidence that will convict the person, persons or Government criminally responsible for the destruction of the American battleship and the death of 258 of its crew.

The suspicion that the Maine was deliberately blown up grows stronger every hour. Not a single fact to the contrary has been produced.

Captain Sigsbee, of the Maine, and Consul-General Lee both urge that public opinion be suspended until they have completed their investigation. They are taking the course of tactful men who are convinced that there has been treachery.

Spanish Government officials are pressing forward all sorts of explanations of how it could have been an accident. The facts show that there was a report before the ship exploded, and that, had her magazine exploded, she would have sunk immediately.

Every naval expert in Washington says that if the Maine's magazine had exploded the whole vessel would have been blown to atoms.

↑ *Remember the Maine!* The accidental sinking of US warship USS *Maine* in Havana harbour saw press magnate Randolph Hearst stir up a war against Spain. It lost its last colonies, in Cuba, Puerto Rico and the Philippines, in the disastrous year of 1898.

historian Marcelino Menéndez Pelayo blamed the country's leaders for a prolonged period of self-destruction. 'We witness today the slow suicide of a people that, deceived a thousand times by wordy sophists, impoverished, run down and laid waste, employs its little remaining strength in destroying itself.' Some even pined for a return to the country's founding myths and 'the Herculean vitality' of the fifteenth century.

A so-called Generation of 1898 emerged to repudiate the catatonic conformism which had accompanied the return of the monarchy, including the Basque philosopher Miguel de Unamuno, who deemed personal envy and Cainism (meaning a violent, fratricidal tendency) as Spain's root problems and saw salvation in the embrace of 'Europe'. The poet Antonio Machado, a young modernist who had been a brilliant pupil at the Institute of Free Teaching's school in Madrid, placed the blame for Spain's decline on a powerful and growing Roman Catholic Church. This educated Spain's middle and upper classes and was growing so fast that its ranks swelled from fewer than 50,000 priests, monks and nuns in the 1860s, to 135,000 seventy years later. The church, Machado declared, was applying 'spiritual asphyxia and Spain will die if its iron grip is not broken'. The Generation of 1898 pledged to revitalize the nation with words, culture, patriotic love and – less convincingly – the discovery of its landscapes by poets like Machado.

Yet some of the greatest talents chose to leave. A young, Málaga-born painter called Pablo Ruiz Picasso, who had trained at the Lonja art school in Barcelona, began splitting his time between the city and Paris at the start of the new century – though Barcelona itself was increasingly in thrall to French culture and sophistication. Most of Picasso's life, indeed, would be spent in France, a country where Spain's greatest twentieth-century artist could do, and paint, as he pleased. In 1912, given the inability of governments to modernize Spain and heal its divisions, Machado wrote a grim greeting to new-born Spaniards that read: 'May God protect you.

One of the two Spains will freeze your heart.'

It was, however, Unamuno who produced the most convincing diagnosis of Spain's ills and revealed the best cure. That resided in the age-old influence of its history as a meeting point of cultures. He wrote in 1902:

> The Castilian soul was great when it exposed us to the four winds and spread throughout the world; later it turned off the valves and we have not yet woken up. Is everything dying? No, the future of our society awaits us within the society of our past history ... and it will not recover strength until awoken by the winds and breezes of the European environment ... Spain waits to be discovered, and only Europeanized Spaniards will discover it.

26
Where Are You, Spain?

As Spaniards wallowed in millennial pessimism, the Catalan poet Joan Maragall penned a famous 'Ode to Spain', which chided it for ignoring Catalonia after the disastrous losses of Cuba and the Philippines in 1898.

> On ets, Espanya? – No et veig enlloc.
> No sents la meva veu atronadora?
> No entens aquesta llengua – que te parla entre perills?
> Has desaprès d'entendre an els teus fills?
> Adéu, Espanya!
>
> (Where are you, Spain? – Nowhere to be seen
> Do you not hear my resounding voice?
> Don't you understand this language, speaking to you amongst dangers?
> Have you stopped listening to your children?
> Farewell, Spain!)

Maragall was a turn-of-the-century product of a long, slow renaissance of writing in Catalan that coincided with and fuelled the rise of localism and nationalism. Catalan literature could look back to a time of medieval glory, when poets and writers like Ramon Llull, Ausias March and Joanot Martorell emerged from the wider region of Catalan language-speakers. Llull was from Majorca, while

March and Martorell (whose chivalric romance *Tirant lo Blanch* was declared 'the best of its kind' by Cervantes) were from Valencia, but the languages known as *valencià* and *mallorquí* are Catalan dialects, despite recent culture war attempts to upgrade them. The long rise of Castilian as Spain's literary language had seen Catalan pushed into the background until the nineteenth century. The father of this prolonged *Renaixença* was Catalonia's unofficial laureate, the late-nineteenth-century poet-priest Jacint Verdaguer.

Verdaguer was Catalonia's equivalent of Alfred, Lord Tennyson. He wrote epic, romantic poetry that praised the supposedly glorious history of Catalonia and the wondrous landscapes that stretched from its Mediterranean coastal lowlands to the Pyrenees. He composed the founding stanzas of Catalan statehood in his epic *El Canigò* in 1877 – a romantic fantasy about the magical, medieval origins of Catalonia. His genius was widely recognized, with Unamuno considering him Spain's finest living poet.

Verdaguer went mad in his later years, performing exorcism rituals on Barcelona's huddled poor from his base in an aristocrat's town palace on Las Ramblas. His literary example, however, inspired not just Maragall but a generation of politicians who wondered just how, or even if, Catalonia fitted into Spain. Barcelona's growing and self-confident industrial bourgeoisie, meanwhile, added economic muscle to this nascent Catalan nationalism.

The father of contemporary Catalanism, former regional premier Jordi Pujol, once stated that after the loss of its self-government *fuero* rights in 1714: 'Catalans returned to their homes and stayed there, without aspiring to anything more than to survive without ambition or any collective project, for 200 years.' Catalonia's Carlists might have disagreed about that, but Maragall's Ode gives some clues as to why there was now a dramatic change. The buoyant imperial Spain of the previous two centuries, with Catalonia at the centre of a textile trade whose exports were only outdone by England, France and the United States, had little more to give.

↑ Amid growing bewilderment over Spain's declining prestige, nationalism took off in regions with their own languages like Galicia, Catalonia and the Basque Country. The latter invented a 'national' flag, modelling its superimposed crosses on Britain's Union Jack.

Like the Basques, in whose region iron smelting and other industries had taken off, the Catalans saw themselves as the engine of Spain, pulling along an increasingly heavy and unproductive load. There were few reasons left, in other words, to kow-tow to Castile.

The cultural resurgence in the Basque Country was even more remarkable because it began from such a low point. Its booming industrial cities with their workforce of so-called *maketo* (or 'outsider') immigrants from rural Castile were already very different to the traditional towns and villages which lived off agriculture and fishing. In political terms, nevertheless, Basque nationalism found fertile ground in the terrain left by the Carlists, with their emphasis on tradition, local rights and the church. Sabino Arana, the father of Basque nationalism, was the eighth child of an ardent Carlist from Bilbao.

Arana was a fervent Roman Catholic who hated the *maketos* of Bilbao's industrial slums. The people of Vizcaya, his home province based on Bilbao, he claimed were 'intelligent and noble ... vigorous and agile', adding that 'the Vizcayan cannot serve, he was born to be *señor* [master]'. Spaniards, on the other hand, were 'inexpressive and harsh ... weak and clumsy' and 'born to be a vassal or a servant'.

Over ten intense years of political activity before he died, aged thirty-eight, in 1903, Arana proved remarkably prolific and successful. He founded the Basque Nationalist Party and sparked a revival of the Basque tongue, Euskara. If both are alive and well today, much of the credit belongs to him.

Euskara is the only surviving pre-Indo-European language on the continent. It has thirteen noun cases, avoids the letters c, q, v, w or y and builds complex, suffix-laden words. In Arana's time Euskara was in full retreat, lacked an agreed standard grammar and was missing basic patriotic terms. He filled the gaps by inventing words: *Euskadi*, the Basque nation; *abertzale*, patriot; *aberri*, fatherland; *lehendakari*, roughly 'person whose job is to lead'; and *ikurrin*, flag (he also designed a Basque flag, based on the Union

↑ Poets led the nationalist surges, with Rosalía de Castro a key figure in Galicia's cultural *Rexurdimento*. She stopped writing in Galician after being criticized for claiming that 'decent' married women invited unknown sailors into their beds if they had been at sea for long periods.

Jack). All are now standard terms in Basque political discourse.

Within four years of his death, Arana's party had won control of the city hall in Bilbao. It was proof that he had managed to square the two apparently contradictory desires which still underpin Spain's complex 'Basque problem'. He gained political recognition of the Basque Country's growing power because of the industrial revolution, while also promoting the protection of the rural Basque culture that same revolution threatened to destroy.

In mostly rural or seafaring Galicia, where almost everyone spoke the Portuguese-tinged Galego, a similar cultural movement known as the *Rexurdimento* helped spark a wave of regionalism and produced the remarkable romantic poet Rosalía de Castro. Her 'Cantares galegos', published in May 1863, revived a literary language which, despite its troubadour past, had long been deemed vulgar and uncultured. In 1881, she found herself in trouble after describing in a newspaper how in Galicia:

> Among some people it is accepted, as a charitable and meritorious act, that should a sailor who has not touched land for a long time arrive at a place where the women are decent and honourable, the wife, daughter or sister of the family which has given the stranger a roof to stay under, allows him, for the space of a single night, to occupy her bed.

Galician regionalists were outraged, and she paid them back by only writing in Castilian Spanish from then on.

The emergence of Galician, Catalan and Basque nationalism highlighted a much deeper problem which was identified by the scholar, poet and critic Juan Valera as early as 1887. 'If by nation we understand a single state with a single political body, we have not yet become a nation, and perhaps never will be one,' he wrote. Twentieth-century Spain would struggle violently over that.

27
A Tragic Week

On 9 July 1909, Spanish workers building a railway line to connect mines in the Rif region with the port at Melilla were attacked by locals, and four were killed. Spain had won de facto control of the north of Morocco five years earlier at the International Conference of Algeciras (and in 1912 completed a carve-up of the country with France when the Spanish Protectorate of Morocco was established, covering the entire Mediterranean coast). Spain still felt humiliated by the loss of Cuba and the Philippines, and the attack sparked a furious reaction that brought war and a call-up of reservists. Many of those called up had young families but were not wealthy enough to raise the 2,000 pesetas (equivalent to more than two years of a manual worker's pay) to buy themselves out. At train stations in Madrid and Zaragoza, there were protests as troops gathered and were sent towards Mediterranean ports. Demonstrations spread to Barcelona on 18 July, as Catalan reservists and conscripts embarked. 'Down with the war. Let the rich go! Everyone, or no one!' the crowd shouted.

A general strike in Barcelona on 26 July brought the city to a halt and turned into a week of street violence, as the local military governor declared a 'state of war'. Anarchists and others, meanwhile, added an anti-clerical note to this class-based, anti-war protest. Barricades went up in cities and towns around Catalonia, while churches and monasteries burned – with thirty set alight on the night of 27 July in Barcelona. Mummified corpses were pulled from church crypts and displayed on the street. Clemente García, a young, mentally ill man, danced through the streets of Barcelona with a nun's corpse removed from one of the convents. That same day, at the Barranco del Lobo, near Melilla, 153 of the reservists who had boarded ship on the 18th were killed and a further 600 wounded in a humiliating defeat.

The church-burning was backed by supporters of the Radical Republican Party of Alejandro Lerroux, a populist demagogue known as the 'Emperor of the Paralelo'. This was the street where the migrant slums full of workers from other parts of Spain and smoke-stack industries of the Poble Sec district met the ancient poverty of the packed Raval quarter. Lerroux's greatest hate, above even Catalan nationalists (since he represented poor immigrants from further south), was the church. 'Destroy its temples, tear aside the veil of novices and elevate them to the category of mothers,' he had once urged his followers, known as the Young Barbarians. Lerroux himself missed Barcelona's 'Tragic Week', however, since he was temporarily in exile.

By the end of the week, Barcelona had been flooded with soldiers, and the fires in 112 buildings extinguished. At least 104 people had died. Repression followed revolt. Some 2,000 people were arrested, and five executed – including Clemente García. More controversially, for the time, the great anarchist thinker and founder of the Escuela Moderna (an atheist, co-educational school hated by the church) Francisco Ferrer, was accused of organizing the uprising and was also executed. Evidence was scant, but authorities had been wanting to get Ferrer ever since his school's librarian, Mateo Morral, had thrown an Orsini bomb hidden inside a bunch of flowers as Alfonso XIII and his English bride Victoria Eugenie (granddaughter of Queen Victoria) waved to crowds in Madrid from their wedding coach on 31 May 1906. His bomb, thrown from a balcony, bounced off a tram cable and killed twenty-five

↑ Police against workers. By the end of the nineteenth century, industrial conflict in Barcelona was already leading to regular confrontations between the Civil Guard police and workers, painted here by Ramón Casas.

people, leaving the monarchs blood-spattered but unharmed.

Ferrer's execution provoked demonstrations in cities as far away as Paris, Buenos Aires and Genoa. It was a sign of the globalization of ideas and ideologies which was making Unamuno's 'four winds' blow into Spain once more. Within a week, Maura was forced to resign. The Tragic Week, and its consequences, were a first political victory for Spain's underclass, and evidence that the sham democracy of the Peaceful Turn could not last.

Miners' strikes in the Basque Country and Huelva, along with local general strikes in Barcelona, Seville, La Coruña and Gijón, were further evidence of working-class muscle being flexed. They produced limited results, but Sundays were finally declared non-working days in 1904, a nascent pensions and social security system was introduced, and fifteen years later the working day was reduced to eight hours.

If Spain's exploited and disenfranchised working class did not fully explode, it was because the country soon entered another boom period. Between 1914 and 1918, it found itself supplying both sides of a world war that it had no need to participate in. This gave a further push to a rapid industrial transformation that had already in 1904 seen automobile production start in Barcelona.

The impact of this next phase of industrialization was felt across Spain. Away from the cities and coasts, parts of Spain's rock-like interior had resisted change. 'You could say that in the *pueblo* where I was born the Middle Ages lasted until the First World War,' the avant-garde film-maker Luis Buñuel said of Calanda, his hometown in Aragón. Henry Buckley, a British correspondent for the *Daily Telegraph* in Madrid, who became the most acute foreign observer after arriving in 1929, nevertheless saw the boom as a wasted chance to overhaul Spain's economy and social model. 'She would undoubtedly have done so if the forces of feudalism had not been too strong,' he said. 'Although money poured into the country and Madrid hotels had gala nights seven days a week at which fortunes were spent on champagne and gaming, the shadow of unrest spread.'

The greatest disaster of the period was the Spanish flu pandemic, which killed 150,000 people between 1918 and 1920. There was nothing specifically 'Spanish' about this flu, but military censors in the warring nations of Europe banned reporting of domestic outbreaks, while Spain – where Alfonso XIII fell very ill – did not. The population, nevertheless, grew by another quarter over the first three decades of the century. Cities sucked in much of that growth, with Barcelona reaching over one million inhabitants and Madrid – which opened a metro system in 1919 – close behind. All this contrasted with the abject poverty of much of rural Spain, which bled population. In fact, two million people (10 per cent of the population) left for the fast-developing former colonies in the Americas, especially Argentina, where the future looked brighter.

Waves of artists and intellectuals accompanied this period of economic growth, becoming more brilliant with each generation.

Two later 'generations' (of 1914 and 1927) picked up the intellectual baton from the pessimistic Generation of 1898 that had lived through the loss of Cuba. They either sought to bring Spain into the fold of European thought, like the philosopher José Ortega y Gasset and composer Manuel de Falla of the 1914 generation, or they rebelled against social and other conventions. The women of the 1927 generation, including philosopher María Zambrano, were known as *las Sinsombrero* – 'the Hatless' – since they refused to cover their heads. Their generation produced some of the world's greatest surrealists, including painter Salvador Dalí and film-maker Luis Buñuel. At one glorious moment, these two coincided in Madrid with the most brilliant member of that generation, playwright Federico García Lorca.

Both Lorca and Falla had looked south again as they sought authentically Spanish culture, much as the *majos* had in Goya's time. They found it, famously, in flamenco and the mysterious inspirational source behind it, *duende*. This untranslatable spirit was described by García Lorca as 'a power, not a work. It is a struggle, not a thought. I have heard an old maestro of the guitar say: "The *duende* is not in the throat; the *duende* climbs up inside you, from the soles of the feet." Meaning this: it is not a question of ability, but of true, living style, of blood, of the most ancient culture, of spontaneous creation ... everything that has black sounds in it, has *duende*.' Gypsies, too, were accepted as part of that – perhaps the first time that they had been placed on the altar of Spanish culture – with Lorca's poetry collection, *Romance Gitano* (*Gypsy Ballads*) and Falla's ballet *Amor Brujo*. The origins of flamenco are lost in history but reflect the fact that – from the very start – Spain's gypsies produced entertainers. They did not, however, bring flamenco with them. This had emerged, centuries later, out of a 'four winds' stew that mixed together gypsy, Arab, African and Jewish music with troubador romances, traditional poetry and, later, beats from Latin America (which is why the different flamenco palos – or rhythmic structures – include some called *colombianas*, *guajiras* and *tangos*). It broke out of its southern confines in the late nineteenth century, when a craze for musical *cafés cantantes* (literally song cafés) began, and flamenco performers were suddenly in demand in cities around the country.

Spain, then, wished to renew itself as it started a new century. Yet its power structures remained the same. Alfonso XIII, the king born after his father died, had finally begun to reign in his own right when he turned sixteen in May 1902. He proved popular to begin with – though he increasingly meddled in military matters, believing himself an expert. Power remained in the hands of a wealthy minority but had started shifting away from the aristocracy and the great landlords towards the new men of industry or finance. Chief amongst these was Juan March, a one-time tobacco smuggler from Majorca whose extensive network of bribery turned many politicians into his servants and saw one contemporary politician claim that he 'for eleven years ... effectively ran Spain'.

By 1914, the Peaceful Turn had begun to wobble. Liberals and conservatives were at war, and their governments failed to pacify either the increasingly demanding workers' organizations or the army's belligerent officer class. The latter increasingly embraced a type of reactionary conservatism previously associated with the Carlists. They were also avowed enemies of the emerging nationalism in Catalonia and other regions. At the same time, tit-for-tat

→ Another assassinated prime minister. José Canalejas was shot by anarchist Manuel Pardiñas while looking into a bookshop window in Madrid in 1912.

SERVICIO 25
BAR SOL
CHOCOLATERIA
SUBIDA al ENTRESUELO
HAY
PESETAS
EL
SE
SORTEA
EL
DIA

killings between anarchists or trade unionists and *pistoleros* hired by factory bosses swept through Barcelona, a city of tinderbox politics.

The tipping point came with a catastrophic military defeat at the hands of the Rif Berbers, led by the formidable Abd el-Krim at Annual in July and August 1921. Survivors of a Spanish army of 18,000 men fled in disarray back to the North African Spanish city of Melilla. Almost 10,000 Spanish soldiers, and another 2,500 colonial troops, were killed, despite being better armed. The defeat rubbed salt into the still open wound left by national humiliation in Cuba and the Philippines two decades earlier. The Peaceful Turn was crumbling, and the position of prime minister had become increasingly dangerous. Anarchists assassinated liberal prime minister José Canelejas and conservative Eduardo Dato in 1912 and 1921 respectively, thereby bringing the number of prime ministers murdered over forty-seven years to four – with another, Antonio Maura, surviving two separate assassination attempts.

Worse still, the king himself had pushed for the ill-judged military advance in North Africa that had ended in a massacre. An official report drawn up by an army general called Juan Picasso (the famous painter's first cousin, once removed) concluded that 'the country has a right to know who is responsible'. Improvisation, over-confidence, poor training and shoddy leadership, he said, were all to blame for one of the worst defeats suffered by a European army in Africa. The suicide of the general in charge, Alfonso XIII's close friend Manuel Fernández Silvestre, meant the monarch's role could be covered up, but newspaper pictures of massacred corpses littering Moroccan hillsides provoked popular indignation. Street protests demanded punishment be meted out to those who were responsible. That was too much for the army, which did not want its cackhandedness, cowardice and corporativism exposed.

On 13 September, General Miguel Primo de Rivera, captain general of Catalonia (whose brother had died at Annual) led a bloodless coup that brought the 'Peaceful Turn', and fake democracy, to an end. Amongst other reasons for his coup, he cited parliamentary demands for the punishment of fellow officers responsible for the Annual massacre. His principal supporters were the monarch, the army and the industrialists of Barcelona, who gathered to wave him off on the train to Madrid after Alfonso XIII agreed to appoint him dictator.

28
Spain's Mussolini

The king hailed Primo de Rivera as 'my Mussolini', in recognition of the flamboyant, strutting fascist appointed to run Italy the previous year. Like Italy's King Victor Emmanuel III, the monarch was terrified of the growing workers' organizations and parties. Spain's dictator was not inspired by the new ideological cocktail that Benito Mussolini, a former socialist, had produced in Italy. In fact, the politically cautious Primo de Rivera was expected to follow the example of previous Spanish strongmen who stepped in when events span out of control and left once order had been restored.

To begin with, it certainly looked like that would happen. Within four years, the war in Morocco had been won. Top-down reforms and large public works were initiated, some to great benefit. Public companies were formed to run everything from the telephone system and tourist hotels (with the Paradores network taking over abandoned castles) to gas stations. The electricity grid, the road network and a state-backed irrigation system all spread across the country. Just as Mussolini made the trains run on time, Primo de Rivera made Spain's economy hum.

He also oversaw a rampant increase in corruption, and brooked no criticism. 'He doesn't even have the brains of a frog: he is the prototype of a frivolous and vain *señorito* [rich kid],' Unamuno complained. When he lowered the dictator's mental capacity to that of a locust in a letter published in an Argentine newspaper, he found

↑ *'My Mussolini'.* King Alfonso XIII annulled democracy and appointed General Miguel Primo de Rivera as the country's first twentieth-century dictator from 1923 to 1930.

himself in trouble, and a military court soon charged him with disrespecting the army. In February 1924, he was arrested, sacked as rector of Salamanca University and sent into internal exile on the Canary Island of Fuerteventura.

The dictator made no attempt to return power to parliament or to hand it to the people. In fact, he seemed intent on consolidating his position – making him more of a Mussolini than the king expected. The Majorcan robber baron Juan March, who was now one of the wealthiest men and most corrupting influences in Spain, was amongst those who benefitted most from the massive, unchecked corruption of the regime. The so-called 'last pirate of the Mediterranean' even had a murder investigation against him (the victim was a business rival and allegedly March's wife's lover) dropped, though he had previously fled to Paris disguised as a priest in order to avoid arrest.

Untrammelled power and a degree of popular support did not see Primo de Rivera resolve the diverse tensions which were stretching and tearing at the country: of workers against bosses; of regions against the centre; and of a bloated officer corps that, once the Moroccan war had been won, had little to do but had gained a reputation for merciless brutality. 'There was no limit to its lust for revenge,' the writer Arthur Barea said after accompanying the new and particularly cruel Spanish Legion as it rampaged through the villages of the Beni Arós region in 1921. 'When it left a village, all that remained were burning buildings and the corpses of men, women and children.'

When Primo de Rivera resigned in 1930, having become unpopular with almost everybody, the king handed his job to a personal favourite, General Dámaso Berenguer (who had been partly responsible for the Annual disaster). His task was to prepare for a return to some sort of parliamentarianism, but he lost control, and a new temporary government had to call municipal elections for 12 April, to be followed in June by a general election.

Municipal elections were the only real barometer of public opinion, since they were much harder to fix. In the cities, Spaniards voted massively for republicanism and its explicit commitment to getting rid of the monarchy, while rural areas, managed by *caciques*, still returned monarchists. It was a killer blow. By the following day, streets were full of people celebrating the end of monarchy. That night, the British journalist Henry Buckley stood outside the royal palace in a heavy overcoat and watched the lights burn. He asked a uniformed doorman what was happening inside and was told that the royal family were 'attending a cinematographic performance in the salon recently fitted up with a sound apparatus'. Even now, as jubilant crowds gathered a mile away in the Puerta del Sol, the king seemed impossibly distant from reality and unaware that he had been abandoned. 'Where are Spain's four hundred generals? Where are the two hundred Grandees?' Buckley asked himself. 'What of this Spain which we are told is so catholic; where are Bishops, friars and the faithful tonight?'

Spain lurched into sudden and enormous change. The following day, Alfonso XIII fled into exile, and the Second Republic was proclaimed without a shot being fired. His English wife Victoria Eugenie left the exiled monarch after he insisted that she choose between him and her favourite travel companions, the Duke and Duchess of Lécera (who were both said to be in love with her). 'I choose them and never want to see your ugly face again,' she spat. Spain's first experiment in proper democracy could now begin. 'How the commentators of Spain have aged!' the great Catalan writer Josep Pla wrote. 'In a single day they have all turned unbearably gaga.'

29
The Second Republic

Joy spilled over amongst those demanding change. The Second Republic was known as '*la niña bonita*', the pretty little girl – glowing, newborn and of uncertain but hopeful future. Suddenly, the country was being run by the people excluded from power for the previous half-century: republicans, leftists, democrats and regionalists.

Their idea of Spain was radically new and won the support of voters at a general election in June 1931, when Spaniards cast ballots freely for the first time. 'Spain is no longer Catholic,' the new prime minister, Manuel Azaña of the Republican Action Party, proclaimed. Women stood as candidates, and three won seats, but suffrage was limited only to men (for the last time). There was no revolution as such, but this time change really was revolutionary.

Now workers' rights, wages, land reform, devolution of power to Catalonia, the Basque Country and other regions and freeing Spain definitively from the yoke of the church topped the political agenda. Women won the vote later in 1931 (thanks to bold campaigners like Clara Campoamor and more than a decade before France or Italy), and divorce was approved. State-run schooling spread into even the smallest villages – a major achievement in

← Prime minister Manuel Azaña ran the first government of the Second Republic founded in 1931, but angered military officers by restricting promotion. He later became the Republic's president.

a country where a third of the population could not read or write.

In this new panorama, the Radical Republican Party (PRR) of Alejandro Lerroux – the former 'emperor' of Barcelona's Paralelo Street, now a moderate conservative – initially found itself as part of a centre-left government, but then became the main opposition to a reconstituted left-wing government (since monarchist and other right-wing parties won so few parliamentary seats). A 1932 charter of regional autonomy for Catalonia, which gave it limited powers of self-government under a restored Generalitat, brought formal recognition of the fact that two centuries of centralist rule had failed to turn Spain into a single, homogenous entity. Similar charters were drawn up four years later for Galicia and the Basque Country but barely had time to be put into effect before war broke out.

A major part of the workers' movement – the anarchists – remained outside the new system and made life difficult with strikes and protests. Organized into the National Workers Federation trade union and the Iberian Anarchist Federation (FAI), the anarchists had a natural enemy in industrialists and business owners, who saw salary costs rising as the new government introduced progressive reforms.

It is ironic that the only organization capable of rapidly founding a nationwide, mass party to participate in a lay republic was the Catholic Church. It was a prime mover behind the foundation of Acción Popular in 1931, which became the seed for the broader Spanish Federation of the Autonomous Right (CEDA) grouping. This damned the country's new leaders as anti-Catholic traitors seeking to destroy the family, snatch away property and sow chaos. It won support not just amongst the rich and the faithful, but also from smallholders and shop owners. Yet when monarchists led by General José Sanjurjo launched a coup in August 1932, it failed spectacularly. Azaña commuted his death sentence, ignoring Mexican president Plutarco Elías Calles's prescient warning that Sanjurjo must be executed 'to avoid a bloodbath'.

Fresh elections were called in 1933 as socialists and republicans split. Standing separately, they suffered a traumatic defeat. Some blamed women for this change, since they had voted for the first time and were more likely to be churchgoers. Now Lerroux's centre-right Radical Republican Party (known as 'the radicals') formed a government backed by CEDA. It was the first of eight right-wing governments formed during two chaotic years that would test the young democracy to its limits.

With no voice in government, while landowners and industrialists were emboldened, workers' movements began plotting revolution. Strikes spread and, eventually, an attempt at revolution emerged from the mining communities of Asturias, in the north, where anarchists and socialists combined in October 1934. This was ferociously put down, with a young general who had become famous in Africa, Francisco Franco, playing a crucial part. The brutal attitude of the officer class in the normally Morocco-based Army of Africa was demonstrated by Lieutenant Colonel Juan Yagüe Blanco, whose men behaved with gleeful sadism, torturing and murdering captive miners. 'They cut off their feet, their hands, their ears, their tongues, even their genitals! A few days later, one of my most trusted officers told me that there were *legionarios* wearing wire necklaces from which dangled human ears from the victims,' the region's shocked commanding officer, General Eduardo López Ochoa, reported. Some 1,500 people were killed.

At the same time, the Catalan regional government also chose to rebel, declaring the existence of a new 'Catalan State' within the Spanish republic. That sparked more fighting, with forty-six people killed across Catalonia. As a result, Catalonia's self-government was suspended.

Lerroux was brought down by corruption scandals (an illegally fixed gambling machine known as the Estraperlo had been introduced to the country thanks to widespread bribery, with Lerroux himself allegedly raking off 25 per cent). When new elections were

↑ Dictator Miguel Primo de Rivera's charismatic son José Antonio brought fascism to Spain with his Falange party, which won few votes but became a lynchpin of the Franco dictatorship.

called for February 1936, the left came together in a Popular Front – which included the small Communist Party of Spain – and won back power. The new government was led by moderate left-wingers who, according to Buckley, were 'quiet, middle-class liberals'.

Almost immediately, the losers began plotting a coup. Since they had the army on their side, this was a far greater threat to Spain's young democracy than a miners' revolt in Asturias. A new fascist party, the Falange (founded by the smooth and charming José Antonio Primo de Rivera, son of the dictator), had failed to win any seats but took violence to the streets. It sparred with socialists, anarchists and the police, provoking retaliation and further violence. Tit-for-tat killings produced a growing death toll, in which many victims were country labourers – since rural zones were controlled by *caciques* and their allies in the Civil Guard rural police force. All this bolstered a right-wing narrative that anarchy and violence were taking hold. Intellectuals on the far right pushed the idea that Spain had lost its way, with Jews and freemasons helping to introduce foreign ideas like socialism and atheism. Rather than open itself to the 'four winds', as Unamuno had urged, it needed to re-establish its own identity and Spanishness ('*hispanidad*'). 'All our ills derive from one alone: the loss of our national idea,' proclaimed the essayist Ramiro de Maeztu y Whitney, who was actually half-British and half-Cuban.

Early in July 1936, the thirty-four-year-old Argentine writer Mika Etchebéhère arrived in Madrid and found that 'an agonizing tension kept everyone awake ... as if they were watching over a dying man'. The government, however, refused to believe that a coup was coming. In June, Prime Minister Santiago Casares Quiroga interviewed a key plotter, the same Lt-Col. Yagüe whose men had behaved atrociously in Asturias, and stated that 'he has given me his word ... and men like Yagüe keep their word'. Demands that Casares Quiroga arrest chief plotter General Emilio Mola were also waved away, since 'Mola is a loyal Republican who deserves the respect of the authorities.'

On 12 July 1936, Falangist gunmen killed a young, left-wing lieutenant called José del Castillo from the Assault Guards police force. This had been set up in 1931 as an urban riot force and counterweight to the conservative, rural Civil Guard. Before his wedding, three weeks earlier, Castillo's bride reportedly received a letter saying: 'Why marry a man who will soon be a corpse?' The following day, his colleagues avenged his death by kidnapping and killing one of the most important right-wing leaders in parliament, the monarchist José Calvo Sotelo.

This murder became a convenient cover for launching a coup that was, in fact, already underway. It brought together the army, Mussolini, the Carlists and other right-wing radicals, including the fascists of the Falange.

30
The 1936 Coup

On 11 July 1936, two days before Calvo Sotelo died, a de Havilland Dragon Rapide aircraft took off from Croydon airport in England, piloted by Captain Cecil Bebb. He had been hired by the plotters to fly to the Canary Islands, pick up General Francisco Franco and take him to North Africa in time to lead the revolt of the Spanish military's most potent force, the colonial Army of Africa, when the coup started on 18 July. Bebb was told to take two young blonde women with him, to make it look like a tourist pleasure jaunt. His daughter and a friend obliged.

In fact, rebels in the North African enclave of Melilla rose a day early, on 17 July, after the local commander, republican loyalist General Romerales Quintero (memorably described as 'the fattest of Spain's 400 generals and one of the easiest to trick'), discovered the plot. He was arrested, and the plotters shot as many people in one night as had died across the country in the previous three months of political violence from which they claimed to be 'saving' Spain. Romerales would be killed later.

The next day, the coup spread across the Canary Islands, Africa and onto mainland Spain, with Seville's garrisons rising at 2 p.m. and placing the notoriously violent (and drunken) General Gonzalo Queipo de Llano in charge. Cádiz, Córdoba and Granada also rose, but the Andalusian countryside remained loyal. The government seemed remarkably unperturbed. 'The coup is bound to fail,' Casares Quiroga told a friend, assuring him that Franco was not among the plotters.

Normally, a coup is over within a few days, if not hours, after rebels capture the major ministries in the capital city and other strategic points. This, however, was a slow-motion coup, which the plotters planned as a short war. That is why it did not reach the two cities of Barcelona and Madrid, home to almost a tenth of the population, until later.

It wasn't until the early morning of 19 July, two days after the coup began in Melilla, that soldiers marched into Barcelona from barracks around the city. Barcelona had been busy preparing for the inauguration that day of the Popular Olympiad, a leftist alternative Olympics designed to rival Hitler's Berlin games. Loyal police and armed workers were expecting the army to rebel, however, and defeated them quickly. Instead of being filled with marching soldiers, the city's streets now swarmed with expropriated cars daubed with the letters of competing trades unions and left-wing parties, their windows bristling with weapons requisitioned from rebel soldiers or snatched from barracks. This was a counter-revolution, meaning that the reactionary generals had provoked their worst nightmare into becoming a reality, with the far left taking control.

The US consul, Lynn Franklin, started the day cabling his superiors about a 'Fascist uprising' and finished it by reporting that at least three churches were burning. 'Many of the Sindicalists' automobiles have rough-looking women in them accompanied by armed men and the sign given by those who pass, on foot or in automobiles, is the raised fist,' he wrote. Bernie Danchik, from the US Olympiad team, was holed up in his hotel, but impressed. 'Sunday – Comes the revolution!' he jotted in his notebook. Like most foreign athletes, Danchik left a few days later, but he was to return as part of a remarkable, 35,000-strong force of volunteers from more than sixty countries which contemporaries compared to the Crusaders and was known as the International Brigades. A fifth of them would die defending the Republic.

The following day, the coup spread to Madrid, but a handful of loyal soldiers and the furious masses who had taken to the streets defeated the rebels there too. The Montaña barracks were stormed, and an angry crowd lynched the rebels, some of whom were hurled to their death from its balconies. Crowds wandered the streets demanding '*Armas! Armas! Armas!*' while a frightened government fretted about what to do. In the end, arms were distributed, the government resigned, and a tub-thumping socialist called Francisco Largo Caballero became prime minister.

A week after the coup, on 25 July, the rebels held their four isolated outposts in Andalusia and a broad stretch of territory in the north that included Navarre, most of Galicia and old Castile, a part of Extremadura and half of Aragón, plus almost all of Spain's islands. Of the big cities, only Seville and Zaragoza were in rebel hands. More importantly, they had also secured the allegiance of most of the army and 85 per cent of its officers. There was, however, one major problem. Franco's Army of Africa – the biggest and most experienced unit of all – was stationed on a different continent. The navy and air force, meanwhile, had mostly stayed loyal, so that the Army of Africa could not be shipped to the mainland.

In his military history of the war, Charles Esdaile describes an apparently advantageous situation for the Republic. 'The government had the population, the enormous gold reserves of the Bank of Spain and the bulk of Spain's manufacturing industry, mineral resources and export crops.' It also had 'fifty of her sixty-five armoured vehicles, 300 of her 400 naval, military and civil aircraft, and twenty-seven of her thirty-one principal naval units.'

Another setback for the rebels came when exiled General

Sanjurjo, who was meant to lead the uprising, took off in a light aircraft from a Portuguese field, only for it to clip some tree-tops and crash. Sanjurjo died, with the pilot (who survived) blaming the weight of the ceremonial uniforms and medals his passenger had packed. It was only after this that Franco became rebel leader and candidate for dictator.

Help for the rebels was on hand from their natural allies abroad – the fascists in Italy and the Nazis in Germany. Mussolini initially held back from sending the arms he had promised before the coup, but on 28 July a dozen Savoia SM.81 aircraft left Italy for Morocco. Two of these crashed in the sea, and one was forced to land in French Morocco – alerting the world to Mussolini's part in the uprising.

On 25 July Adolf Hitler returned from watching a performance of Richard Wagner's *Siegfried* at the Bayreuth Festival. Emissaries from Franco awaited him and explained that they urgently needed to transport the 35,000 experienced men of the Army of Africa to mainland Spain. Inspired by the opera he had just seen, Hitler ordered his Luftwaffe to carry out the biggest military airlift the world had ever seen. He dubbed it Operation Magic Fire after a passage from Wagner's opera in which Siegfried wades through flames to rescue Brünnhilde. Twenty large Junkers Ju 52 transport aircraft and nine of the Italian Savoias began to ferry troops at the end of July, with Franco himself arriving on 6 August (while a naval force also managed to deliver 1,600 men). A faltering coup thus became a civil war which was not just a Spanish conflict, but part of the global clash of ideologies that would lead to another world war three years later.

Once on the mainland, Franco's experienced forces tore through a chaotic Republican army made up of untried militia units formed by political parties and trades unions. They applied to Spanish citizens the same ferocity usually meted out to opponents in the

el generalisimo

JUNTA DELEGADA DE DEFENSA
DE MADRID
DELEGACION DE PROPAGANDA Y PRENSA

Moroccan wars. In Badajoz, many hundreds of Republican loyalists were executed in the bullring. Yagüe claimed to have killed even more: 'Of course we shot them ... Was I meant to take 4,000 reds with me as my column advanced?' Portuguese journalist Mário Neves, who saw hundreds of burned corpses in the cemetery, vowed never to return to the city. 'It is impossible to remain calm in the face of such horrible scenes,' he wrote. In Navalcarnero, on the road to Madrid, American journalist John Whitaker saw Franco's senior Moroccan officer Major Mohammed Ben Mizzian hand over two young 'red' women to forty of his colonial troops, admitting that they would be dead within hours.

By early November 1936, Franco's troops were at the gates of Madrid, the government had fled to Valencia and General Mola was boasting that he would soon be drinking coffee on the city's central Gran Vía. Remarkably, however, Franco's forces were stopped at Madrid, in part because the International Brigades had just arrived.

The time bought at Madrid and at battles near the city in places like Jarama and Guadalajara, allowed the Republic to reorganize its army and receive arms, tanks, advisers and aircraft from Joseph Stalin's Soviet Union. This was the legitimate government's sole significant backer, apart from Mexico. Britain, France and the United States, meanwhile, began their cowardly policy of appeasing Hitler and Mussolini with a non-intervention pact that was brazenly ignored by the dictators. The Non-Intervention Committee became 'the most cynical and lamentably dishonest group that history has known', according to an American envoy.

Hitler sent his expeditionary Condor Legion of the Luftwaffe to help Franco and experiment with tactics and equipment. German

← The Roman Catholic Church, army and landowners backed *generalísimo* Francisco Franco as he and other generals overthrew democracy in the Spanish Civil War of 1936–9, bringing in a dictatorship that lasted until his death in 1975.

bombers razed the historic Basque town of Guernica in April 1937, in one of the world's first fire-bombings of a civilian target. Mussolini sent 75,000 troops and fascist militiamen, in three divisions, while also carrying out a bombing campaign against Barcelona that targeted civilian neighbourhoods, killing 3,000 people in a precursor to the London Blitz. 'Terror is the most effective weapon of the air force,' one of his generals recommended, foreseeing the tactics of the Second World War. 'It should be launched against enemy populations, destroying cities, their centres and all means of life, submitting it to a nightmare that forces surrender.' For the first time ever, newspaper readers around the world became used to seeing photographs of dead women and children, or of homes ripped in half by bombs, spilling their innards.

After it halted the advance on Madrid, which did not fall until the end of the war, the Republican army was slowly rolled back on other fronts. The Battle of Brunete in July 1937, a Republican offensive near Madrid, showed that Franco's air force had almost complete superiority in the air. Two-thirds of his air force was made up of Italian or German aircraft and pilots. They experimented with the technique of Blitzkrieg, as aircraft led attacks, followed by tanks and then by motorized troops. In the north of Spain, these tactics brought victory by the autumn of 1937. By April 1938, Franco's troops had also reached the Mediterranean and the mouth of the Ebro river, splitting Republican Spain in two. The Republic delayed defeat by launching a bloody and epic attack across the Ebro in Catalonia in July 1938. The hope of the Republican prime minister Juan Negrín was that this might keep the war alive until the predicted larger, European war broke out.

Franco, meanwhile, was not interested in negotiating a surrender. He wanted to inflict absolute defeat and, behind the lines of his conquered territory, set about liquidating opposition. Falangist death squads rounded up civilians (like playwright and poet Federico García Lorca, shot outside Granada in August 1936), while military firing squads and concentration camps dealt with those captured by his army or police. Some 130,000 people were shot or died in Francoist hands. In the chaotic early months of the war, there was bloody repression behind the Republican lines too. Almost 50,000 people were killed, including at least 6,845 churchmen and nuns (and almost a third of all monks in the Republican zone) by anarchists or others, though it was never quite as systematic or extensive as the Francoist purges, which continued after the war with a further 50,000 executions.

When Franco finally declared victory on 1 April 1939, it was by virtue of conquest. Spanish society was to be divided between 'winners' and 'losers' for the next thirty-six years, until the dictator finally died.

↑ Pablo Picasso painted his giant *Guernica*, one of the most famous anti-war paintings of all time, for the Spanish Republic's Pavilion at the 1937 Paris Expo. The Basque town had been partially destroyed on 26 April that year by incendiary bombs dropped by Adolf Hitler's Condor Legion, which fought alongside General Franco's forces during the civil war.

31
El Caudillo

Francisco Franco Bahamonde was a naval officer's son, who was unable to follow family tradition and go to sea. Instead, he joined the army as a fourteen-year-old military cadet. His high-pitched voice and skinny, short frame saw colleagues give him the nickname of *Cerillita*, or Little Matchstick (though when he plumped out later in life, they called him *Paca la Culona*, or Big-Arsed Fanny). Like almost everybody, they underestimated the iron will hidden by his unimpressive aspect. What he lacked in brains and imagination, Franco made up for in ambition and fearlessness. It was enough to make him the most important person in Spain's bloody and repressive twentieth century.

As a young officer in Morocco, he displayed considerable physical courage time and time again. The consequences were war wounds, a lucky escape from death, rapid promotion and meteoric fame. He arrived in Spain's narrow sliver of North Africa as a nineteen-year-old second lieutenant in 1912 and left as a thirty-three-year-old general in 1926. 'This is where the idea of rescuing Spain was born,' Europe's youngest general admitted later. 'Without Africa I can barely explain who I am to myself.'

In 1920, when Spain created its own version of the French Legion, the Legión Española, with a battle-cry of 'Long live death!', he was an obvious choice to be one of its commanders. The Legion mostly recruited Spaniards and, indeed, came to be seen as the supreme expression of a chest-beating Spanish masculinity based on fearlessness, violence and disdain for weakness or 'introversion' of any kind. Its members were known as 'The Bridegrooms of Death'.

The new Spain was born out of extreme notions of colonial pride, violence and martial vigour. It also reflected the small-minded Roman Catholicism of Franco himself, whose idea of religion was based on obedience rather than love. That did not stop him from stamping on Spanish coins that he was dictator 'por la gracia de Dios', 'by God's will'. In short, Franco was the perfect reactionary. He wanted a return to social cohesion based on fear and the obedience owed to church, landowners, police and those who sacrificed themselves for the fatherland, meaning the army. He was still relatively young – aged forty-three – as well as notoriously cold and difficult to read. 'Only his eyes show life and cleverness,' Alfonso XIII's son and heir Juan de Borbón (who Franco never allowed to rule), said of him. 'One is the master of what one does not say, and the slave of what one does,' Franco himself observed, to explain why he spoke so little. He was a skilled exponent of *retranca*, a deliberate ambivalence that trips up other people and is reputed to be a mark of people from Galicia.

As a man accustomed to military violence, without empathy and incapable of understanding fear, he felt no compunction about using terror to impose a new, highly personal regime. This was, in some ways, an imitation of the absolutist monarchies of the past, but with a massive increase in violent repression and little of the Enlightenment thought that those regimes encouraged to bring innovation or progress. A sluggish conservatism and a heavy-handed love of 'order' stymied early attempts by even those close to him to bring Spain properly into the twentieth century. It did not help that he refused to see himself as a politician, since this was a profession that he despised. Nor was he keen on intellectuals who questioned the supposed virility of his regime.

Miguel de Unamuno had been appalled by anarchist atrocities

early in the war and was prepared to give Franco a chance. Within months he discovered his mistake, as friends were detained or shot. In a famous public row with Franco's former Foreign Legion commander General Millán Astray at Salamanca University late in October 1936, Unamuno denounced the 'uncivil war' and warned Franco that military victory alone did not confer moral authority, and that he must *convencer*, convince, rather than *vencer*, win. José Millán Astray allegedly shouted: 'Death to intelligence!' and Unamuno, once more, was sacked as rector and remained shut up in his house until his death ten weeks later. Another philosopher, José Ortega y Gasset, warned that with Unamuno's voice now permanently muted, 'I fear that this country is entering a period of terrible silence.' He was right.

In the years after Franco's victory, Spaniards bore the burden of this inward-looking, nationalistic and ruthless pattern of thought. Its most lethal and tragic expression was the vengeance inflicted on the war's losers. In the first few years of his dictatorship (and final months of the war), half a million Spaniards fled the country while another 260,000 were in prison camps. Of the latter group, more than 50,000 were shot in the years after his victory. Historian Paul Preston puts the total number of executions, during and after the war, at 130,000. All in all, more than 300,000 people had died because of the war provoked by Spanish reactionaries and fascists.

A retroactive Law of Political Responsibility meant that left-wing officials who had held elected office in the Republic could be jailed and fined. The Law of Repression of Freemasons and Communists added to Franco's arsenal of totalitarian laws. In some ways, it was as if a far bloodier version of the Inquisition had returned, since even the families of those who had broken the 'natural laws' of Spain were punished and paid fines for the crimes of the dead. Even the notorious SS Reichsführer Heinrich Himmler, on a wartime visit, tried to counsel Franco against exacting revenge on the working class. Preston calls Franco's strategy an 'investment in state terror', in which an early, heavy dose produces long-lasting fear and a cowed population. It was also, in the words of the Falangist leader Dionisio Ridruejo, 'a complete extirpation of the political forces that had sustained the Republic'.

When Franco took power, his fascist allies were emboldened to ramp up their aggressive annexationist policies. The Spanish Civil War had shown the weakness of the liberal democracies in response to their aggression. Exactly five months after Franco had declared victory, Hitler invaded Poland and started the Second World War.

Franco's regime relished its proximity to the great new power that was Nazi Germany and supplied it with crucial materials during the Second World War, especially the tungsten it used for armour-piercing shells. Spain did not join the Axis, but Franco sent a volunteer division – the so-called Blue Division – to fight for Hitler against the Soviet Union.

A totalitarian Spain emerged, in which Franco was backed by a single 'movement' created by fusing the fascist Falange, the ultra-Catholic Carlists and other rightist factions. Since the very idea of participatory or pluralistic politics was anathema to Franco, he refused to call it a 'party'. Instead, it was known as the Falange Española Tradicionalista y de las Juntas de Ofensiva Nacional Sindicalista (FET y de las JONS), or Traditionalist Spanish Falange and the Juntas of the National Syndicalist Offensive. Together with a single state-run union, the Spanish Trade Union (OSE), which was also known as the 'vertical union' (Sindicato Vertical), and the regime's military and bureaucratic apparatus, this formed the backbone of a corporatist state, similar to that of Mussolini's Italy. To begin with, Spain's own fascists – the Falange – had oversight of the country's labour force as they jostled for power with the army and monarchists. Mines, railways, telephone and petrol stations were nationalized. State companies were set up in sectors as diverse as petrochemicals, cars and steel.

Franco's regime was militaristic, nationalist and Roman

Catholic. That meant one state (and, so, no regional governments), one official language and one church. It also meant, above all, one leader. Propaganda transformed a *generalísimo* enamoured of his quasi-royal status and the protocol that accompanied it, into everything from a 'visionary Caesar' to the 'guardian of the West'. He was compared to El Cid, Charlemagne, Napoleon, Alexander the Great, and the Archangel Gabriel. It was, his followers believed, a moment of great national resurgence and recovery from what a future Francoist minister and historian Manuel Fraga claimed had been a long-standing conspiracy between England and France, which had 'viciously kicked Spain as it lay on the ground prostrate'.

Divorce was banned, abortion punished and religious censorship reinstated. The new Spain's motto was 'One, Great and Free!' There was nothing 'great' however, about this war-ravaged country. It was poor, damaged and had buried too many of its people, while putting many more in jail or forcing them into exile. Franco's first few years went down in history as 'the years of hunger'. In terms of calories consumed per person, Spain did not return to the levels of 1935 until twenty years later. The economy only recovered its pre-war size after a dozen years of misery in which black market trading and corruption became rife. Amongst those who thrived during these miserable years were officers who plundered and sold military supplies as well as the Majorcan financier Juan March, who had bankrolled Franco during the war and was on his way to becoming one of the world's wealthiest people (some reports ranked him at number six globally). In terms of GDP per capita, Spain lagged far behind parts of its former empire, like Argentina or Uruguay, for several decades.

The leading figure of this early totalitarian phase of Francoism was the Caudillo's brother-in-law, Ramón Serrano Suñer. In the bloody, hate-filled days of the late 1930s and early 1940s,

↑ Franco originally declared himself a 'totalitarian' and backed his ally Adolf Hitler to win the Second World War, only changing path when an Allied victory looked inevitable.

he helped Franco design his new state. The quick-witted, tall and elegant Serrano Suñer provided an unflattering contrast to his squat, pot-bellied brother-in-law. 'Beside the Don Quixote of his brother-in-law, the Caudillo often appears to be Sancho Panza,' France's Marshal Pétain observed.

Serrano Suñer initially combined leadership of the Falange with the interior ministry and then, in 1940, the foreign ministry. He was crucial in keeping Spain close to the Axis powers. He saw Mussolini as a genius of the kind who appears 'once every two or three thousand years'. In 1940, he brought Himmler to Madrid, decorating the city with swastikas. At an October 1940 meeting between Hitler and Franco in a railway wagon at Hendaye, in occupied France, Serrano Suñer helped strike a secret deal by which Spain would join the Second World War on the Axis side at a time of 'common agreement'. That never happened, not least because Franco made wild demands for Spanish ownership of Gibraltar, Morocco and French Cameroon – though the Francoist regime would later claim this ability to sit out the world war was proof of the dictator's subtle and cautious genius.

By 1945, with Franco's allies defeated in Europe, Spain was a pariah. As the biggest, fascist-style state left in Europe it was banned from the United Nations until 1955. 'Having been helped to power by fascist Italy and Nazi Germany, and having patterned itself along totalitarian lines, the present regime in Spain is naturally the subject of distrust,' President Franklin Roosevelt declared. 'We do not forget Spain's official ... assistance to our Axis enemies at a time when the fortunes of war were less favourable to us, nor can we disregard the activities, aims, organizations and public utterances of the Falange.'

Spain could have gained hugely, in economic terms, from its non-participant role in the Second World War. This, however, did not happen. A self-inflicted decision to isolate Spain was to blame. 'Spain is a privileged country that can survive off its own resources. We have all we need ... we do not need to import anything,' Franco said as he set off towards the Quixotic chimera of autarky, or self-reliance. As a result, a poor and backward country remained that way for most of the first half of Franco's thirty-six-year rule. During that period he received some 7.5 million dollars worth of presents, while his family grew wealthy and his wife hoarded jewels or melted down the gold medals they were given by municipal authorities on their travels. Some ministers also grew rich as a culture of corruption – denounced by the more purist Falangists – ran through the regime. Petty corruption, often driven by desperation or because it was the only way to compete, became rife at all levels of society while also serving to spread fear and exercise control. It was up to Francoist authorities, after all, to either act against perpetrators, turn a blind eye or take a cut.

Franco's regime lasted so long, however, that there was time for it to mutate several times over. The iron grip of the state was never fully relaxed, but there were three distinct periods, delivering different kinds of economic progress and repression.

The first phase of totalitarian, terror-based autarky began to change towards the end of the Second World War, when Franco realized he had backed the losing side. As the German and Italian armies were rolled back, the dictator was left with little choice but to soften his regime. In this second phase, he dropped some of the glaringly fascist ceremonial trappings borrowed from Italy and Germany. In 1947, Franco declared himself dictator for life of a Spain that was 'Catholic, social and representative'. He gave himself, alone, the task of choosing a successor, who was meant to come from the royal family. Referendums were allowed, but strictly controlled and nobody believed the 95 per cent approval for his dictatorship-for-life law in 1947.

For Spaniards, the change was merely a move from the years of hunger to the 'grey years', when the regime remained vindictive, cultural life was dull and repressive, and many families had relatives in prison camps. From 1940 to 1958, indeed, some prisoners were forced to work on building a huge monument called the Valley of the Fallen in the hillside 50 kilometres from Madrid. Nominally this was for all Civil War victims, but its main use was as a propaganda tool for Franco, the Falange and the regime. A 150-metre-high blue-grey granite cross rises from a rocky outcrop here while, beneath it, a 260-metre-long underground basilica (with a 22-metre-high, mosaic-clad interior dome) is bored into the rock. Some 33,000 corpses were transported to shabby side chambers, where they continue to lie today. Only José Antonio Primo de Rivera – the founder of Spain's fascist Falange – is buried in full sight, in the basilica itself, though Franco's corpse accompanied him for almost half a century before being forcibly removed by a socialist government in 2019. A new 'Democratic Memory' law due to be passed in 2022 was expected to expel Primo de Rivera from his tomb and may lead to closure of the Benedictine monastery that is attached to the basilica.

Relief for the people of Spain came from a changing world order and the new divisions produced by the Cold War. As an avowed anti-communist, Franco was courted by the USA, which established military bases in Spain after 1953 and helped it join the UN. Spain was back in the club of respectable nations, and Spanish Morocco was given independence (mainly because France had already decided to leave its part of Morocco). Internally, the opposition became bolder. The first major protests against the regime broke out in universities, with street battles between students and Falangists in 1956. By the mid-1950s, the country was suffering an inevitable economic crisis that exposed the frailty of Franco's plans for self-reliance and autarky.

A third and final phase of Francoism, the so-called development era, began a quarter of a century after the end of the civil war, as the ideals of Spanish exceptionalism were scrapped. A group of young economists from the ultra-Catholic Opus Dei movement (founded by Spanish priest Jose María Escrivá in 1928), were appointed to reform the economy. Liberalization, stability and pent-up demand catapulted Spain into runaway growth as it became a 'tiger economy'. Between 1961 and 1964, growth averaged 8.7 per cent a year. From 1966 to 1971, it continued at 5.6 per cent. Industry flourished, and with it the cities. Spaniards were almost two-and-a-half times richer in 1975 than they had been in 1960. Despite this, almost 2 million Spaniards emigrated between 1960 and 1973. In comparative terms, Spain still could not match European growth since 1936, but the speed of change brought remarkable improvements to material well-being. This 'Spanish miracle' was accompanied by massive urban migration, with 4 million Spaniards abandoning the countryside (though half of them emigrated to French factories, Swiss restaurants or jobs elsewhere in Europe).

By the early 1970s, then, Spain was turning into a modern country in almost all ways except for a glaringly damaging one – it was run by a dictator. In 1969, he had appointed thirty-one-year-old Prince Juan Carlos as his heir. Juan Carlos was the grandson of Alfonso XIII and had been tutored under Franco's close guidance since the age of ten. The compliant Juan Carlos was expected to keep the dictatorship going, and Franco, who only had one daughter, came to see him as 'the son that he had never had'. As tourism took off, however, and millions of wealthier Europeans arrived in caravans, trains and planes, Spaniards increasingly saw that their country was an anachronism. When the tourism ministry invented the advertising slogan 'Spain is different' it was greeted with scorn. Spain was a dictatorship. That was what made it different.

Spanish women were especially aware of all this. Their oppression under Franco was extraordinary and largely unmatched in the rest of Europe. Spain's civil code explicitly stated that: 'The husband must protect his wife and she must obey her husband.' Without her husband's permission she could not work, open a bank account, start a business, sign contracts or sue in court. She could not leave home for any length of time without the risk of losing her children, who effectively belonged to her husband under *patria potestad* rules. Divorce was out of the question, and adultery a crime punishable with prison sentences (though, bizarrely, not for the husband unless it was under his own roof, public knowledge or he was cohabiting with the other woman).

On 20 December 1973, Franco's right-hand man and prime minister, Admiral Luis Carrero Blanco, left daily Mass at the Jesuit order's San Francisco de Borja church in Madrid in his official black Dodge Dart 3700 GT sedan. A few minutes later, an 80-kilo bomb planted under the road outside blew the car over the five-story building and into a patio behind the church, killing Carrero

Blanco, his driver and bodyguard. The assassination, known as 'Operation Ogre', was carried out by Euskadi Ta Askatasuna (ETA, or Basque Homeland and Freedom), an armed separatist organization that was one of a handful of groups to use violence against the dictatorship. It marked, at least psychologically, an end to the regime's invulnerability.

Spaniards were divided about their dictator. More than three decades of dictatorship had followed the civil war, and supporters considered Franco's reign to be a tremendous success. It had certainly brought a halt to the wild political fluctuation of the previous 100 years, but the price paid for that had been huge. Basic freedoms were glaringly absent and trouble built in the 1970s, as strikes spread, underground parties operated in factories and companies, and small radical groups opted for violence. In a 1970 church-run poll, 30 per cent of Spaniards wanted Franco's regime to continue after his death, while half wanted a Republic and the rest opted for monarchy.

Additional proof that the outside world had changed came when the Roman Catholic Church (under the relatively liberal Pope Paul VI) formally apologized for its role in the civil war in 1971. The regime, however, reacted to unrest by returning to its repressive, violent roots. The Basque Country, especially, was targeted, with ETA's violence being answered by repeated, localized states of exception for the Basque provinces of Guipúzcoa and Vizcaya.

One of the most barbaric forms of state murder – the garotte – was restored. In 1974 and 1975, three members of a Marxist-Leninist group called FRAP (Revolutionary Antifascist Patriotic Front), two militants from ETA (which killed forty-seven people between 1968 and 1975) and an anarchist called Salvador Puig Antich were executed. This provoked international outrage, and pressure for change grew from within and outside Spain. The simplest way for this to happen was for the aged dictator to die, but he resisted.

In 1975, Spaniards spent much of their time discussing news bulletins about the dictator's health and wondering what would happen when he was gone. On 20 November, Franco finally died in hospital of natural causes at the age of eighty-two. Celebrations were discreet and tinged with fear. 'Above the skyline of the Collserola mountains, champagne corks soared into the Autumn twilight. But nobody heard a sound,' writer Manuel Vázquez Montalbán said of the Catalan capital, Barcelona. Up to half a million Spaniards filed past his open coffin in Madrid's Palacio de Oriente. Not all were there, as the joke went, to see if he was really dead. Few heads of state attended his funeral, with Chilean dictator Augusto Pinochet as the most prominent. Almost four decades of one-man rule were over. A fixed part of most Spaniards' world had disappeared, and that was unsettling. What would come next?

32
A Return to Democracy

When Prince Juan Carlos had accepted his nomination as Franco's heir in 1969, he praised the 1936 coup against democracy that had sparked the civil war.

> I receive from his Excellency the Head of State, Generalísimo Franco, the political legitimacy that emerged from July 18, 1936, amidst so much sad but necessary sacrifice and suffering so that our Patria could rejoin the path of destiny. The work of setting it on the right path and showing clearly the direction it must go has been carried out by that exceptional man whom Spain has been immensely fortunate to have, and will be fortunate to have for years to come, as the guide of our policy. My hand will not tremble to do all that is necessary to defend the principles [of the *Movimiento*] and laws that I have just sworn.

When Franco died, and a red-eyed Juan Carlos oversaw the funeral at the Valle de Los Caídos of a man for whom he felt true affection, the dictator's supporters expected more of the same. On 27 November 1975, the king formally received a dictator's powers. 'This is not a restoration of monarchy but the establishment of a new Francoist monarchy,' one ardent Francoist claimed. As if to confirm this, Juan Carlos immediately reappointed the hardliner Carlos Arias Navarro – who had sobbed as he announced Franco's

↑ King Juan Carlos I had been appointed by Franco as his political heir, but he reneged on their agreement and ushered in democracy with the help of prime minister Adolfo Suárez (pictured above). He was a former senior Francoist and governed from 1976 to 1981.

death on television – as prime minister.

It turned out, however, to be something very different. Some people on the left hoped the young king would be swiftly ejected on the grounds that he represented two things that Spaniards now loathed: dictatorship and monarchy. Democracy, they thought, could only be achieved once he was out of the way. In fact, Juan Carlos turned out to be a skilful political operator with a talent for picking people who might bring change.

In July 1976, he appointed as his prime minister Adolfo Suárez, an ambitious but relatively unknown forty-three-year-old Falangist technocrat who had been leader of the single party, or Movimiento Nacional. Suárez led a process by which, using the existing laws of Francoism, the rubber-stamp parliament agreed to its own dissolution and to new elections in which a wide range of parties could take part. In June 1977, Spain celebrated its first free elections since 1936.

Out of gratitude, and fearful of change going too fast or encouraging a military coup, Spaniards elected Suárez, who had formed a centre-right party called Union of the Democratic Centre (UCD), to lead them. The following year, they approved a new constitution at referendum. Spain was to have a monarch, but with power vested in parliament. Juan Carlos had shed his powers, while also restoring his family's role and privileges. In fact, he continued to wield considerable influence over politics for the next few years.

The most difficult sticking points were the demands for autonomy from regions like the Basque Country and Catalonia – reflecting the origins of Spain as a collection of nations. A country which had spent four decades declaring itself to be 'One, Great and Free' found itself incapable of recognizing them as 'nations' in their own right. Instead, a deliberately ambiguous solution was found. The constitution recognized 'the right to autonomy of the nationalities and regions of which it is composed, and the solidarity among them all'. The chosen term, 'nationalities', was a fudge designed to avoid the word (or recognize the existence of) 'nations'. In order to assuage the military and others who might still be offended, the constitution also spoke of the 'indissoluble unity of the Spanish nation, the common and indivisible country of all Spaniards'. The army's mission included, and still includes, the obligation to defend Spain's 'territorial integrity'. Some, inevitably, worried that this gave the military the right to prevent any division of the country. Many in the army agreed.

After four decades of dictatorship, Spain transformed itself into a democracy in just four years. This was not an entirely peaceful process. ETA and radical, armed left-wing groups like the First of October Anti-Fascist Resistance Groups (GRAPO) continued to assassinate policeman and politicians, while right-wing extremists killed five labour lawyers in their offices in Madrid on 24 January 1977. In all, more than 591 people died in political violence over the seven years after Franco's demise, including fifty-eight demonstrators killed by police or right-wing thugs.

Moving from dictatorship to democracy required a series of compromises that stored up problems for later. The main architects of change were Francoists who, overnight, declared themselves democrats. Many people doubted the motives of these co-called 'jacket changers', with good reason. There was no change to land or business ownership. Wealthy elites who had prospered under the Francoist regime, in other words, remained rich – no matter how corrupt their money. An amnesty covered regime thugs who had committed crimes on behalf of the dictatorship. Police torturers, politicians and those in charge of repression could not be prosecuted. This was combined with an amnesty for political prisoners from leftist, regionalist or separatist groups. It was to be, in the words of one parliamentary deputy, 'an amnesty for everyone, a forgetting by everyone for everyone'. In ethical terms this meant that nobody was held responsible for the suppression of democratic and individual rights over the previous thirty-six years, yet alone the bloodbath of the Civil War. Schools, meanwhile, were encouraged not to teach either the civil war or Francoism. Recent history was swept under carpet. Spain was to look forwards, not back.

The immediate benefits of all this were evident. Despite the years of economic growth, Franco had built a meagre welfare state. Public spending grew from 24 per cent of GDP on his death to 40 per cent by 1980. Public health care, education and pensions all benefitted. With socialists, communists and regionalists from Catalonia and the Basque Country now sitting in parliament, only a few violent groups like ETA remained outside the new structure.

The greatest threat to democracy, however, was the army. This was the deepest repository of resentment over what some saw as trickery by their new commander-in-chief, King Juan Carlos, who had reneged on his oaths of loyalty to Francoism. Fear of a coup explains why Spaniards did not make too vigorous demands of their new democracy. Just having it seemed like a miracle, and rapidly brought massive change in every sphere – including, at its most banal, a sudden explosion of sex and nudity in Spanish films, known as the *destape*, or 'great uncovering'.

Military discontent finally exploded on 23 February 1981. Civil Guard Lieutenant Colonel Antonio Tejero burst into the debating chamber of the Spanish parliament wearing his shiny, tricorn patent leather hat and accompanied by 200 men armed with rifles and submachine guns. The armed intruders took the country's elected deputies hostage. They had been debating a change of prime minister, with Leopoldo Calvo-Sotelo (nephew of the right-wing leader José Calvo Sotelo, assassinated in 1936) of the UCD tapped to replace the now unpopular Suárez. A television camera was kept running, conserving an exact record as the intruders peppered the ceiling with gunfire and Tejero ordered: '*Al suelo!*', 'To the floor!' His men, more confusingly, shouted '*En nombre del Rey!*', 'In the king's name!'

Juan Carlos halted the coup, using his position as commander-in-chief to keep wavering generals loyal. He donned military uniform for a live television broadcast, denouncing the 'actions or attitudes of anyone who wants to interrupt by force the democratic process that was decided when, by referendum, the constitution was voted on by the Spanish people'. Tejero and his men surrendered after thirty-six hours, leaving a bar and café bill of 7,000 euros.

Some plotters had genuinely believed they had the king's backing, and questions remain about whether Juan Carlos unintentionally encouraged them. Some also thought opposition politicians were ready to form a government of national unity led by a mysterious character known as Elefante Blanco, or White Elephant, who was probably the former Juan Carlos aide General Alfonso Armada. He and two dozen other plotters were jailed.

The failed coup marked a watershed in Spain's young democracy. On the one hand, it showed that the military were not as

↑ Centrist Adolfo Suárez and socialist Felipe González were the major figures of the first two decades of Spain's new democracy, with the latter (on the right) winning four elections to govern from 1982 to 1996.

large a threat as they were supposed to be (though another coup attempt in October 1982 was quietly dismantled in advance). It also brought an end to the period of government by the now fractured UCD party, with Calvo-Sotelo surviving less than two years as prime minister. At elections in October 1982, a huge turnout of 80 per cent of voters swept the Spanish Socialist Workers Party (PSOE) of forty-year-old Felipe González to power. For the first time since 1936, Spain had a left-wing government. It was also the first time that a single party had won an absolute majority.

Democracy entered a phase of consolidation, accompanied by swift social change. González stayed in power for thirteen years, and the old Francoists mostly disappeared from sight, with only former minister Manuel Fraga – who had founded the conservative opposition People's Alliance and helped negotiate the new constitution – as a reminder of those who had once exercised absolute power.

33
The Red Rose

When Felipe González leaned out of a window in Madrid's Palace Hotel on the evening of 28 October 1982 and waved a red rose at the crowd celebrating in the street, it seemed Spain had finally buried a twentieth-century past of dictatorship, repression and fratricidal war. 'It may seem trivial to put it this way, but those elections were like the ritualistic death of the father; new faces appeared and the fresh air of freedom blew through all parts of Spanish society,' recalls the historian Santos Juliá. Spain's timid social transformation, which had started before Franco's death, was about to gain wings.

Although González was young, he had already spent almost a decade as party leader, having been elected aged thirty-two at a conference held near Paris while the party was still banned (he was codenamed Isidoro, after the medieval saint from his home city of Seville). He had been a crucial participant in negotiations during the transition to democracy and in 1979 stood down as leader for six months in order to persuade his party to drop Marxism – which it did – and then take him back. Together with his deputy, Alfonso Guerra, he now exercised total control over his party, making decision-making simpler but, in effect, presidential.

One reason for the socialist landslide was that the economy had run into trouble. Inflation was running at 15 per cent, and one in six people were unemployed. With an absolute majority in parliament, however, González was free to act as he wished.

Those who feared a wave of nationalizations or huge tax hikes were surprised. In France, President François Mitterrand had just had to reverse his moves towards deeper socialism, an experience that served as a warning to a government of young men (with an average age of around forty and no women). Instead, González picked orthodox social democratic finance ministers, who took tough decisions about shutting loss-making state industries. In fact, they oversaw a sell-off of state businesses like the Seat car company (to Volkswagen) or truck-maker Enasa (to a Fiat subsidiary). They also weakened Spanish labour protection (which had been strong under Franco, making people almost unsackable) by introducing short-term contracts. These became the chosen vehicle of many employers, who preferred not to hire people on full-time contracts with their heavy costs for firing people. In many ways, indeed, González was a pro-markets precursor to the Third Way of Tony Blair in the United Kingdom.

In 1985, Spain took an historic step. For decades, if not centuries, it had lamented its status as Europe's laggard. In an attempt to belittle their southern neighbours, nineteenth-century French commentators had claimed that 'Africa starts at the Pyrenees', and Spaniards fretted that this still summed up Europe's view of their country. Unamuno, meanwhile, had long proposed that the solution to Spain's problems must come from a closer embrace of Europe. On 12 June 1985, Spain signed an agreement to join the European Economic Community (EEC), as the European Union was then known. This was then a club of a dozen countries, almost all of them much wealthier than Spain. Earlier attempts by the Franco regime to join the EEC had been blocked, and the decision was a reward for the country's embrace of democracy.

The move satisfied a desire among Spaniards to be seen as Europeans, while also bringing easier access to European markets, capital and the structural or cohesion funds given to poorer countries and regions. González himself negotiated the creation of the

CONTEMPORARY SPAIN'S SEVENTEEN AUTONOMOUS REGIONS
WITH THEIR PROVINCES, AND ITS TWO NORTH AFRICAN CITIES
CANTABRIAN SEA
FRANCE
A Coruña
OVIEDO
SANTANDER
Bilbao
Donostia-San Sebastián
SANTIAGO DE COMPOSTELA
Lugo
GALICIA
ASTURIAS
CANTABRIA
PAÍS VASCO/EUSKADI
VITORIA-GASTEIZ
PAMPLONA
NAVARRE
ANDORRA
León
Ourense
Pontevedra
LOGROÑO
Burgos
LA RIOJA
Huesca
Girona
CATALUÑA/CATALUNYA
Palencia
VALLADOLID
CASTILLA Y LEÓN
Soria
ZARAGOZA
ARAGÓN
Lleida
BARCELON
Zamora
Segovia
Salamanca
Tarragona
COMUNIDAD DE MADRID
Guadalajara
Ávila
Teruel
Castelló de la Plana/Castellón de la Plana
MADRID
TOLEDO
CASTILLA-LA MANCHA
Cuenca
COMUNITAT VALENCIA
PORTUGAL
Cáceres
EXTREMADURA
VALENCIA
PALMA DE MALLORCA
LISBON
MÉRIDA
Albacete
Badajóz
Ciudad Real
Alicant/Alicante
REGIÓN DE MURCIA
Córdoba
Jaén
ANDALUCÍA
MURCIA
Huelva
SEVILLE
Granada
Málaga
Almería
Cádiz
MEDITERRANEAN SEA
AUTONOMOUS CITY OF CEUTA
AUTONOMOUS CITY OF MELILLA
N
0 50 100
KM
ATLANTIC OCEAN
CANARY ISLANDS
LA PALMA
LANZAROTE
FUERTEVENTURA
TENERIFE
SANTA CRUZ DE TENERIFE
LA GOMERA
GRAN CANARIA
LAS PALMAS DE GRAN CANARIA
HIERRO
0 200 400
KM

cohesion funds, which went to countries (like Spain) with per capita income below 90 per cent of the EU average.

In the first year of membership (1986) alone, the proportion of exports to the EU jumped from 53 to 60 per cent, while West Germany overtook the US as the main source of imports, and the value of EU goods arriving in Spain grew by one-third. The move also required Spain to align its economy with EU countries'. An improved tax regime saw sales tax introduced in 1986, while the number of income tax payers increased to 11 million by 1992 (compared to 300,000 in 1970).

González's tacking towards the political centre produced some remarkable U-turns. He had come to power, for example, pledging to take Spain out of NATO (which it had joined early in 1982) but instead called a March 1986 referendum in which he personally argued for Spain to remain in the bloc. Such was his prestige among voters (he threatened to resign if they voted 'no'), that they followed his urgings.

During the long socialist tenure, there was also a gradual decentralization of Spanish government. In order to meet demands for greater self-government from Catalonia, the Basque Country and Galicia without offending anyone else, a nationwide system of devolved administration was set up. The framework for this had been established before the socialists reached power, with Spain split into seventeen so-called 'autonomous communities' which, over time, gained control of the bigger parts of public spending – notably health and education – though with limited law-making powers. Two city enclaves in North Africa, Ceuta and Melilla, also gained some autonomy.

This was not federalism, but it went a long way towards such a system. In simple terms, big decisions were to be taken in Madrid and put into effect by the regional governments. This seemed to satisfy most people, and both Catalans and Basques, for example, voted at referendum in favour of charters giving them semi-autonomous government. Among other things, they made both Catalan and Euskara the language of schools (or part of it), reversing an historic decline in their use.

The real triumph of this period, however, was the change to women's lives, and how this allowed women to change Spain. The initial changes had been brought in by Suárez. Adultery laws were removed in 1978, and civil code rules restricting women's rights over their children or family money scrapped in 1981, when divorce was finally introduced (though, tellingly, alimony payments were not legally enforceable). Women grabbed their new freedoms with fervour. By the late 1980s women made up a majority of university students, had broken into the armed forces and would go on to dominate professions like medicine. Soon they had outstripped women from, say, Italy in terms of their weight in the workforce. They also had far fewer children, with the birth-rate sinking below two children per family in the early 1980s. Women gained so much in so little time, indeed, that they skipped some key battles, leaving them in charge of the home and subject to rampant machismo in their new jobs. 'Spain has leapt from pre-feminism into post-feminism without having really experienced the feminist upheaval which elsewhere took place in between,' the *Guardian* correspondent John Hooper commented in *The New Spaniards*, first published in 1987. 'Spanish society was never lectured by a Gloria Steinem or Germaine Greer. As a consequence, profoundly sexist attitudes have survived into an era in which women are acquiring much genuine freedom and equality.'

Once more, as in Goya's time, Spain embraced its most southern version – and the lisping argot of Andalusia and of the gypsies made its way into the patois of youth culture in cities like Madrid and Barcelona. Flamenco gained new adepts and, with the remarkable singer José Monje Cruz, known as Camarón de la Isla, began to fuse with rock, jazz and other musical forms. The socialist boom era was accompanied, at least in Madrid, by a movement that

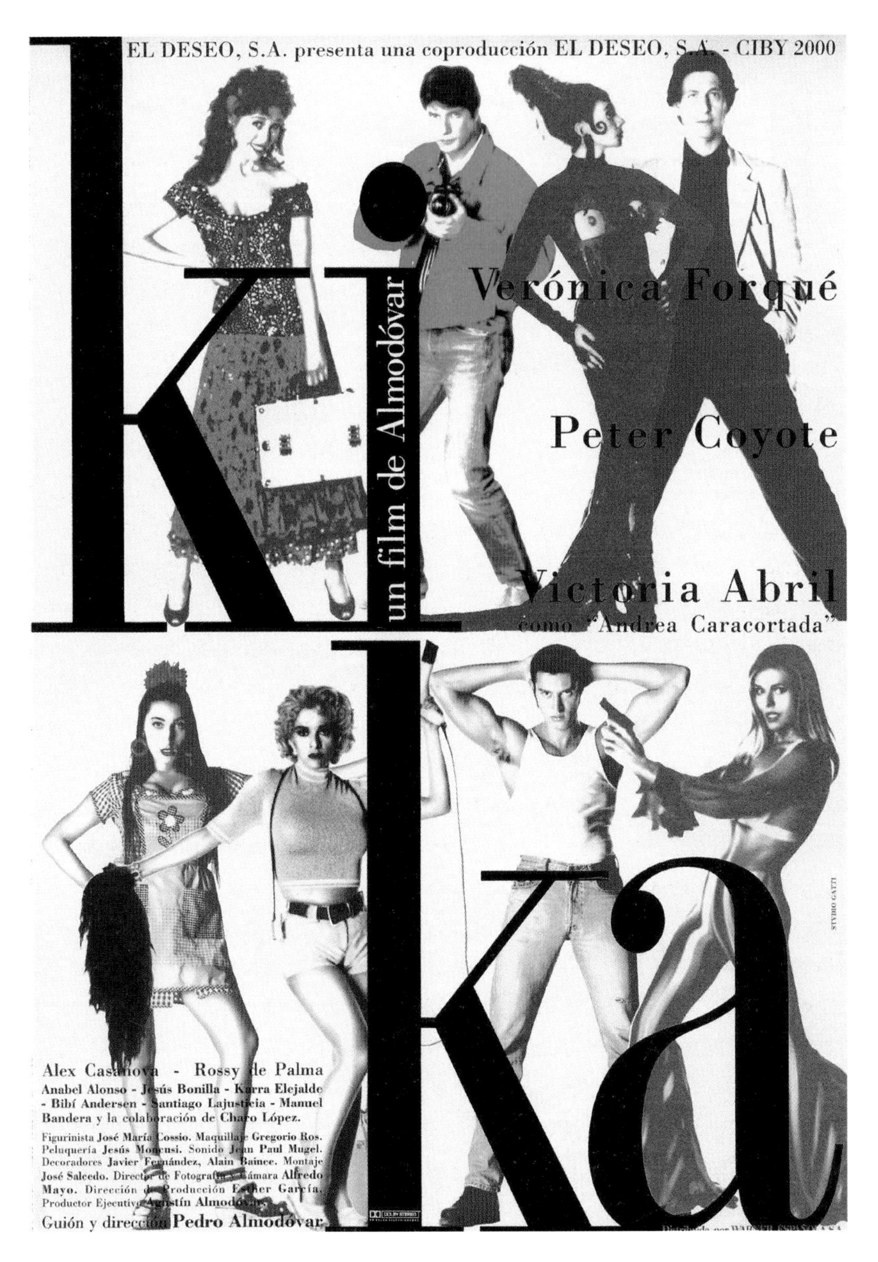

↑ With democracy safe, Spain launched into a dizzying period of cultural and social ferment, characterized by film director Pedro Almodóvar's extravagant dramas, like *Kika* (1993).

was more social than cultural and became known as the *movida madrileña* (with 'from Madrid to Heaven' – *De Madrid al Cielo* – as its slogan). In simple terms, this was about the right to party, and that was what Spanish youth (and the not so young) did relentlessly thorough the 1980s and into the 1990s. The *movida* produced only a handful of cultural icons, with Oscar-winning film-maker Pedro Almodóvar as its star, encapsulating the anything-goes attitude in colourful, crazy and gender-challenging films featuring actors like Antonio Banderas, Victoria Abril, Marisa Paredes or the transgender Bibiana Fernández. Unfortunately, the *movida* era was also accompanied by a massive influx of heroin, which wiped out some of its brightest young stars and left streets and metro stations full of desperate junkies who often resorted to knife crime to find the money they needed.

After winning three absolute majorities in a row, González went into elections in 1993 looking like a loser. The economy had stalled, despite (or because) of a massive amount of public spending. In 1992, Barcelona hosted the Olympic Games, Seville held an Expo, and Madrid was the EU's cultural capital of the year. International glory, however, had not generated domestic joy. As the economy shrank, unemployment grew to a record 24 per cent in 1993.

Two sprawling, overlapping problems turned voters against González. The first was corruption. Some socialists evidently saw politics as a path to self-enrichment, as if nothing had changed from the corrupt days of Franco, Primo de Rivera or the nineteenth-century Peaceful Turn regimes. At the same time, politicians indulged openly in nepotism and cronyism – with González's deputy, Alfonso Guerra, eventually resigning over a contract given to his brother to work as his 'assistant' from Seville, from where he allegedly doled out government largesse. The array of socialist scandals became dizzying. The governor of the Bank of Spain, for example, was revealed to have his own secret tax-opaque bank accounts, while the Socialist Party itself was taking illegal donations from major companies.

The example set by politicians was repeated throughout society. Companies continued to run two sets of accounts – a fake for the tax authorities, and honest ones for themselves. Senior executives in banks expected extra, undeclared 'bonus' payments in foreign accounts. Little surprise, then, that tradesmen and shopkeepers routinely offered their clients the option of paying in 'black' money, without sales tax, rather than helping to fund a state that – despite having a socialist government – consistently spent a smaller percentage of its income on social welfare than other European countries.

The novelist Juan Benet recalled officials in González's Moncloa Palace offices claiming that corruption was a necessary evil. 'Corruption is the oil of the system. It lubricates the wheels so that they turn smoothly and do not screech. It is only necessary to make sure that it does not go beyond a certain level,' they said. It was a dangerous philosophy, not least because – by any standards – that level was so easily surpassed.

At the same time, it became clear that Spain's police and spy services had long been fighting a murderous dirty war against ETA in which innocent victims died and due process was flouted. A young magistrate called Baltasar Garzón began to investigate and produced evidence that state money was used to set up, finance and recruit foreign mercenaries (including Italian fascists) into a police-controlled group known as GAL (Grupos Antiterroristas de Liberación). Between 1983 and 1987 these death squads killed thirty people and injured a similar number in attacks carried out in south-west France, where ETA's command and logistics structure was based. Perhaps one-third of the victims, including an elderly shepherd, two gypsies and a teenage girl, had nothing to do with ETA.

The dirty, unaudited money floating around the interior ministry also fuelled corruption – paying illegal bonuses, gifts and favours. Eventually journalists revealed that even the first civilian head of the Civil Guard police force, socialist politician Luis Roldán, and some senior officers had been taking backhanders from construction companies who built barracks for the paramilitary rural force. The scandal became more farcical when Roldán fled, was tracked down to Laos and eventually gave himself up at Bangkok airport. By then, he had amassed a fortune of 14 million euros. A middleman, the former government spy Francisco Paesa, then faked his own death and cremation in Thailand, complete with death notices in the newspapers and a commission for a month of daily Gregorian Masses to be said in his name at the medieval monastery where El Cid had deposited his wife Ximena.

With newspapers reporting ever more extravagant excesses by socialist politicians, almost everyone was surprised when González won a fourth term in June 1993, even if it was no longer with an absolute majority. One reason for his victory was a last-minute signing to the socialist ticket – the same Judge Baltasar Garzón who had been such a scourge of the government's cover-up of the dirty war.

Garzón was given a junior minister's job in the interior ministry, and soon discovered just how corrupt it had become. 'There was a room full of watches, ties, scarves, pens ... that were for giving away as presents; and another room full of paintings. The truly amazing thing, however, was that it all disappeared in twenty-four hours,' he told a biographer. A cleaning lady brought him a million pesetas (6,000 euros) she had found lying in the drawer of an unoccupied desk. He resigned in disgust after ten months and was allowed to return to his courthouse, where he once more began investigating the same government he had just served in. Years later, he would also investigate rampant corruption in the People's Party and, in what was a poorly disguised case of political revenge, be suspended as punishment for his overzealousness in pursuing ETA cases.

By 1996, the socialist party was so deep in the mud of corruption that the regionalists from Catalonia who propped up the minority government withdrew support. Fresh elections were called and, for the first time since democracy was restored, Spaniards voted in a party that unambiguously declared itself to be right-wing (rather than 'centrist' like Suárez), and José María Aznar of the People's Party became prime minister. An era had come to an end during which a transformed Spain had turned its back on conservative social and political mores. What, then, could the return of the right bring with it?

34
The Right Returns

It is often said that Spain's civil war is one of the few wars whose history was written by the losers. Much the same can be said of the once omnipotent Francoism, which became a byword for thuggish backwardness and cast a pall of suspicion over the new democratic right embodied by the People's Party (PP). It did not help that this was led by the former Francoist minister Manuel Fraga until a muddled handover eventually saw José María Aznar become party leader in 1989, aged just thirty-six. Dour and uncharismatic, he struggled to make an impression until he won popular respect by showing courage and dignity after surviving an ETA bomb attack on his armour-plated car in 1995.

The elections of 1996 were a reminder that, while nationalists in Catalonia and the Basque Country mistrusted the People's Party, they were all conservative Christian Democrats. Socialists and the communist-led United Left coalition might have formed a government had they not hated one another so intensely, and if they had enjoyed the support of Jordi Pujol's nationalist Catalan Convergence and Union coalition. Instead, Pujol chose to back a minority government led by Aznar – who pledged not to serve more than two terms (compared to González's four).

Aware of the lingering suspicion of the PP's origins and hobbled by the minority status of his government, Aznar trod warily. A quid pro quo agreement with the Catalan nationalists allowed the corrupt Pujol to stay in charge of the Generalitat, now at the head of a minority government with PP support. He thus stretched his period as regional president to an astonishing twenty-four years. Pujol passed new language laws to reinforce Catalan while regional governments as a whole won greater tax-raising powers and could now borrow money on the markets. Nor did Aznar reverse some major socialist measures that his party had opposed, like abortion or the ramped-up pensions that had multiplied fivefold under González.

On 21 October 2000, a left-wing journalist called Emilio Silva returned to his family's home town of Priaranza del Bierzo, in northern León, with a large mechanical digger. His aim was to find the body of his grandfather – a left-wing civilian – and a dozen men who had been shot alongside him after Franco's soldiers took control of the town in 1936. They were buried in a mass grave beside a large walnut tree. The bones duly appeared, in the spot where everybody knew that a mass grave lay. Forensic scientists with experience in Chile or Kosovo matched one set of bones to his grandfather, who was reburied in the cemetery.

Although the original aim of his expedition had not been to spark a war over historical memory, this is what eventually happened, with Silva as one of its main combatants at the head of the Recovery of Historical Memory group. Slowly, during the Aznar years, a movement took off to find the hundreds of mass graves containing victims of death squads which – to the surprise of many Spaniards – lay scattered around the country. They were evidence of Franco's terrifying repression, but also of the fact that his victims had been unable to recover the bodies during his dictatorship and that, so far, Spain's democracy had also forgotten them. They also provided a useful way of testing whether Aznar's new-look right was prepared to abandon any defence of Francoism, and a club to beat his party with if – as it turned out – they did not respond to demands that the state set about finding

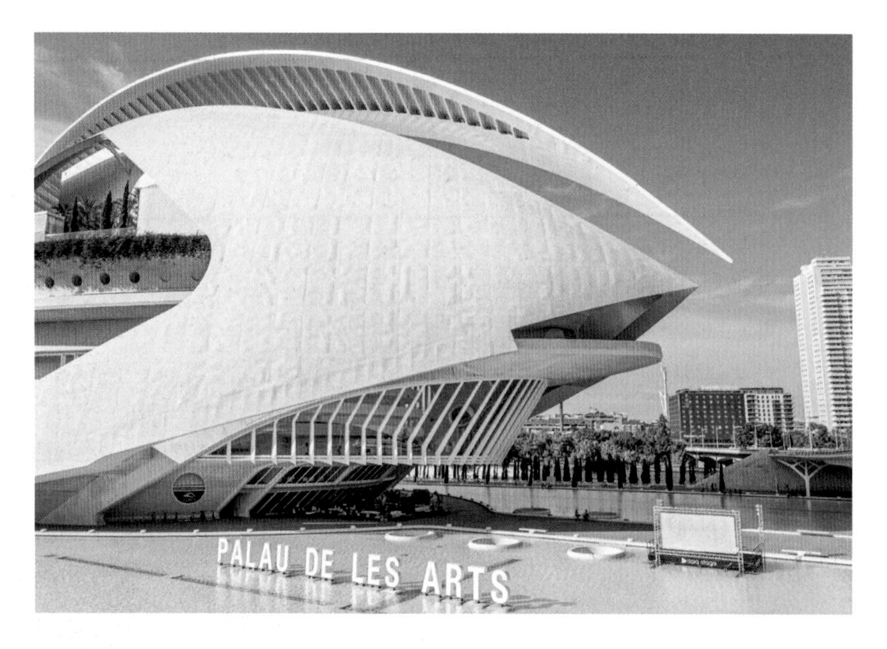

↑ The booming economy of the late 1990s and early 2000s brought landmark architectural projects such as the Palace of the Arts in Valencia (above), by Santiago Calatrava, and the Guggenheim Museum in Bilbao (opposite), by Frank Gehry, designed to project Spain's image as a self-confident, modern country.

the thousands of corpses buried in roadside graves. In fact, it was historical memory (over which Spain's politicians would continue to fight for the next two decades) that showed up the divide between Aznar's right and González's left, which, in economic terms, were looking increasingly similar.

Aznar based his policies on hitting a target that Spaniards supported wholeheartedly – qualifying for membership of the eurozone. This came into being in 1999 but required candidate countries to rein in interest rates, inflation, public debt and deficit. That was achieved promptly, and a fresh economic spurt saw Spanish income levels begin to catch up with the rest of the EU.

The new boom was accelerated by a combination of liberal

economic policies – eurozone banks could now invest (or lend money) in Spain – with an easing of building restrictions in 1998 that provoked a construction frenzy. The sector, which was already busy building roads and high-speed railways with EU money, grew massively, eventually accounting for 10 per cent of the economy. Low interest rates (and mortgages) and high employment brought an explosion in demand for new housing. Banks saw a gold mine, too, lending generously to mortgagees and, above all, to property developers and speculators. Spain's large network of locally based savings banks, which were often controlled by politicians seeking to artifically boost local economies, line their own pockets or dispense largesse, began to offer 100 per cent mortgages and underwrite highly speculative land purchases.

At the same time, Spain's partially privatized state-owned companies found they could also borrow money cheaply and embarked on a shopping spree across Latin America in an attempt to build themselves into multinationals. This was largely successful, and the same companies – like phone operator Telefonica – eventually found themselves with sufficient muscle to buy up competitors in other European countries.

As a new century dawned, Spain found it did not have enough workers for the first time ever. Migrants arrived en masse – especially from Latin America – boosting the population by 10 per cent over a decade and enriching Spain's cultural mix. In 2003, Spain took in one-third of all immigrants into the European Union. Many found jobs almost immediately on building sites. Their wages fuelled more growth, especially in construction as they also bought newly built apartments.

Aznar rode the booming economy to an absolute parliamentary majority in elections in 2000. His government's new motto was that it was rightist '*sin complejos*', meaning it had shed the complexes associated with Francoism. With the economy still booming, it was only the more independent-minded regions like Catalonia and the Basque Country (whose parties no longer held the balance of power in parliament, as they had done for the previous seven years) that complained. In the meantime, the People's Party proved to be even more corrupt than the socialists, though it would take time before the police and courts caught up with it. Even a visit and open-air Mass by Pope Benedict XVI was used as an excuse to scam public money. 'In Spain, no one has ever been afraid to be corrupt,' Baltasar Garzón, who did his best to pursue official graft, lamented. 'Given that its existence was taken for granted, corruption is not something that has bothered the average citizen. This indifference has ensured that its roots have grown deep and solid and sustain a structure of interests that is very difficult to bring down.' A court system in which cases took up to a decade to come to trial meant that voters could not punish corrupt politicians directly, since those who were found out were usually out of power and could be easily disowned by their parties.

A successful crackdown on ETA, which was broken by a series of police raids on its command structure in France, helped increase Aznar's popularity, and when he announced that he would not lead his party into 14 March 2004 elections, it seemed obvious that his appointed heir, Deputy Prime Minister Mariano Rajoy, would win. A combination of hubris and terror dashed that prospect.

35
Bombs in Al-Andalus

Clara Escribano, a child cancer nurse at one of Madrid's main hospitals, boarded a train in the commuter suburb of Santa Eugenia early on 11 March 2004. She did not get far. As the train left the platform, a bomb exploded inside her carriage. 'I must have passed out because I was the only one left in there when they took me out,' she recalled later. Clara was fortunate to survive. Seventeen other people in her carriage were killed by the force of the explosion or the shrapnel unleashed by the bomb.

Within the space of seven minutes, nine other bombs tore through commuter trains around the Spanish capital, killing 191 people and injuring 1,800. Three more bombs failed to explode. Each contained 12 kilos of Spanish-made Goma 2 explosives, with nuts and screws as shrapnel and a mobile phone alarm attached to a detonator. This was Europe's worst terror attack since the downing of a Pan Am airliner above the Scottish town of Lockerbie by Libyan agents in 1988. Most of those killed were early-morning shift workers – cleaners and the like – or schoolchildren and teachers heading into the city.

The bombs were planted by a group of young Islamist radicals living in Madrid, many with a history of petty crime. Coming two and a half years after the 9/11 Twin Towers attacks in New York and given that Aznar had joined George W. Bush and Tony Blair as one of the chief proponents of a so-called global war against terror,

↑ On 11 March 2004, a dozen bombs killed 191 people on Madrid commuter trains. Islamist radicals planted the bombs but, with elections due, the right-wing People's Party (PP) government of José María Aznar tried to pin the blame on Basque separatist terror group ETA. Voters evicted the PP from power three days later.

it was reasonable to assume that Islamist radicals were involved. Aznar's government insisted otherwise, claiming it had irrefutable evidence that ETA was to blame. In electoral terms, given that Spaniards were due to vote at a general election three days later, this was the most favourable possible version of what had happened for Aznar. He had been tough on ETA, accusing others of going soft. An attack of such extraordinary magnitude would have proved that his hardline attitude towards the Basque terrorist group had always been correct. Yet ETA had never committed an atrocity quite as bloody, ambitious or random as this.

As evidence grew about the true identity of the bombers, Aznar's government denied the obvious. Three days later, following massive street demonstrations, his party was voted out of power in the general election. If that had been the terrorists' aim (and we cannot ask them, since they blew themselves up when surrounded by police in a Madrid apartment block two weeks later), then the attack was devastatingly successful. More importantly, Aznar's obstinate cunning had backfired.

The victorious socialist leader José Luis Rodríguez Zapatero began with a dramatic change in foreign policy, as Spain immediately withdrew from the US-led coalition in Iraq. Apart from that, the country continued to ride its economic boom and the soft but significant cultural changes brought in by Zapatero's government – including gay marriage (the first nominally Catholic country to pass such a law and amongst the first in the world to include full rights for same-sex partners or adoption) and express divorce – helped him win a second term four years later, just as the world tipped into the financial crash of 2008.

Spain was, initially, fortunate. It was not badly exposed, since its banks had been banned from buying the sub-prime packages of risky US mortgages that provoked the crisis. Soon, however, Spain succumbed to a more lethal risk – its very own property bubble. As this burst, a cycle of doom took grip. Banks had loaned too much to property speculators and developers, who now defaulted. Building work ground to a halt, 4.5 million workers lost their jobs, and the malaise spread.

Banks began to crash. Regional savings banks fell like dominoes, victims to the corrupt system which had seen them run by politicians who helped friends, distributed favours and gave risky loans to property developers. 'The combination of mismanagement, hubris and greed, coupled with a banking system that lent according to political not financial criteria, proved disastrous,' Tobias Buck, the *Financial Times* writer in Madrid, said. As Spain searched for money to bail banks out, financial markets worried that the country would itself go bust and charged ever higher interest rates.

This was the first crisis since the euro had been introduced, and Spain could no longer use the classic trick of devaluing its currency to escape problems and cut debt, since this was now the euro (which it shared with many other European countries). Zapatero's mild socialist government, which had an equal number of men and women in the cabinet and had just made a promise of increased social spending on the old and needy, could only now function with the help of the European Union. As a result, Spain became a rule-taker from an EU dominated by Chancellor Angela Merkel's centre-right German government.

Zapatero was forced to introduce austerity measures as the country struggled to provoke 'internal devaluation' by lowering salaries and shrinking government spending. Whereas *mileurista* workers had complained in 2008 that they could not live off salaries of 1,000 euros a month, a new generation considered itself lucky to earn that much, or to have a job at all. Income inequality grew in what was already the most unequal major economy in Europe after the United Kingdom. It took nine years, until 2017, for the economy to return to pre-crash size. By that stage, labour costs had fallen by 14 per cent. Wage earners, in other words, were poorer and had a smaller share of the same-sized pie.

Spain's national soccer team, usually a source of national disappointment, provided some cheer to an otherwise dire situation – becoming the champions of Europe in both 2008 and 2012, and winning the World Cup in Johannesburg in 2010. The combined power of the two great domestic clubs, Real Madrid and Barcelona, finally provided a generation of remarkable football players, led by the likes of Xavi Hernandez, Andrés Iniesta and Pep Guardiola. With those two clubs taking the European Champions League seven times between them in the decade from 2008 and rivalling

Manchester United to be the wealthiest team on the planet, Spain's position as a footballing superpower contrasted dramatically with its otherwise declining fortunes.

As discontent with the economy spread, spontaneous demonstrations erupted and brought the peaceful occupation of town and city squares by so-called *indignados* – the indignant ones – who appeared out of nowhere on 15 May 2011 to take control of Madrid's Puerta del Sol. These protests were remarkable both for their peaceful nature (except in Barcelona, where the Generalitat sent baton-wielding police to clear them from Plaza Catalunya), their lack of a unifying message and their failure to provoke change. Six months later, indeed, the squares were empty and voters had brought the conservative People's Party back into power at the November 2011 elections.

The situation had become unsustainable. Spain's problems threatened the survival of the euro itself, forcing the EU to offer a rescue package in exchange for more austerity. Bank losses were passed to the state, forcing ordinary Spaniards to pay through their taxes for the excesses of bankers, politicians and speculators. Corruption, indeed, was soon revealed to be the one thing that had been smoothly passed on from the Francoist period (and before) in even the highest spheres.

36
Out with the Old?

On 18 June 2018, Iñaki Urdangarín, the son-in-law of King Juan Carlos, stepped through the doors of the jail at Brieva in Ávila. The former Olympic handball medalist's five-year prison sentence for embezzlement, fraud, prevarication, influence peddling and tax dodging showed just how far corruption remained part of the Spanish state.

In retrospect, it should have been no surprise that a senior member of the royal family had been caught up in corruption. It ran rampant through the upper echelons of business and politics, and soon hit King Juan Carlos himself. Three ministers from Aznar's People's Party government eventually ended up in jail – though the court system worked so slowly that this took years. Even a refurbishment of the PP's headquarters building was found to have been financed with illegal donations. Former finance minister Rodrigo Rato was the most high-profile crook, along with a significant part of the PP's regional government of Valencia.

The royal family, meanwhile, came under ever closer scrutiny for its cavalier, and potentially illegal, behaviour. In simple terms, representative democracy and monarchy – the two key institutions of the post-Franco regime – appeared to have become rotten. A growing number of Spaniards felt duped by the people who had led them.

Urdangarín had become involved with the corrupt branch of the PP, which poured money into non-profit organizations that he used as a front. As he was the king's son-in-law, and the royal family was considered untouchable, he expected to get away with it. His fellow crooks saw that the safest place to practise corruption was in the royal family's shadow – a place where few officials were prepared to shine any light. Fortunately, corruption had not reached the court system. Prosecutors became increasingly tough on political graft and illegal cronyism, even though punishments arrived years after politicians had retired – allowing their parties to claim that the crimes belonged to a bygone era.

By the time Urdangarín was jailed, King Juan Carlos himself had been forced to abdicate. While the rest of Spain hunkered down to survive the financial crisis in 2012, the married monarch had to be flown home from an elephant-hunting trip to Botswana with a former lover after twisting an ankle. He apologized, but the monarchy's standing was so battered that only abdication in 2014 – in favour of his son Felipe – could save it.

Six years later, on 3 August 2020, the eighty-two-year-old former monarch fled to Dubai and self-imposed exile, amid questions about a $100 million payment into a secret Swiss bank account by Saudi Arabia's royal family. Newspapers reported that this was for help given in negotiating a contract for Spanish companies to build a $6.7 billion high-speed railway line from Medina to Mecca, though proof was missing. The married king had given most of the money to the same former lover – a glamorous German businesswoman called Corinna Larsen – with whom he had gone elephant-hunting. She then refused to give it back, since that would have been money-laundering.

From his new hideaway, Juan Carlos also admitted tax dodging to the extent of 678,000 euros – based on spending by his family using credit cards off accounts held by a Mexican businessman. There were reports, too, of regular trips by Swiss bankers to drop off bags containing hundreds of thousands of euros at the royal palace, with machines installed there to count the notes.

State pollster CIS stopped measuring the popularity of the royal family after it dipped into negative figures in 2015. It was a clear sign that the monarchy was in trouble and that mainstream politicians (who controlled the pollster) wanted to hide this. By early 2022, official polling had still not recommenced, leaving the press and the Catalan regional government's pollster to ask Spaniards what they really thought about the monarchy. The results showed overall disapproval.

The decaying state of Spanish politics and its main institutions was a cross-party affair. Just as the PP's Valencia government was found to be crooked, so too was the socialist government of Andalusia. Catalan nationalists also regularly swindled tax-payers, cheating on party financing rules and, in the case of Jordi Pujol, hiding money from the tax authorities in foreign banks.

Appalled by all this, Spaniards looked for something new. For many that meant voting either for the far-left Podemos party, which picked up the legacy of the *indignados* and emerged powerfully in 2014, or for a new anti-corruption and anti-Catalan nationalist centre-right party called Ciudadanos (Citizens). By 2018, they had been joined by Vox, the first successful far-right party since Franco's death.

The traditional two-party system had lost credibility. Unlike the fake democracy of the nineteenth-century *turno pacífico*, however, a simple solution to this structural crisis emerged naturally from the voting urns. By 2020, governments across the nation – from the Socialist-Podemos national government led by Prime Minister Pedro Sánchez to regional governments in Andalusia, Valencia and elsewhere, were coalitions of some kind. This added a texture and subtlety to Spanish politics which appeared to improve it (only time will tell), since it limited opportunities for corruption or other abuses.

In Catalonia, the same disenchantment with the status quo drove people towards separatism. This resurgent nationalism had already received a boost after a new charter of autonomy was

ES A

↑ The sudden emergence of the left-wing populist Podemos party in 2014 broke up a two-party system in which power had been exercised either by the Socialist Party (PSOE) or the right-wing People's Party (PP). As several more successful new parties, including the radical right-wing Vox, emerged across the spectrum, Spanish politics shifted into a new era of coalitions.

first watered down in parliament by Zapatero, then passed narrowly at referendum in 2006 before finally having parts of it annulled by the Constitutional Court at the urging of Rajoy's People's Party.

By 2016, Catalonia had a separatist government led by Carles Puigdemont, which had been elected to carry out an illegal independence referendum. When it tried to do this on 1 October 2017, peaceful voters found their way blocked by police and, if they refused to leave voting centres, risked being beaten. Pictures of middle-aged and elderly people being mistreated by baton-wielding police officers spread rapidly around the globe, local health services dealt with 1,000 people (mostly, but not entirely, with minor injuries), and Spain's reputation took a blow. The results of the poll were meaningless, since only separatists campaigned, and unionist voters stayed home.

When Puigdemont unilaterally declared a deliberately ambiguous (and, ultimately, ineffectual) form of independence and promptly fled the country, the stand-off turned to farce. The government invoked a clause in the constitution which allowed it to take control of the regional government. Catalans, meanwhile, remained equally divided on independence. Tempers frayed, and families split. It became clear that Spain's adored constitution made independence possible to request, but impossible to achieve without the support of both the socialists and the People's Party. Since the former were not keen, and the second was utterly opposed, this could never happen. Given that Catalans wished to remain European Union citizens and would lose this status if they stopped being Spanish, the confrontation seemed absurd. It was as if they demanded the freedom to decide on something that, ultimately, they did not want. The only way to prove that, of course, is with a referendum which only central government can call and, unless there is massive change, never will.

The politicians who organized the referendum were sent to jail for sedition or went into exile. While Catalan separatists felt sure they had natural justice on their side, their campaign of civil disobedience failed. Few people outside Catalonia believed the laws that effectively block independence were so manifestly unfair that they needed changing. This, in part, is because Catalans voted massively in 1978 for the same constitution that now constrains them, with 61 per cent in favour and only three per cent voting against it (a third of Catalan voters did not take part, while the Basques and Galicians produced majority boycotts of the poll). That has left Spain at an impasse. Only the Basque independence campaign of ETA and its allies – admittedly more violent and less popular – provides guidance as to how this might end. In that case, the Spanish state showed an unlimited ability to resist pressure until, exhausted, ETA melted away (it officially dissolved in 2018, but gave up violence eight years earlier after killing 864 people over 50 years). By the time the socialist-led coalition government of Prime Minister Pedro Sánchez handed out pardons to jailed Catalan politicians in 2021, the independence surge was already losing steam. Yet the desire for independence in both Catalonia and the Basque Country will never disappear completely. It could still, indeed, reappear with even greater strength in the future.

In some ways, the Catalan confrontation revealed a mature democracy, though badly in need of fine-tuning. Nothing broke. Yet the 1978 constitution that gave Spaniards freedom, prosperity and membership of the European democracies club clearly needed updating. The wide consensus necessary for that, however, did not yet exist. Nor was there any sign that it could come in the near future.

Between 2020 and 2022, the great Covid-19 pandemic swept the world. Spain initially suffered worse than many other countries in Europe, almost certainly because Spaniards live closely packed together, are intensely sociable and enjoy physical contact. Twenty-three of the thirty-three most densely populated square kilometres in Europe are in Spain, in major cities like Barcelona and Madrid. They provided a perfect human ecosystem for the virus to spread.

The pandemic also pointed up weaknesses in specialist health care, reduced because of austerity, and data gathering due to decentralization. It remains to be seen whether solutions will be found. A country where tourism accounts for 12 per cent of GDP and which is also Europe's second-largest producer of cars (after Germany) suffered greater economic damage than those around it. Recovery was expected to be based, to a large extent, on drawing deeply from special EU funds. It remains to be seen, too, whether any recovery will be evenly distributed or will increase the growing gap between the rich and the rest.

No society remains still for ever. Spaniards love to criticize their own country but have lived in peace and with previously unimaginable levels of prosperity for half a century. Fundamental disagreements remain, and there is still no accepted national narrative, but they are not set on destroying those gains. Within Europe, poorer former communist bloc countries are catching up or (in the case of the Czech Republic) have overtaken them, partly because they inherited better education systems or are closer to economic powerhouses like Germany or Scandinavia. As Spain entered the second decade of the twenty-first century, indeed, it remained unclear whether it would ever catch up with more mature Western European democracies that have built resilient and prosperous societies based on equity, education and empathy.

With the country divided about history, identity and the basic dilemma of whether Spain is a single nation or a collection of them, further progress may take time. Yet there are still many dreams that all Spaniards share. The vast majority want, in some form, for the windows to the world that Franco and others tried to shut to remain open so that Miguel de Unamuno's 'four winds' can blow in. Strictly speaking, some only want a single wind to come from Europe, but the enthusiasm for that project remains palpable. For anyone seeking a new point of unity, or even a viable national narrative, it is a good place to start.

Acknowledgements

I owe thanks to the many historians of Spain who I have read and spoken to over the years, but especially to Martin Minchom for casting an eye over an early version of this text. Any mistakes, however, are my own. Special thanks also go to Neil Belton and Matilda Singer at Head of Zeus, to Georgina Capel and, as ever, to Katharine Blanca Scott.

Recommended reading

For those who want to dig deeper into the history of Spain, this selected reading list covers just about everything.

History
Beevor, Antony, *The Battle for Spain: The Spanish Civil War 1936–1939*
Carr, Raymond, *Spain, 1808–1975*
Cervantes, Fernando, *Conquistadores: A New History*
Elliott, J. H., *Empires of the Atlantic World: Britain and Spain in America 1492–1830*
Elliott, J. H., *Imperial Spain 1469–1716*
Esdaile, Charles, *The Peninsular War: A New History*
Fernández-Armesto, Felipe, *Columbus*
Fletcher, Richard, *Moorish Spain*
Graham, Helen, *The Spanish Civil War: A Very Short Introduction*
Hooper, John, *The New Spaniards*
Kamen, Henry, *Golden Age Spain*
Kamen, Henry, *The Spanish Inquisition: A Historical Revision*
MacKay, Angus, *Spain in the Middle Ages: From Frontier to Empire 1000–1500*
Parker, Geoffrey, *Emperor: A New Life of Charles V*
Parker, Geoffrey, *Imprudent King: A New Life of Philip II*
Preston, Paul, *A People Betrayed: A History of Corruption, Political Incompetence and Social Division in Modern Spain 1874–2018*
Preston, Paul, *Franco*
Preston, Paul, *Juan Carlos: Steering Spain from Dictatorship to Democracy*
Tremlett, Giles, *Ghosts of Spain: Travels Through a Country's Hidden Past*
Tremlett, Giles, *The International Brigades: Fascism, Freedom and the Spanish Civil War*
Tremlett, Giles, *Isabella of Castile: Europe's First Great Queen*

Culture, Society, Sport
Cumming, Laura, *The Vanishing Man: In Pursuit of Velázquez*
Gibson, Ian, *The Shameful Life of Salvador Dali*
Hensbergen, Gijs van, *Gaudí*
Hughes, Robert, *Barcelona*
Hughes, Robert, *Goya*
Irwin, Robert, *The Alhambra*
Kurlansky, Mark, *The Basque History of the World*
Lowe, Sid, *Fear and Loathing in La Liga: Barcelona vs Real Madrid*
Minder, Raphael, *The Struggle for Catalonia: Rebel Politics in Spain*

Index

Illustrations and captions are denoted by *italics*.

Image credits

p. 12, Cameron Spencer/ Getty Images
p. 16, MiguelMPhotography/ Shutterstock
p. 18, saiko3p/Shutterstock
p. 22, Museo de Altamira y D. Rodríguez/Wikimedia
p. 26, Universal History Archive/Universal Images Group/Getty Images
p. 34–5, pablopicasso/ Shutterstock
p. 45, PHAS/Universal Images Group/Getty Images
p. 48–9, John Turp/Getty Images
p. 57, Universal Images Group North America LLC / Alamy
p. 61, Wikimedia Commons/Museu Nacional d'Art de Catalunya
p. 68, akg-images / Album / Prisma
p. 69, akg-images / Erich Lessing
p. 76–7, Madrugada Verde/ Shutterstock
p. 80–1, agefotostock / Alamy
p. 94, Stefano Bianchetti/ Corbis/Getty Images
p. 104, Wikimedia Commons/Museum of Fine Arts, Budapest
p. 109, Heritage Image Partnership Ltd/Alamy
p. 117, Wikimedia Commons/Museo del Prado
p. 118–19, Lukasz Janyst/ Shutterstock
p. 122–3, Granger Historical Picture Archive/ Alamy
p. 126, akg-images
p. 130, Heritage Image Partnership Ltd/Alamy
p. 136–7, eldar nurkovic/ Shutterstock
p. 139, Wikimedia Commons/Hospital de la Santa Caridad
p. 141, Wikimedia Commons/Museo del Prado
p. 143, Metropolitan Museum of Art/ Purchase, Fletcher and Rogers Funds, and Bequest of Miss Adelaide Milton de Groot (1876–1967), by exchange, supplemented by gifts from friends of the Museum, 1971
p. 160, Wikimedia Commons/Museo del Prado
p. 161, Wikimedia Commons/Museo del Prado
p. 166 Leemage/Corbis/ Getty Images
p. 168, Patrick Ward/ Popperfoto/Getty Images
p. 172, Prisma/Universal Images Group/Getty Images
p. 176–7, Wikimedia Commons/Museo del Prado
p. 179, Wikimedia Commons/Museo del Prado
p. 182, Fine Art Images/ Heritage Images/Getty Images
p. 188, Jose Lucas/Alamy
p. 196, Wikimedia Commons/Lima Art Museum
p. 204, Archivo General de Indias, MP-INGENIOS,66/Archivos Españoles
p. 209, PRISMA ARCHIVO/Alamy
p. 213, Album/Alamy
p. 221, History and Art Collection/Alamy
p. 225, Wikimedia Commons/Museo Zumalakarregi Museoa
p. 226, Granger Historical Picture Archive/Alamy
p. 231, Photo 12/ Universal Images Group/Getty Images
p. 233, Wikimedia Commons/ Fundación Rosalía de Castro
p. 237, Heritage Image Partnership Ltd/Alamy
p. 241, Heritage Image Partnership Ltd/Alamy
p. 245, Photo12/UIG/Getty Images
p. 248, ullstein bild/Getty Images
p. 252, Keystone-France/ Gamma-Keystone/Getty Images
p. 258, Wikimedia Commons
p. 262–3, Picasso, Guernica, 1937 © Succession Picasso/DACS, London 2022
p. 269, Heinrich Hoffmann/ ullstein bild/Getty Images
p. 277, Album/Alamy
p. 281, Gianni Ferrari/ Cover/Getty Images
p. 287, Album/Alamy
p. 294, Jeff Greenberg/ Education Images/ Universal Images Group/ Getty Images
p. 295, Alisia Luther/ Shutterstock
p. 299, Getty Images
p. 306–7, Pedro Rufo/ Shutterstock